Siegel's
CIVIL PROCEDURE

*Essay and Multiple-Choice
Questions and Answers*

D1401444

By

BRIAN N. SIEGEL

J.D., Columbia Law School

and

LAZAR EMANUEL

J.D., Harvard Law School
General Counsel, Emanuel Publishing Corp.

Siegel's Series

Published by

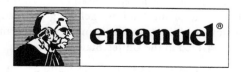

emanuel®

Siegel's Civil Procedure, 4th Edition (1998)
Emanuel Publishing Corp. • 1865 Palmer Avenue • Larchmont, NY 10538

ISBN 1-56542-351-8

About the Authors

Professor Brian N. Siegel received his *Juris Doctorate* from Columbia Law School, where he was designated a Harlan Fiske Stone Scholar for academic excellence. He is the author of *How to Succeed in Law School* and numerous works pertaining to preparation for the California Bar examination. Professor Siegel has taught as a member of the adjunct faculty at Pepperdine School of Law and Whittier College School of Law, as well as for the UCLA Extension Program.

Lazar Emanuel is a graduate of Harvard Law School. In 1950, he became a founding partner of the New York firm now known as Cowan, Liebowitz & Latman. From 1960 through 1971, he was president of Communications Industries Corp., multiple licensee of radio and television stations in the Northeast. Since 1987, he has served as Executive Vice President and General Counsel of Emanuel Publishing Corp. He has edited many of the publications in the Professor Series of study aids and in the Siegel's series of Essay and Multiple-Choice Question & Answer books.

Acknowledgment

The authors gratefully acknowledge the assistance of the California Committee of Bar Examiners which provided access to questions upon which many of the questions in this book are based.

Introduction

Although your grades are a significant factor in obtaining a summer internship or permanent position at a law firm, no formalized preparation for finals is offered at most law schools. Students, for the most part, are expected to fend for themselves in learning the exam-taking process. Ironically, law school exams ordinarily bear little correspondence to the teaching methods used by professors during the school year. They require you to spend most of your time briefing cases. Although many claim this is "great preparation" for issue-spotting on exams, it really isn't. Because you focus on one principle of law at a time, you don't get practice in relating one issue to another or in developing a picture of the entire course. When exams finally come, you're forced to make an abrupt 180-degree turn. Suddenly, you are asked to recognize, define and discuss a variety of issues buried within a single multi-issue fact pattern. In most schools, you are then asked to select among a number of possible answers, all of which look inviting but only one of which is right.

The comprehensive course outline you've created so diligently and with such pain, means little if you're unable to apply its contents on your final exams. There is a vast difference between reading opinions in which the legal principles are clearly stated, and applying those same principles to hypothetical exams and multiple choice questions.

The purpose of this book is to help you bridge the gap between memorizing a rule of law and ***understanding how to use it*** in the context of an exam. After an initial overview describing the exam writing process, you will be presented with a large number of hypotheticals which test your ability to write analytical essays and to pick the right answers to multiple-choice questions. ***Do them — all of them!*** Then review the suggested answers which follow. You'll find that the key to superior grades lies in applying your knowledge through questions and answers, not rote memory.

In the sample answers (both to the essays and to the multiple choice), you will notice references to *Emanuel* on *Civil Procedure*. The reference tells you where in the outline to find the relevant discussion. Thus, a reference to "Ch. 1–IV(E)(2)(a)" means Chapter 1, section (Roman numeral) IV, capital letter E within that section, number 2, paragraph a. This notation is perhaps less convenient than page numbers, but it helps us keep the reference constant from one edition of a book to the next.

GOOD LUCK !

Table of Contents

Preparing Effectively for Essay Examinations

Essay Questions

Essay Answers

Multiple Choice Questions

Answers to Multiple Choice Questions

Tables and Index

Preparing Effectively for Essay Examinations[1]

To achieve superior scores on essay exams, a student must (i) learn and understand "blackletter" principles and rules of law for each subject, and (ii) analyze how those principles of law arise within a test fact pattern. One of the most common misconceptions about law school is that you must memorize each word on every page of your casebooks or outlines to do well on exams. The reality is that you can commit an entire casebook to memory and still do poorly on an exam. Reviewing hundreds of student answers has shown us that most students can recite the rules. The ones who do **best** on exams understand how problems (issues) stem from the rules which they have memorized and how to communicate their analysis of these issues to the grader. The following pages cover what you need to know to achieve superior scores on your law school essay exams.

The "ERC" Process

To study effectively for law school exams you must be able to **"ERC"** (**E**lementize, **R**ecognize, and **C**onceptualize) each legal principle listed in the table of contents of your casebooks and course outlines. **Elementizing** means reducing the legal theories and rules you learn, down to a concise, straightforward statement of their essential elements. Without a knowledge of these precise elements, it is not possible to anticipate all of the potential issues which can arise under them.

For example, if you are asked, "what is self-defense?", it is **not** sufficient to say, "self-defense is permitted when, if someone is about to hit you, you can prevent him from doing it." This layperson description would leave a grader wondering if you had actually attended law school. An accurate elementization of the self-defense principle would be something like this: "Where one reasonably believes she is in imminent danger of an offensive touching, she may assert whatever force she reasonably believes necessary under the circumstances to prevent the offensive touching from occurring." This formulation correctly shows that there are four separate, distinct elements which must be satisfied for this defense to be successfully asserted: (i) the actor must have a **reasonable belief** that (ii) the touching which he seeks to prevent is **offensive**, (iii) the offensive touching is **imminent**, and (iv) the actor must use no greater force than she **reasonably believes is necessary under the circumstances** to prevent the offensive touching from occurring.

---

1. To illustrate the principles of effective exam preparation, we have used examples from Torts and Constitutional Law. However, these principles apply to all subjects. One of the most difficult tasks faced by law students is learning how to apply principles from one area of the law to another. We leave it to you, the reader, to think of comparable examples for the subject-matter of this book.

Recognizing means perceiving or anticipating which words within a legal principle are likely to be the source of issues, and how those issues are likely to arise within a hypothetical fact pattern. With respect to the self-defense concept, there are four *potential* issues. Did the actor reasonably believe that the person against whom the defense is being asserted was about to make an offensive contact upon her? Was the contact imminent? Would the contact have been offensive? Did the actor use only such force as she reasonably believed was necessary to prevent the imminent, offensive touching?

Conceptualizing means imagining situations in which each of the elements of a rule of law have given rise to factual issues. *Unless a student can illustrate to herself an application of each element of a rule of law, she does not truly understand the legal principles behind the rule!* In our opinion, the inability to conjure up hypothetical problems involving particular rules of law foretells a likelihood that issues involving those rules will be missed on an exam. It is therefore *crucial* to (i) *recognize* that issues result from the interaction of facts with the appropriate words defining a rule of law; and ii) develop the ability to *conceptualize* fact patterns involving each of the words contained in the rule

For example, an illustration of the "reasonable belief" portion of the self-defense principle in tort law might be the following:

> One evening, A and B had an argument at a bar. A screamed at B, "I'm going to get a knife and stab you!" A then ran out of the bar. B, who was armed with a concealed pistol, left the bar about 15 minutes later. As B was walking home, he suddenly heard running footsteps coming up from behind him. B drew his pistol, turned and shot the person advancing toward him (who was only about ten feet away when the shooting occurred). When B walked over to his victim, he recognized that the person he had killed was not A (but was instead another individual who had simply decided to take an evening jog). There would certainly be an issue whether B had a reasonable belief that the person who was running behind him was A. In the subsequent wrongful-death action, the victim's estate would certainly contend that the earlier threat by A was not enough to give B a reasonable belief that the person running behind him was A. B could certainly contend in rebuttal that given the prior altercation at the bar, A's threat, the darkness, and the fact that the incident occurred within a time frame soon after A's threat, his belief that A was about to attack him was "reasonable."

An illustration of how use of the word "imminent" might generate an issue is the following:

> X and Y had been feuding for some time. One afternoon, X suddenly attacked Y with a hunting knife. However, Y was able to wrest the knife away From X. At that point X retreated about four feet away from Y and screamed: "You were lucky this time, but next time I'll have a gun and you'll be finished." Y, having good reason to believe that X would subsequently carry out his threats (after all,

X had just attempted to kill Y), immediately thrust the knife into X's chest, killing him. While Y certainly had a reasonable belief that X would attempt to kill him the *next time* the two met, Y would probably *not* be able to successfully assert the self-defense privilege since the "imminency" element was absent.

A fact pattern illustrating the actor's right to use only that force which is reasonably necessary under the circumstances might be following:

> D rolled up a newspaper and was about to strike E on the shoulder with it. As D pulled back his arm for the purpose of delivering the blow, E drew a knife and plunged it into D's chest. While E had every reason to believe that D was about to deliver an offensive impact on him, E probably could not successfully assert the self-defense privilege because the force he utilized in response was greater than reasonably necessary under the circumstances to prevent the impact. E could simply have deflected D's prospective blow or punched D away. The use of a knife constituted a degree of force by E which was *not* reasonable, given the minor injury which he would have suffered from the newspaper's impact.

"Mental gymnastics" such as these must be played with every element of every rule you learn.

Issue-Spotting

One of the keys to doing well on an essay examination is issue-spotting. In fact, issue spotting is *the* most important skill you will learn in law school. If you recognize all of the legal issues, you can always find an applicable rule of law (if there is any) by researching the issues. However, if you fail to perceive an issue, you may very well misadvise your client about the likelihood of success or failure. It is important to remember that (1) an issue is a question to be decided by the judge or jury; and (2) a question is "in issue" when it can be disputed or argued about at trial. The bottom line is that if *you don't spot an issue, you can't discuss it*.

The key to issue-spotting is to approach a problem in the same way as an attorney would. Let's assume you're a lawyer and someone enters your office with a legal problem. He will recite the facts to you and give you any documents that may be pertinent. He will then want to know if he can sue (or be sued, if your client seeks to avoid liability). To answer your client's question intelligently, you will have to decide the following: (1) what theories can possibly be asserted by your client; (2) what defense or defenses can possibly be raised to these theories; (3) what issues may arise if these theories and defenses are asserted; (4) what arguments can each side make to persuade the factfinder to resolve the issue in his favor; and (5) finally, what will the *likely* outcome of each issue be. *All the issues which can possibly arise at trial should be discussed in your answer.*

How to Discuss an Issue

Keep in mind that ***rules of law are the guides to issues*** (i.e., an issue arises where there is a question whether the facts do, or do not, satisfy an element of a rule); a rule of law ***cannot dispose of an issue*** unless the rule can reasonably be ***applied to the facts.***

A good way to learn how to discuss an issue is to start with the following mini-hypothetical and the two student responses which follow it.

Mini-Hypothetical

A and B were involved in making a movie which was being filmed at a bar. The script called for A to appear to throw a bottle (which was actually a rubber prop) at B. The fluorescent lighting at the bar had been altered, the subdued blue lights being replaced with rather bright white lights. The cameraperson had stationed herself just to the left of the swinging doors which served as the main entrance to the bar. As the scene was unfolding, C, a regular patron of the bar, unwittingly walked into it. The guard who was stationed immediately out-side the bar, had momentarily left his post to visit the restroom. As C pushed the barroom doors inward, the left door panel knocked the camera to the ground with a resounding crash. The first (and only) thing which C saw, how-ever, was A (who was about 5 feet from C) getting ready to throw the bottle at B, who was at the other end of the bar (about 15 feet from A). Without hesita-tion, C pushed A to the ground and punched him in the face. Plastic surgery was required to restore A's profile to its Hollywood-handsome pre-altercation form.

Discuss A's right against C.

Pertinent Principles of Law:

1. Under the rule defining the prevention-of-crime privilege, if one sees that someone is about to commit what she reasonably believes to be a felony or misdemeanor involving a breach of the peace, she may exercise whatever degree of force is reasonably necessary under the circumstances to prevent that person from committing the crime.

2. Under the defense-of-others privilege, where one reasonably believes that someone is about to cause an offensive contact upon a third party, she may use whatever force is reasonably necessary under the circumstances to prevent the contact. Some jurisdictions, however, limit this privilege to situations in which the actor and the third party are related.

First Student Answer

"Did C commit an assault and battery upon A?

"An assault occurs where the defendant intentionally causes the plaintiff to be reasonably in apprehension of an imminent, offensive touching. The facts state that C punched A to the ground. Thus, a battery would have occurred at this point. We are also told that C punched A in the face. It is reasonable to assume that A saw the punch being thrown at him, and therefore A felt in imminent danger of an offensive touching. Based upon the facts, C is liable for an assault and battery upon A.

"Were C's actions justifiable under the defense-of-others privilege?

"C could successfully assert the defense of others and prevention of crime privileges. When C opened the bar doors, A appeared to be throwing the bottle at B. Although the "bottle" was actually a prop, C had no way of knowing this fact. Also, it was necessary for C to punch A in the face to assure that A could not get back up, retrieve the bottle, and again throw it at B. While the plastic surgery required by A is unfortunate, C could not be successfully charged with assault and battery."

Second Student Answer

"Assault and Battery:

"C committed an assault (causing A to be reasonably in apprehension of an imminent, offensive contact) when A saw C's punch about to hit him, and battery (causing an offensive contact upon A) when he (i) C knocked A to the ground, and (ii) C punched A.

"Defense-of-Others/Prevention-of-Crime Defenses:

"C would undoubtedly assert the privileges of defense-of-others (where defendant reasonably believed the plaintiff was about to make an offensive contact upon a third party, he was entitled to use whatever force was reasonably necessary to prevent the contact); and prevention-of-crime defense (where one reasonably believes another is about to commit a felony or misdemeanor involving a breach of the peace, he may exercise whatever force is reasonably necessary to prevent that person from committing a crime).

"A could contend that C was not reasonable in believing that A was about to cause harm to B because the enhanced lighting at the bar and camera crash should have indicated to C, a regular customer, that a movie was being filmed. However, C could probably successfully contend in rebuttal that his belief was reasonable in light of the facts that (i) he had not seen the camera when he attacked A, and (ii) instantaneous action was required (he did not have time to notice the enhanced lighting around the bar).

"A might also contend that the justification was forfeited because the degree of force used by C was not reasonable, since C did not have to punch A in the face after A had already been pushed to the ground (i.e., the danger to B was no longer present). However, C could argue in rebuttal that it was necessary to knockout A (an individual with apparently violent propensities) while the opportunity existed, rather than risk a drawn-out scuffle in which A might prevail. The facts do not indicate how big A and C were; but assuming C was not significantly larger than A, C's contention will probably be successful. If, however, C was significantly larger than A, the punch may have been excessive (since C could presumably have simply held A down)."

Critique

Let's examine the First Student Answer first. It mistakenly phrases as an "issue" the assault and battery committed by C upon A. While the actions creating these torts must be mentioned in the facts to provide a foundation for a discussion of the applicable privileges, there was no need to discuss them further because they were not the issue the examiners were testing for.

The structure of the initial paragraph of First Student Answer is also incorrect. After an assault is defined in the first sentence, the second sentence abruptly describes the facts necessary to constitute the commission of a battery. The third sentence then sets forth the elements of a battery. The fourth sentence completes the discussion of assault by describing the facts pertaining to that tort. The two-sentence break between the original mention of assault and the facts which constitute this tort is confusing; the facts which call for the application of a rule should be mentioned *immediately* after the rule is stated.

A more serious error, however, occurs in the second paragraph of the First Student Answer. While there is an allusion to the correct principle of law (prevention of crime), the **rule is not defined**. As a consequence, the grader can only guess why the student thinks the facts set forth in the subsequent sentences are significant. A grader reading this answer could not be certain that the student recognized that the issues revolved around the **reasonable belief** and **necessary force** elements of the prevention-of-crime privilege. Superior exam-writing requires that the pertinent facts be **tied** directly and clearly to the operative rule.

The Second Student Answer is very much better than the First Answer. It disposes of C's assault and battery upon A in a few words (yet tells the grader that the writer knows these torts are present). More importantly, the grader can easily see the issues which would arise if the prevention-of crime-privilege were asserted (i.e., "whether C's belief that A was about to commit a crime against B was reasonable" and "whether C used unnecessary force in punching A after A had been knocked to the ground"). Finally, it also utilizes all the facts by indicating how each attorney would assert those facts which are most advantageous to her client.

Structuring Your Answer

Graders will give high marks to a clearly-written, well-structured answer. Each issue you discuss should follow a specific and consistent structure which a grader can easily follow.

The Second Student Answer above basically utilizes the *I-R-A-A-O format* with respect to each issue. In this format, the *I* stands for the word *Issue*, the *R* for *Rule of law*, the initial *A* for the words *one side's Argument*, the second *A* for *the other party's rebuttal Argument*, and the *O* for your *Opinion as to how the issue would be resolved.* The *I-R-A-A-O* format emphasizes the importance of (1) discussing *both* sides of an issue, and (2) communicating to the grader that where an issue arises, an attorney can only advise her client as to the *probable* decision on that issue.

A somewhat different format for analyzing each issue is the *I-R-A-C format.* The "*I*" stands for *"Issue;"* the "*R*" for *"Rule of law;"* the "*A*" for *"Application of the facts to the rule of law;"* and the "*C*" for *"Conclusion." I-R-A-C* is a legitimate approach to the discussion of a particular issue, within the time constraints imposed by the question. The *I-R-A-C format* must be applied to each issue; it is not the solution to an entire exam answer. If there are six issues in a question, for example, you should offer six separate, independent *I-R-A-C* analyses.

We believe that the *I-R-A-C* approach is preferable to the *I-R-A-A-O* formula. However, either can be used to analyze and organize essay exam answers. Whatever format you choose, however, you should be consistent throughout the exam and remember the following rules:

First, *analyze all of the relevant facts.* Facts have significance in a particular case *only as they come under the applicable rules of law.* The facts presented must be analyzed and examined to see if they do or do not satisfy one element or another of the applicable rules, and the essential facts and rules must be stated and argued in your analysis.

Second, you must communicate to the grader the *precise rule of law* controlling the facts. In their eagerness to commence their arguments, students sometimes fail to state the applicable rule of law first. Remember, the "*R*" in either format stands for "Rule of Law." Defining the rule of law *before* an analysis of the facts is essential in order to allow the grader to follow your reasoning.

Third, it is important to treat *each side of an issue with equal detail.* If a hypothetical describes how an elderly man was killed when he ventured upon the land of a huge power company to obtain a better view of a nuclear reactor, your sympathies might understandably fall on the side of the old man. The grader will nevertheless expect you to see and make every possible argument for the other side. Don't permit your personal viewpoint to affect your answer! A good lawyer never does! When discussing an issue, always state the arguments for each side.

Finally, don't forget to *state your opinion or conclusion* on each issue. Keep in mind, however, that your opinion or conclusion is probably the *least* important part of an exam answer. Why? Because your professor knows that no attorney can tell her client exactly how a judge or jury will decide a particular issue. By definition, an issue is a legal dispute which can go either way. An attorney, therefore, can offer her client only her best opinion about the likelihood of victory or defeat on an issue. Since the decision on any issue lies with the judge or jury, no attorney can ever be absolutely certain of the resolution.

Discuss All Possible Issues

As we've noted, a student should draw *some* type of conclusion or opinion for each issue raised. Whatever your conclusion on a particular issue, it is essential to anticipate and discuss *all of the issues* which would arise if the question were actually tried in court.

Let's assume that a negligence hypothetical involves issues pertaining to duty, breach of duty, proximate causation and contributory negligence. If the defendant prevails on any one of these issues, he will avoid liability. Nevertheless, even if you feel strongly that the defendant owed no duty to the plaintiff, you *must* go on to discuss all of the other potential issues as well (breach of duty, proximate causation and contributory negligence). If you were to terminate your answer after a discussion of the duty problem only, you'd receive an inferior grade.

Why should you have to discuss every possible potential issue if you are relatively certain that the outcome of a particular issue would be dispositive of the entire case? Because at the commencement of litigation, neither party can be *absolutely positive* about which issues he will win at trial. We can state with confidence that every attorney with some degree of experience has won issues he thought he would lose, and has lost issues on which he thought victory was assured. Since one can never be absolutely certain how a factual issue will be resolved by the factfinder, a good attorney (and exam-writer) will consider **all** possible issues.

To understand the importance of discussing all of the potential issues, you should reflect on what you will do during the actual practice of law. If you represent the defendant, for example, it is your job to raise every possible defense. If there are five potential defenses, and your pleadings only rely on three of them (because you're sure you will win on all three), and the plaintiff is somehow successful on all three issues, your client may well sue you for malpractice. Your client's contention would be that you should be liable because if you had only raised the two additional issues, you might have prevailed on at least one of them, and therefore liability would have been avoided. It is an attorney's duty to raise **all** legitimate issues. A similar philosophy should be followed when taking essay exams.

What exactly do you say when you've resolved the initial issue in favor of the defendant, and discussion of any additional issues would seem to be moot? The answer is simple. You simply begin the discussion of the next potential issue with something like, "Assuming, however, the plaintiff prevailed on the foregoing issue, the next issue would be…" The grader will understand and appreciate what you have done.

The corollary to the importance of raising all potential issues is that you should avoid discussion of obvious non-issues. Raising non-issues is detrimental in three ways: first, you waste a lot of precious time; second, you usually receive absolutely no points for discussing a point which the grader deems extraneous; third, it suggests to the grader that you lack the ability to distinguish the significant from the irrelevant. The best guideline for avoiding the discussion of a non-issue is to ask yourself, "would I, as an attorney, feel comfortable about raising that particular issue or objection in front of a judge"?

Delineate the Transition From One Issue to the Next

It's a good idea to make it easy for the grader to see the issues which you've found. One way to accomplish this is to cover no more than one issue per paragraph. Another way is to underline each issue statement. Provided time permits, both techniques are recommended. The essay answers in this book contain numerous illustrations of these suggestions.

One frequent student error is to write a two-paragraph answer in which all of the arguments for one side are made in the initial paragraph, and all of the rebuttal arguments by the other side are made in the next paragraph. This is **a bad idea**. It obliges the grader to reconstruct the exam answer in his mind several times to determine whether all possible issues have been discussed by both sides. It will also cause you to state the same rule of law more than once. A better-organized answer presents a given argument by one side and follows that immediately in the same paragraph with the other side's rebuttal to that argument.

Understanding the "Call" of a Question

The statements *at the end of* an essay question or of the fact pattern in a multiple-choice question is sometimes referred to as the "call" of the question. It usually asks you to do something specific like "discuss," "discuss the rights of the parties," "what are X's rights?" "advise X," "the best grounds on which to find the statute unconstitutional are:," "D can be convicted of:," "how should the estate be distributed," etc. The call of the question should be read carefully because it tells you exactly what you're expected to do. If a question asks, "what are X's rights against Y?" or "X is liable to Y for:..." you don't have to spend a lot time on Y's rights against Z. You will usually receive absolutely no credit for discussing facts that are not required by the question. On the other hand, if the call of an essay question is simply "discuss" or "discuss the rights of the parties" then *all* foreseeable issues must be covered by your answer.

Students are often led astray by an essay question's call. For example, if you are asked for "X's rights against Y" or to "advise X", you may think you may limit yourself to X's viewpoint with respect to the issues. This is *not correct*! You cannot resolve one party's rights against another party without considering the issues which might arise (and the arguments which the other side would assert) if litigation occurred. In short, although the call of the question may appear to focus on one of the parties to the litigation, a superior answer will cover all the issues and arguments which that person might *encounter* (not just the arguments she would *make*) in attempting to pursue her rights against the other side.

The Importance of Analyzing the Question Carefully Before Writing

The overriding *time pressure* of an essay exam is probably a major reason why many students fail to analyze a question carefully before writing. Five minutes into the allocated time for a particular question, you may notice that the person next to you is writing furiously. This thought then flashes through your mind, "Oh, my goodness, he's putting down more words on the paper than I am, and therefore he's bound to get a better grade." It can be stated *unequivocally* that there is no necessary correlation between the number of words on your exam paper and the grade you'll receive. Students who begin their answer after only five minutes of analysis have probably seen only the most obvious issues, and missed many, if not most, of the subtle ones. They are also likely to be less well organized.

Opinions differ as to how much time you should spend analyzing and outlining a question before you actually write the answer. We believe that you should spend at least 12-18 minutes analyzing, organizing, and outlining a one-hour question before writing your answer. This will usually provide sufficient time to analyze and organize the question thoroughly *and* enough time to write a relatively complete answer. Remember that each word of the question must be scrutinized to determine if it (i) suggests an issue under the operative rules of law, or (ii) can be used in making an argument for the resolution of an issue. Since you can't receive points for an issue you don't spot, it is usually wise to read a question *twice* before starting your outline.

When to Make an Assumption

The instructions on an exam may tell you to *"assume"* facts which are necessary to the answer. Even where these instructions are *not* specifically given, you may be obliged to make certain assumptions with respect to missing facts in order to write a thorough answer. Assumptions should be made when you, as the attorney for one of the parties described in the question, would be obliged to solicit additional information from your client. On the other hand, assumptions should *never be used to change or alter the question.* Don't ever write something like "if the facts in the question were …, instead of …, then … would result." If you do this, you are wasting time on facts which are extraneous to the problem before you. Professors want you to deal with *their* fact patterns, not your own.

Students sometimes try to "write around" information they think is missing. They assume that their professor has failed to include every piece of data necessary for a thorough answer. This is generally *wrong.* The professor may have omitted some facts deliberately to see if the student *can figure out what to do* under the circumstances. In some instances, the professor may have omitted them inadvertently (even law professors are sometimes human).

The way to deal with the omission of essential information is to describe (i) what fact (or facts) are missing, and (ii) why that information is important. As an example, go back to the "movie shoot" hypothetical we discussed above. In that fact pattern, there was no mention of the relative strength of A and C. This fact could be extremely important. If C weighed 240 pounds and was built like a professional football linebacker, while A tipped the scales at a mere 160 pounds, punching A in the face after he had been pushed to the ground would probably constitute unnecessary force (thereby causing C to forfeit the prevention-of-crime privilege). If the physiques of the parties were reversed, however, C's punch to A's face would probably constitute reasonable behavior. Under the facts, C had to deal the *"knockout"* blow while the opportunity presented itself. The last sentences of the Second Student Answer above show that the student understood these subtleties and correctly stated the essential missing facts and assumptions.

Assumptions should be made in a manner which keeps the other issues open (i.e., necessitates discussion of all other possible issues). Don't assume facts which would virtually dispose of the entire hypothetical in a few sentences. For example, suppose that A called B a "convicted felon" (a statement which is inherently defamatory, *i.e.*, a defamatory statement is one which tends to subject the plaintiff to hatred, contempt or ridicule). If A's statement is true, he has a complete defense to B's action for defamation. If the facts don't tell whether A's statement was true or not, it would ***not*** be wise to write something like, "We'll assume that A's statement about B is accurate, and therefore B cannot successfully sue A for defamation." So facile an approach would rarely be appreciated by the grader. The proper way to handle this situation would be to state, "if we assume that A's statement about B is not correct, A can not raise the defense of truth." You've communicated to the grader that you recognize the need to assume an essential fact and that you've assumed it in such a way as to enable you to proceed to discuss all other potential issues.

Case Names

A law student is ordinarily ***not*** expected to recall case names on an exam. The professor knows that you have read several hundred cases for each course, and that you would have to be a memory expert to have all of the names at your fingertips. If you confront a fact pattern which seems similar to a case which you have reviewed (but you cannot recall the name of it), just write something like, "One case held that …" or "It has been held that …" In this manner, you have informed the grader that you are relying on a case which contained a fact pattern similar to the question at issue.

The only exception to this rule is in the case of a landmark decision. Landmark opinions are usually those which change or alter established law.[2] These cases are usually easy to identify, because you will probably have spent an entire class period discussing each of them. *Palsgraf v. Long Island Rail Road* is a prime example of a landmark case in Torts. In these special cases, you may be expected to remember the case by name, as well the proposition of law which it stands for. However, this represents a very limited exception to the general rule which counsels against wasting precious time trying to memorize case names.

---

2. The only subject to which this does not apply is Constitutional Law, since here virtually every case you study satisfies this definition. Students studying Constitutional Law should try to associate case names with holdings and reproduce them in their exam answers.

How To Handle Time Pressures

What do you do when there are five minutes left in the exam and you have only written down two-thirds of your answer? One thing *not* to do is write something like, "No time left!" or "Not enough time!" This gets you nothing but the satisfaction of knowing you have communicated your personal frustrations to the grader. Another thing *not* to do is insert the outline you may have made on scrap paper into the exam booklet. Professors rarely will look at these items.

First of all, it is not necessarily a bad thing to be pressed for time. The person who finishes five minutes early has very possibly missed some important issues. The more proficient you become in knowing what is expected of you on an exam, the greater the difficulty you may experience in staying within the time limits. Second, remember that (at least to some extent) you're graded against your classmates' answers and they're under exactly the same time pressure as you. In short, don't panic if you can't write the "perfect" answer in the allotted time. Nobody does!

The best hedge against misuse of time is to *review as many old exams as possible*. These exercises will give you a familiarity with the process of organizing and writing an exam answer, which, in turn, should result in an enhanced ability to stay within the time boundaries. If you nevertheless find that you have about 15 minutes of writing to do and five minutes to do it in, write a paragraph which summarizes the remaining issues or arguments you would discuss if time permitted. As long as you've indicated that you're aware of the remaining legal issues, you'll probably receive some credit for them. Your analytical and argumentative skills will already be apparent to the grader by virtue of the issues that you have previously discussed.

Write Legibly

Make sure your answer is legible. Students should *not* assume that their professors will be willing to take their papers to the local pharmacist to have them deciphered. Remember, your professor may have 75-150 separate exam answers to grade. If your answer is difficult to read, you will rarely be given the benefit of the doubt. On the other hand, a legible, well-organized paper creates a very positive mental impact upon the grader.

Many schools allow students to type their exams. If you're an adequate typist, you may want to seriously consider typing. Typing has two major advantages. First, it should help assure that your words will be readable (unless, of course, there are numerous typos). Second, it should enable you to put a lot more words onto the paper than if your answer had been handwritten. Most professors prefer a typed answer to a written one.

There are, however, a few disadvantages to typing. For one thing, all the typists are usually in a single room. If the clatter of other typewriters will make it difficult for you to concentrate, typing is probably *not* wise. To offset this problem, some students wear earplugs during the exam. Secondly, typing sometimes makes it difficult to change or add to an earlier portion of your answer. You may have to withdraw your paper from the carriage and insert another. Try typing out a few practice exams before you decide to type your exam. If you do type, be sure to leave at least one blank line between typewritten lines, so that handwritten changes and insertions in your answers can be made easily.

If you decide against typing, your answer will probably be written in a "bluebook" (a booklet of plain, lined, white paper which has a light blue cover and back). It is usually a good idea to write only on the odd numbered pages (i.e., 1, 3, 5, etc.). You may also want to leave a blank line between each written line. Doing these things will usually make the answer easier to read. If you discover that you have left out a word or phrase, you can insert it into the proper place by means of a caret sign ("^"). If you feel that you've omitted an entire issue, you can write it on the facing blank page. A symbol reference can be used to indicate where the additional portion of the answer should be inserted. While it's not ideal to have your answer take on the appearance of a road map, a symbol reference to an adjoining page is much better than trying to squeeze six lines into one, and will help the grader to discover where the same symbol appears in another part of your answer.

The Importance of Reviewing Prior Exams

As we've mentioned, it is *extremely important to review old exams.* The transition from blackletter law to essay exam can be a difficult experience if the process has not been practiced. Although this book provides a large number of essay and multiple-choice questions, *don't stop here*! Most law schools have recent tests on file in the library, by course. We strongly suggest that you make a copy of every old exam you can obtain (especially those given by your professors) at the beginning of each semester. The demand for these documents usually increases dramatically as "finals time" draws closer.

The exams for each course should be scrutinized *throughout the semester.* They should be reviewed as you complete each chapter in your casebook. Generally, the order of exam questions follows the sequence of the materials in your casebook. Thus, the first question on a law school test may involve the initial three chapters of the casebook; the second question may pertain to the fourth and fifth chapters, etc. In any event, *don't wait* until the semester is nearly over to begin reviewing old exams.

Keep in mind that no one is born with the ability to analyze questions and write superior answers to law school exams. Like any skill, it is developed and perfected only through application. If you don't take the time to analyze numerous examinations from prior years, this evolutionary process just won't occur. Don't just **think about** the answers to past exam questions; take the time to **write the answers down**. It's also wise to look back at an answer a day or two after you've written it. You will invariably see (i) ways in which the organization could have been improved, and (ii) arguments you missed.

As you practice spotting issues on past exams, you will see how rules of law become the sources of issues on finals. As we've already noted, if you don't **understand** how rules of law translate into issues, you won't be able to achieve superior grades on your exams. Reviewing exams from prior years should also reveal that certain issues tend to be lumped together in the same question. For instance, where a fact pattern involves a false statement made by one person about another, three potential theories of liability are often present — defamation, invasion of privacy (false, public light) and intentional infliction of severe emotional distress. You will need to see if any or all of these apply to the facts.

Finally, one of the best means of evaluating if you understand a course (or a particular area within a subject) is to attempt to create a hypothetical exam for that topic. Your exam should contain as many issues as possible. If you can write an issue-packed exam, you probably know that particular area of law. If you can't, then you probably haven't yet acquired an adequate understanding of how the principles of law in that subject can spawn issues.

As Always, a Caveat

The suggestions and advice offered in this book represent the product of many years of experience in the field of legal education. We are confident that the techniques and concepts described in these pages will help you prepare for, and succeed, at your exams. Nevertheless, particular professors sometimes have a preference for exam-writing techniques which are not stressed in this work. Some instructors expect at least a nominal reference to the **prima facie** elements of all pertinent legal theories (even though one or more of those principles is **not** placed into issue). Other professors want their students to emphasize public policy considerations in the arguments they make on a particular issue. Because this book is intended for nationwide consumption, these individualized preferences have **not** been stressed. The best way to find out whether your professor has a penchant for a particular writing approach is to ask her to provide you with a model answer to a previous exam. If an item is not available, speak to upperclass students who received a superior grade in that professor's class.

One final point. While the rules of law stated in the answers to the questions in this book have been drawn from commonly used sources (i.e., casebooks, hornbooks, etc.), it is still conceivable that they may be slightly at odds with those taught by your professor. In instances where a conflict exists between our formulation of a legal principle and the one which is taught by your professor, *follow the latter!* Since your grades are determined by your professors, their views should always supersede the views contained in this book.

Essay Exam Questions

Question 1

APOW owns and operates a nuclear power plant. For one hour on each of three successive days, the plant emitted heavy radiation over the surrounding area which has a population of 10,000. Several individuals injured by the radiation emitted on the third day brought a class action for "damages" in an appropriate federal district court against APOW on behalf of all those injured on one or more of the three days. After describing the relevant facts, the complaint alleged only that APOW was responsible for "wrongful conduct". Jurisdiction was based properly and exclusively on diversity of citizenship.

1. APOW moved to dismiss the complaint for failure to state a claim upon which relief could be granted. The motion was denied.

2. APOW then opposed plaintiffs' motion to certify the class, arguing that there was no common issue and that plaintiffs' claims were not typical of the class. Certification was granted.

3. During discovery, plaintiffs requested that APOW produce a memorandum concerning possible legal liability for nuclear power accidents, prepared by APOW's legal staff prior to the accident, but following minor accidents at another company's nuclear power plant. APOW objected. The state in which the action was brought had abolished its own work product doctrine a year earlier. The court held that the memorandum could be discovered.

Were the court's rulings correct? Discuss.

Question 2

Owner was the driver, and Rider a passenger in Owner's expensive auto when it collided on a State X highway with a pickup truck driven by Trucker, a citizen of adjoining State Y. Both vehicles were damaged. Rider, Trucker and Owner were injured.

Owner, a citizen of State X, sued Trucker in a federal district court in State X, claiming $80,000 in property damage to his auto. In his answer, Trucker denied negligence and asserted contributory negligence. After a non-jury trial, the court expressly found that Trucker was not negligent. Judgment was entered for Trucker and has become final.

Subsequently, Rider commenced a $400,000 personal injury suit against Owner in an appropriate State X court. State X has adopted the Federal Rules of Civil Procedure. Prior to trial, Owner timely moved that the suit be dismissed on the ground that Trucker was an indispensable party and had not been made a defendant. After a hearing, the court denied Owner's motion.

Before trial, Trucker timely petitioned to intervene as a plaintiff and the court granted the petition over Owner's objection.

Trucker's complaint in intervention sought $200,000 for personal injury and property damage against Owner, who counterclaimed for $150,000 in personal injury damages. Rider was permitted to assert a $400,000 cross-complaint against Trucker, over Trucker's objection.

None of the claims asserted is barred by a statute of limitations.

1. In the State X court action, did the court correctly rule that:

    a. Trucker was not an indispensable party?

    b. Trucker could intervene?

    c. Rider could cross-complain against Trucker?

Discuss.

2. In the State X court action, what effect, if any, should the federal district court action have on:

    a. Rider's claim against owner?

    b. Rider's cross-complaint against Trucker?

    c. Trucker's claim against Owner?

    d. Owner's counterclaim against Trucker?

Discuss.

Question 3

Seler, a citizen of State S, and Byer, a citizen of State B, met in State B, and signed a written contract by which Seler agreed to sell Whiteacre, located in State W, to Byer. The contract provided that the purchase price of Whiteacre was $85,000. Seler returned to State S and sent Byer a deed conveying good title to Whiteacre.

Byer did not send Seler any money, but brought an action against Seler for reformation of the contract to correct an alleged error in the contract price. Byer alleged that the agreed price was $37,500, and that the $85,000 figure in the contract was a typographical error. The action was brought in a federal district court in State B. Subject matter jurisdiction was based on diversity. Personal jurisdiction over Seler was based on service of process under State B's long-arm statute.

A. Seler moved to dismiss the action, alleging lack of personal and subject matter jurisdiction. The motion was denied.

B. Seler then filed an answer asserting that the written contract accurately stated the agreed price. In addition, he counterclaimed for the $85,000 purchase price set forth in the contract and demanded a jury trial. Byer answered the counterclaim and moved to strike the demand for jury trial. The motion was denied.

C. Seler then served Byer with interrogatories demanding responses to the following questions: "(1) Have you had Whiteacre appraised? (2) If so, state by whom, state the appraised value or values, and attach copies of all written reports received from all appraisers." Over Byer's timely objections to the interrogatories, the court ordered disclosure only of the identity of appraisers and their appraised values.

D. At trial, Byer testified that the agreed price was $37,500 and that the $85,000 figure in the written contract was a typographical error. An appraiser testified on behalf of Byer that the value of Whiteacre when the contract was signed was, at most, $42,200. Byer rested his case. Seler testified that the agreed price was $85,000, and judgment was entered accordingly. Byer promptly moved for judgment notwithstanding the verdict (JNOV is now called "judgment as a matter of law"); and, in the alternative, for a new trial. The court granted the motion for judgment notwithstanding the verdict. No other motions were made during or after trial.

1. Did the court rule correctly on the motion to dismiss? Discuss.

2. Did the court rule correctly on the motion to strike the demand for a jury trial? Discuss.

3. Did the court rule correctly on the objection to the interrogatories? Discuss.

4. Was the evidence admitted at trial such that the court was correct in granting the motion for judgment notwithstanding the verdict? Discuss.

5. What procedural argument or arguments should Seler have made in opposition to the motion for judgment notwithstanding the verdict? Discuss.

Question 4

Daw had just spent five days of vacation in State X and was on his way home to State A when his car collided with a vehicle driven by Paul. The collision occurred in State Y, ten miles beyond the State X border.

Paul, a citizen of State X, filed an action against Daw in a State X state court. Paul alleged that he had suffered $700 in property damage when his car was struck by Daw's car. Daw was served at his home in State A and moved to quash service of process on the ground that the court lacked personal jurisdiction over him. The motion was denied.

Daw then filed an answer that denied negligence on his part and alleged contributory negligence.

Paul served interrogatories on Daw which requested the substance of a conservation that Daw had with his wife and his attorney's investigator soon after the accident. When Daw refused to answer those interrogatories, Paul moved to compel answers, and the court granted the motion. A $700 default judgment was entered against Daw when he refused to comply with the discovery order. State X follows the Federal Rules of Civil Procedure with regard to discovery sanctions. Daw did not appeal the judgment, which then became final.

Paul filed a complaint against Daw in the United States district court in State X for $78,000 for personal injuries arising out of the accident. In his answer, Daw denied negligence and alleged contributory negligence. He also counterclaimed for damages for personal injuries resulting from the accident.

Both Paul and Daw moved for summary judgment based on *res judicata* and collateral estoppel.

1. Was the State X court correct in denying Daw's motion to quash? Discuss.

2. Was the State X court correct in granting a default judgment against Daw? Discuss.

3. How should the United States district court rule on:

   a. Paul's motion for summary judgment on his complaint and on Daw's counterclaim? Discuss.

   b. Daw's motion for summary judgment on Paul's complaint? Discuss.

Question 5

Two years ago, Worker was injured by a defectively constructed machine while he was working in an industrial plant in State A. The machine had been manufactured by Macco, a State B corporation. While Worker was being treated for his injuries in Hospital in State A, Doctor, Worker's physician, prescribed medicine to which Worker was allergic. Worker's condition worsened gradually after that, but it was not clear whether his decline was due to the medicine or his injuries.

Worker sued Hospital in a state court in State A for negligence. Hospital's defenses were (1) it was not responsible for the acts of Doctor, since he was an independent contractor, (2) Doctor had not been negligent, and (3) Worker's present condition was caused by his injury, not the medicine. The trial court, sitting without a jury, found that Doctor had not acted negligently and that Doctor was not an agent of Hospital. The court made no finding on the cause of Worker's worsened condition. Judgment was entered for Hospital. No appeal was taken.

One month ago, Worker died and Worker's widow, Paula, who had lived in State A for five years, returned to her original home in State C. As executrix of her husband's estate duly qualified in State C, she has now filed suit in a state court in State C against Macco for the wrongful death of her husband. She has also filed suit against Doctor in a state court in State A for the damages she sustained as a result of the death of her husband. None of these suits is barred by a statute of limitations.

Macco makes sales in forty states and maintains an office in State C. During the past ten years, Macco has sold its products in State C. Its annual sales volume in that state is between $400,000 and $500,000. The machine that injured Worker was originally sold to a corporation in State A, which sold it to Worker's employer.

A statute in State C provides: "The courts of this state may exercise jurisdiction over a person and property to the full extent permitted by the Constitution of the United States."

1. Assuming appropriate objection by Macco, may State C exercise jurisdiction over Macco in Paula's suit as executrix? Discuss.

2. What effect, if any, does Worker's suit in State A have on:

   a. Paula's action in State C against Macco? Discuss.

   b. Paula's action in State A against Doctor? Discuss.

Question 6

Paul, a citizen of State X, brought suit against Dave, a citizen of State Y, in the U.S. district court in State Y for property damage caused to Paul's car when Dave's car ran into it in State Y. Jurisdiction was based on diversity of citizenship. The action was filed two weeks before the expiration of the period of State Y's one-year statute of limitations for negligent torts.

One month later, Paul filed an amended complaint that added a claim for personal injury arising out of the car accident. Dave moved to dismiss the personal injury claim. Because State Y had no rule allowing an amendment to relate back to the time of the original pleading under any circumstances, the district court granted Dave's motion, holding that the personal injury claim was barred by the State Y statute of limitations.

Dave next filed a third-party complaint impleading Insco, which he alleged was his auto insurer. Dave claimed Insco owed him the duty to defend against Paul's suit and to reimburse him for any loss. Insco, a State Y corporation, moved to dismiss the third-party complaint on the following grounds: (a) the third-party complaint was not authorized under the Federal Rules of Civil Procedure; (b) the district court lacked subject matter jurisdiction; and (c) the insurance policy had been fraudulently obtained. The district court dismissed Dave's third-party complaint.

At trial, over objection, the district court admitted the testimony of Dave's witness, Wit. Wit had not been listed by Dave in the pre-trial order prepared pursuant to the Federal Rules of Civil Procedure. Though Dave could not demonstrate a valid reason why he had not included Wit in the pre-trial order, the district court was of the view that no prejudice had resulted to Paul, since he had been aware of Wit's existence.

Did the district court err in:

1. Granting Dave's motion to dismiss the personal injury claim? Discuss.

2. Dismissing Dave's third-party complaint impleading Insco? Discuss.

3. Admitting the testimony of Wit? Discuss.

Question 7

On March 15, 1987, Pat brought suit against Truco, a corporation, as sole defendant, in the United States district court in State Red. The State Red statute of limitations for personal injury claims caused by negligence is two years.

The complaint alleged that Pat "resided" in State Red at the time of the events complained of and had become a "resident" of State White on March 1, 1987; that Truco was a citizen of State Red; and that on March 20, 1986, in State Red, Dan, a citizen of State Red and an employee of defendant Truco, negligently drove a motor vehicle, striking Pat and causing various personal injuries. The complaint sought a damage judgment against Truco for $100,000. Truco moved to dismiss the complaint on the following grounds: (1) lack of subject matter jurisdiction, and (2) failure of the complaint to join Dan as a defendant.

After its motions were denied, Truco's answer denied all of the allegations of Pat's complaint, except that its citizenship is in State Red, and that Dan was negligent.

At the pre-trial conference, Pat and Truco stipulated that (1) plaintiff's actual damages were $85,000, and (2) Truco would be liable to Pat if Dan was an employee of Truco.

At trial on February 1, 1990, undisputed testimony admitted into evidence established that Pat was a citizen of State White at the time the complaint was filed, and that on March 20, 1986, when the accident occurred in State Red, Dan was driving a car owned by Truco with defendant's permission, but was *not* employed by Truco.

After each party rested, (1) Truco moved for a directed verdict, (now called "judgment as a matter of law"), based on the stipulation and evidence introduced at trial, and (2) Pat moved for (a) permission to amend her complaint to insert a claim based upon a statute of State Red imposing liability upon the owner of a motor vehicle for the negligence of a driver operating the vehicle with the owner's permission, and (b) a directed verdict in her favor against Truco on the complaint as amended, for $85,000.

How should the court have decided:

1. Truco's initial two motions to dismiss,

2. Truco's motion for a directed verdict, and

3. Pat's post-trial motions?

Discuss.

Question 8

Albert is a touring professional golfer domiciled in State Red. Par Golf Clubs, Inc. is incorporated and has its central administrative office in State Red, but its major manufacturing facility is located in State Green. Par pays Albert $25,000 per year for Albert's endorsement of a set of golf clubs which it manufactures in State Red and sells through independent retailers in every state. Albert uses these clubs in the tournaments in which he plays throughout the United States. Whenever he is interviewed, he specifically endorses the clubs.

Harold lives in State White. He is a weekend golfer. While at a golf tournament in State Red, he heard Albert's endorsement of the Par Golf Clubs, and purchased a set from a golf shop in State Red.

While in State White, Harold was using one of the clubs for the first time. As a result of a metallurgical defect, the head of the club flew off the shaft and seriously injured Francis and Robert, both of whom are residents of State Green and were on a golfing holiday with Harold in State White.

Francis sued Par and Albert in a state court in State White. Par was sued as the manufacturer and Albert as the endorser of a defective product. Francis' complaint was based on theories of negligence and strict liability in tort. Two copies of the summons and complaint were personally delivered to Albert, who was "served personally and also on behalf of Par." At the time, Albert was physically present and playing in a tournament in State White. A copy of the complaint and summons was also personally delivered to the president of Par while he was on vacation in Hawaii. State White statutes authorize such service in actions for injuries received within the state.

1. Assuming all appropriate objections are properly made, may State White take jurisdiction over Albert and Par? Discuss.

2. Assuming Albert and Par desire to remove Francis' case to the U.S. district court in State Red, what arguments should Francis make in opposition? Discuss.

3. Assuming a final judgment on the merits is obtained in *Francis v. Albert and Par Golf Clubs, Inc.*, in a subsequent action by Robert in State Green, what use may Robert make of the judgment? What use may Par and Albert make of the judgment? Discuss.

Question 9

Pete, a citizen of State A, saw an advertisement in a newspaper published in adjoining State B, but distributed also in State A. It described a new chemical process just developed by Devco, a State C corporation, which has its principal office in State C. The advertisement claimed the new process would revolutionize the industrial dye industry and urged readers to purchase stock in Devco. Pete wrote Devco requesting more information about the new process. Devco sent Pete promotional brochures which directed persons interested in buying Devco stock to consult Bull, a stockbroker.

Bull is a State A citizen, but his brokerage office is in State B. Most of Bull's business has been selling Devco stock, for which Devco has paid him a commission. Devco did no business in either State A or State B. Pete purchased 20,000 shares of Devco stock through Bull. Pete is the only Devco shareholder who is domiciled in State A. Shortly after Pete purchased his stock, it was found that the new chemical process developed by Devco had no commercial value. As a result, the value of Pete's Devco stock declined.

Pete sued Devco in the United States district court in State A, alleging jurisdiction based on diversity of citizenship. The complaint purported to state a claim for relief based solely on common law fraud and contained a demand for a jury trial.

Devco then moved for dismissal of the complaint on the ground that the court lacked personal jurisdiction over it. Under State A law, a court has jurisdiction over a foreign corporation only if it is doing business in the state. The motion was denied, the court holding that it had jurisdiction to the full extent permitted by Fifth Amendment due process.

Devco moved to have Bull joined as a party defendant. The motion was granted. Bull then moved for dismissal of the action against him on the ground that the district court in State A lacked subject matter jurisdiction. The motion was granted.

Devco answered the complaint and moved to strike Pete's demand for jury trial on the ground that factual issues in the case involved very complex scientific matters beyond the intellectual capabilities of the average juror, and therefore it had no adequate remedy at law. The district court struck Pete's jury trial demand and set the case for a bench trial.

1. Did the district court in State A have personal jurisdiction over Devco? Discuss.

2. Did the district court in State A have subject matter jurisdiction over the action against Bull? Discuss.

3. Assuming the district court in State A had subject matter jurisdiction over the claim against Bull, was the court correct in ordering Bull joined as a party defendant? Discuss.

4. Did the district Court err in striking Pete's demand for a jury trial? Discuss.

Question 10

Valco is a corporation incorporated in State B. Its principal office and sole manufacturing plant is in State A. It manufactures pressure valves for compressed air tanks. It purchases from Mity, a corporation, the "collars" affixed to the pressure valves which are used to attach the valve to the air tank. Mity is incorporated and has its sole place of business in State A.

The Valco pressure valve on a piece of machinery owned by Peter and Quincy and used by them in State C, exploded. Peter and Quincy were seriously injured. At all times Peter was a citizen of State C. At the time of the explosion Quincy was a citizen of State A, but after the accident he moved to State B, where he is now domiciled.

Peter and Quincy wish to assert claims against Valco and Mity on the theory that the valve exploded because of a defective collar. Valco has informed Peter and Quincy that it will claim that written notice had been sent to them and to all other users of this model valve, recalling the valves; and that Peter and Quincy ignored the notice.

1. If Peter, as sole plaintiff, institutes an action against Valco, as sole defendant, in the United States district court in State C, may Valco object to the failure by Peter to join Mity as a defendant? May Valco bring Mity into the case as a defendant and, if so, how? Discuss.

2. If Peter and Quincy institute an action against Valco and Mity in the United States district court in State C for $100,000 damages each, what issues may be raised as to joinder of parties plaintiff, joinder of parties defendant, joinder of causes of action, jurisdiction over the defendants and jurisdiction over the subject matter? How should the trial court rule on each issue? Discuss.

3. If an action by Peter, as sole plaintiff, against Valco and Mity is commenced and tried in the United States district court in State A, should the trial court apply State A law, State C law or federal law on the issues of (a) whether plaintiff must plead freedom from contributory fault, and (b) who has the burden of persuasion on the issue of contributory fault? Discuss.

Question 11

Don Pickles was a teenage comedian. In early September, Merv Griffey, a talent agent, took Don under his wing, and in 2 months made Don a star. In early December, Merv told Don that he had booked him to give a performance at the Palladium in California on New Year's Eve. Don immediately advised Merv that he had a verbal agreement with Mr. Bigbucks, a prominent New York attorney, to play at the latter's New Year's Eve Party (where Don had previously performed). Merv advised Don to "cancel out" Bigbucks since "verbal contracts are unenforceable," which Don immediately did via telegram. Don and Merv both lived in Chicago, Illinois.

Two weeks later, when in Massachusetts en route to New Jersey to visit his girlfriend, Don stopped at a roadside restaurant. As he exited his car, he was served with a summons and complaint in an action filed by Bigbucks against Don and the Palladium Corporation in the U.S. district court for Massachusetts. The complaint alleged that Don was liable for breach of contract and that the Palladium Corporation was liable in the amount of $75,000 for inducing breach of the Don-Bigbucks agreement. Bigbucks asked for an injunction precluding Don from playing at the Palladium because his remedy at law was inadequate. Bigbucks premised this assertion on the grounds that Bigbucks had already invited many of his major clients to the party, and would "lose face" if Don played somewhere else. The Palladium is located in California, owned by Palladium Corporation, a New York corporation (where its Board of Directors meets monthly). Palladium Corporation was served by delivering a copy of the summons and complaint to the president's personal secretary at its corporate offices in New York.

Don answered by denying all but the jurisdictional allegations of Bigbucks' complaint (i.e., he admitted that he was an Illinois citizen). Don also filed a third party complaint against Merv for misadvising him as to his legal obligations to Bigbucks. Palladium Corporation filed an answer denying Bigbucks' allegations and a third-party complaint against Merv, claiming that Merv never advised them of an outstanding contract for Don's services. Palladium Corporation also filed a *forum non conveniens* motion, asking that the matter be transferred to the appropriate U.S. district court in California, but this motion was denied.

Before Merv was served with Don's third-party complaint, Don called him and complained about being "in the middle of a federal case." Don advised Merv that unless the latter "got him out of this mess, he was going to find another agent." Don also advised Merv to "come see him right away" in Boston, Massachusetts. Immediately after Merv arrived at the airport, Don asked Merv if the Palladium show was going to be cancelled or not. When Merv said "No," Don motioned to a process server who handed Merv the third-party complaint and summons. The Palladium Corporation served Merv by mailing a certified letter containing a copy of the summons and complaint to his office in Chicago. Merv's secretary signed for it and later gave the documents to him. This type of service was permissible under Massachusetts law. Merv responded to the third-party complaints by making the appropriate motions to dismiss them. When these motions were denied, he filed an answer denying liability to both Don and the Palladium Corporation.

The trial judge determined that she would hear the request for injunctive relief first (as was permissible under Massachusetts law), since this was the "lynchpin" issue. At trial, Don raised the defense of minority against Bigbucks' action, even though he had not stated it as an affirmative defense in this answer. The court, upon objection by Bigbucks, held that this defense was at variance with the pleading and could not now be raised. The court also held that Bigbucks was entitled to the relief he sought from Don. The jury decided that (1) Bigbucks was entitled to recover on his claim against the Palladium Corporation, and (2) Don and the Palladium Corporation were entitled to prevail on their third-party claims against Merv.

Discuss the issues which could be raised on appeal.

Question 12

Ped is a citizen of State A. Driver is a citizen of State D. Health is a corporation incorporated in State H. Its sole place of business is a hospital in State A. Ped was injured when struck by a motor vehicle operated by Driver in State A and hospitalized in the Health hospital. His injuries were allegedly aggravated as a result of the hospital's negligence.

Ped sued Driver and Health in a State A court, claiming damages in the sum of $100,000 and alleging that he was uncertain which defendant was responsible for which portion of his damages.

Upon Health's timely petition, the case was removed to the United States district court in State A. Thereafter, Ped moved to have the case remanded to the applicable state court in State A. Ped's motion was granted.

After remand, Health demurred on the grounds of improper joinder of several causes of action. The demurrer was overruled.

Both Health and Driver filed answers denying liability and damages. Ped then filed timely requests for admissions asking that each defendant admit liability, reserving for trial only the issue of damages. Both defendants filed timely objections on the grounds that the requests called for legal conclusions. The objections were sustained.

Following a jury trial, a verdict was returned in favor of Ped and against both defendants in the sum of $43,652.89. Ped moved for a new trial on the issue of damages and, in the alternative, on all issues. He supported his motion by the affidavits of five jurors who stated that: (1) immediately after entering the jury room, the jurors took a ballot on the issue of whether Ped should recover and the vote was 12 to 0 in favor of Ped and against both defendants; (2) each juror then wrote down his/her idea of the amount of the recovery; the figures were totaled, divided by 12, and the result was $43,652.89; and (3) all jurors then agreed that their verdict would be $43,652.89. Based upon defendants' objections, the court refused to consider the affidavits and denied Ped's motion for a new trial.

Discuss the correctness of the court's rulings, setting forth the arguments which might reasonably be made in support of and in opposition to each of the following:

1. Health's motion to remand;

2. Health's demurrer;

3. Ped's request for admissions; and

4. Ped's motion for a new trial.

Question 13

Abel, an African American citizen of State Red, attempted to rent an apartment in a building in State Red owned by Cozy Nook, Inc., a State Red corporation. Abel's offer to rent was refused, and the apartment was rented to Dod for a term of two years.

Abel then obtained housing in State White, and sued Cozy Nook in a State White court of general jurisdiction, alleging a racially motivated denial of housing in violation of a federal statute. The complaint prayed for money damages and a mandatory injunction requiring defendant to give plaintiff possession of the apartment plaintiff had offered to rent or a similar apartment in the same building. Cozy Nook maintained a bank account in State White at Bank, but had no other business dealings in that state. This account was attached by Abel after notice and a hearing attended by Cozy Nook's president. The president of Cozy Nook was also (pursuant to State White law) personally served in State White with notice of the summons and complaint in the main action.

The federal statute authorized actions to be brought in "appropriate state or local courts of general jurisdiction," as well as federal court. The statute has been construed by the U.S. Supreme Court to require trial by jury in federal court suits. State White law does not provide for a jury trial in such cases.

Cozy Nook:

A. Moved to dismiss the action on the grounds that:

    1. Dod was not a party;

    2. The court lacked jurisdiction over the person;

    3. Proper service had not been accomplished;

    4. State White was an inconvenient forum; and

B. Made a timely demand for jury trial if the action was not dismissed.

How should the court rule on each ground set forth in the motion to dismiss and on the demand for jury trial?

Discuss.

Question 14

Tinselware, Inc., an Arizona corporation, sells widgets only in Phoenix, Arizona. Maureen, an employee of Tinselware, initiates telephone negotiations with Don, hoping he will purchase widgets for resale in California. Don, domiciled in San Francisco, responds to Maureen's telephone call by driving to Phoenix.

While in Phoenix, Don buys seventy-five thousand widgets at one dollar each. After returning to California, Don discovers that the widgets do not function properly. He files a breach of contract action against Tinselware in the U.S. district court in San Francisco.

Summons and complaint are hand delivered to Maureen in Arizona, on behalf of Tinselware, Inc. Don then mailed a copy of the summons and complaint to the president of Tinselware (a permissible means of service of process under California law).

Tinselware successfully moved to have the action dismissed because of (1) lack of subject matter and personal jurisdiction, and (2) lack of proper service. If Tinselware's motions had been denied, it would have attempted to have the action transferred to the U.S. district court in Nevada so that each party could travel an approximately equal distance to attend trial. Don then filed a new complaint against Maureen in the U.S. district court in San Francisco. However, the applicable statute of limitations had run after dismissal of the first suit and prior to refiling the second suit, so his action was dismissed.

1. Was the court's dismissal of the original action on each of the grounds stated correct?

2. Could the court have transferred the action to a federal district court in Nevada?

3. Was the dismissal of Don's action against Maureen correct?

Question 15

Defendant airliner, carrying passengers and cargo from Boston to Philadelphia, skidded off the runway during takeoff, causing minor injuries to all the passengers. There were forty passengers aboard from various states. Pete was one of the passengers. Pete is domiciled in Arizona, but owns several apartment houses in Los Angeles, California (which is in the central district of California).

Pete files a diversity class action against Defendant in U.S. district court in the central district of California. Pete seeks a $80,000 recovery for his minor personal injuries and to recover for injuries suffered by each of the other passengers. There is some non-conclusive indication that Donald Company's engine may have malfunctioned during takeoff, causing the accident. Donald Company is a Delaware corporation. Its principal place of business is in Massachusetts.

Defendant is incorporated in Massachusetts. However, the majority of its flights originate and land on the west coast, and the defendant's main booking terminal and reservation center is in Arizona. Defendant would prefer to defend in Massachusetts, where the crash occurred and it believes juries are less liberal.

Defendant made the following motions:

1. That the court is not competent;

2. That a class action is not appropriate;

3. That venue is not proper; and

4. That if venue is proper, the action should be transferred to the appropriate federal district court in Massachusetts.

Defendant has also impleaded the Donald Company.

Discuss the likely outcome of Defendant's motions and its impleader action.

Question 16

Paul sued Doe in the appropriate U.S. district court in State X for personal injuries, including a broken leg, allegedly caused by Doe's negligent operation of a motor vehicle. Suit was filed January 2, 1990. The injuries were alleged to have been, and in fact were, received on March 1, 1989. Thereafter the following took place:

On July 1, 1990, Paul filed a motion for leave to file an amended complaint, setting forth that in the previous month, while doing exercises prescribed by his doctor to strengthen the leg that was broken, he fell and suffered a fracture of the *other* leg, for which he claimed additional damages of $10,000. The court denied the motion. A one-year statute of limitations is applicable to all actions in State X.

On July 25, 1990, Doe filed an answer denying liability and alleging, as a further and separate defense, that on February 20, 1990, in consideration of the sum of $10,000 paid to Paul by Doe, Paul had executed a release of all claims he had against Doe. Paul then asked for and was granted leave to file a second amended complaint adding a count for rescission of the release on the grounds of fraud. Doe filed an appropriate answer to the second amended complaint, denying any fraud.

Doe applied for an order requiring Paul to submit to a physical examination and to furnish copies of all of his medical and hospital reports since the date of the accident and for one year prior thereto. The court issued the order over Paul's objection that the matters were privileged and not relevant.

Paul timely demanded a jury trial. Doe thereafter moved that the issues raised by the second amended complaint be tried first, by the court (without a jury). Doe's motion was granted.

Discuss the correctness of the court's ruling on each of the following:

1. Paul's motion for leave to file his first amended complaint.

2. Paul's motion for leave to file his second amended complaint.

3. Doe's application for an order for a physical examination and copies of his medical reports.

4. Doe's motion for an initial trial before the court (without a jury) on the issues raised by the second amended complaint.

Question 17

Smith, a citizen of State X, was an employee of Zonco, a corporation which was incorporated and had its principal place of business in State X. A truck owned by Zonco, while driven by Smith, struck Paul, a citizen of State Y. Paul was injured and sued Zonco for $150,000 in the U.S. district court in State X, alleging that Zonco and Smith were negligent. Smith was not made a party defendant.

Zonco made a motion to dismiss the complaint for failure to join Smith. The motion was overruled. Thereafter, Zonco answered, denying the negligence of either Zonco or Smith, and further denying that Paul was injured.

Paul then served Zonco with a notice to produce a written statement made and signed by a co-worker of Smith who was riding with Smith at the time of the accident. The statement had been obtained by an adjuster for Zonco's insurance carrier. Zonco refused to produce the statement and the court sustained that refusal.

Paul took the deposition of Smith at which Smith testified under oath that (1) Paul was crossing the intersection in the pedestrian crosswalk with the green light, and (2) the truck driven by Smith ran into Paul because the brakes failed. Paul filed the deposition with a motion for summary judgment on the issue of liability, reserving for the jury only the question of damages. The motion was denied.

The action was tried before a jury. At the conclusion of the evidence, Zonco moved for a directed verdict ("judgment as a matter of law"). There was uncontradicted testimony introduced at trial that Smith was employed by Zonco and Paul had suffered a severe, painful injury as a consequence of the accident, and that his special damages for medical and hospital bills and loss of earnings were $80,000. The jury returned a verdict in the sum of $85,000. Zonco moved for a judgment notwithstanding the verdict. This motion was denied. Paul moved for a new trial solely on the issue of damages. The trial judge ordered that the motion should be granted, unless Zonco consented to an increase in the judgment to $95,000.

Discuss the arguments which might reasonably have been made to the trial court in support of, and in opposition to, the court's rulings on:

1. Zonco's motion to dismiss for failure to join Smith;
2. Paul's notice to produce;
3. Paul's motion for summary judgment;
4. Zonco's motion for judgment notwithstanding the verdict; and
5. Paul's motion for a new trial.

Question 18

On January 25, Paul (an inventor) sued Dumbo, Inc. (a manufacturer of video games) in the U.S. district court in Ohio. Paul is a citizen of that state. Dumbo is incorporated in Delaware. Its principal place of business is in Pennsylvania. However, it maintains a warehouse in Ohio, (from which it sells its products directly to local retailers) where it does approximately 5% of its gross sales.

Paul's complaint contends that he invented a new video game (called "Enemy Attack") which Dumbo had produced and sold in violation of Paul's common law copyright rights. Paul sought damages of $100,000 and an injunction prohibiting Dumbo from making any further sales of the game. Pursuant to Ohio law, service of process was made upon Dumbo by personally serving each member of its board of directors.

On February 10, Dumbo filed an FRCP 12(b) motion to dismiss Paul's complaint on the grounds that (1) it failed to state a claim upon which relief could be granted, (2) the court lacked personal jurisdiction over it, and (3) service of process was improper because it was not accomplished pursuant to the FRCP. The initial contention was supported by a Points and Authorities which asserted that no case had, as yet, extended common law copyright rights to video games. Dumbo's motion was denied.

On February 20, Dumbo answered Paul's complaint, contending that, while it had entered into an agreement with Paul for the rights to distribute the "Enemy Attack" video game, it had been sued by Susan on the grounds that Paul had "stolen" the game from her. As a result, Dumbo had been obliged to pay Susan $80,000 for the rights to "Enemy Attack" after its attorneys determined her action was probably meritorious. Additionally, Dumbo claimed it had "loaned" Paul a computer and numerous electronic components which he said were necessary to create the game; but Paul had sold these items to other persons. In addition to its answer, Dumbo's response contained a counterclaim, demanding reimbursement of the $80,000 paid to Susan and an additional $10,000 (reflecting the alleged value of the materials delivered to Paul). Dumbo's answer and counterclaim were delivered to Paul's attorney on February 23.

On March 14, Dumbo requested the clerk of the court to enter a default on its counterclaim. The clerk did so. On March 16, Dumbo asked for a judgment on the default in the amount of $90,000 (as per its counterclaim), and the judgment was so entered.

On April 20, Dumbo moved for a judgment on the pleadings with respect to Paul's claim, contending that (1) by failing to answer its affirmative defense of material breach, Paul had admitted the assertions contained therein, and (2) by reason of the default judgment which had now become final, Paul was barred from denying Dumbo's defense that Paul materially breached their agreement.

Paul replied that (1) the default judgment was prematurely entered, and is therefore invalid, and (2) pursuant to FRCP 60(b), Paul should be relieved of the default judgment because a summer clerk, to whom Paul's attorney had given the answer and counterclaim for the purpose of making copies, had accidentally misplaced the item in the copying room. As a result, Paul's attorney failed to note on his calendar the date when a response to Dumbo's counterclaim was made.

Discuss the court's rulings on Dumbo's FRCP 12(b) motion, and the likely outcome of:

1. Dumbo's motion for judgment on the pleadings, and

2. Paul's motion to be relieved from Dumbo's default judgment.

Question 19

Salco is a corporation, incorporated and having its principal place of business in State A. Its sole business is the sale of products by mail order. It advertises its products in national magazines. None of these magazines is published in State B. Salco employs no agents or salespeople.

Poe, a citizen of State B, commenced a class action in a competent State B court against Salco for fraud and misrepresentation in the sale of certain hi-tech alarm clocks to him and other citizens of State B. He alleged that 300 such clocks were sold to citizens of State B, and that he and each such person was damaged in the sum of $250. He asked for actual damages in the amount of $75,000, and punitive damages in the sum of $25,000,000. In accordance with State B law, process was served on Salco by sending a copy of the complaint and summons by registered mail, return receipt requested, to the president of Salco at its principal place of business in State A.

Salco filed a petition for removal from the State B court to the United States district court in State B. After removal, Salco filed a 12(b) motion to dismiss the matter. The motion was denied. Poe then filed a motion to remand to the State B court on the ground that the complaint did not state a claim within the jurisdiction of the United States district court.

The motion was denied. Salco then moved for a more definite statement. This motion was also denied. The action then proceeded to trial. Judgment on the merits was rendered in favor of Salco.

After the judgment was final, Jones, a citizen of State B, filed an action in a State B court against Salco, based on the same claims of fraud and misrepresentation in the sale to him of one of the 200 alarm clocks. Salco filed a motion to dismiss upon the ground that the judgment in *Poe v. Salco* was a bar to the action by Jones. The motion was granted.

1. Was the United States district court correct in its rulings on:

   a. The FRCP 12(b) motion to dismiss the case;

   b. The motion to remand in *Poe v. Salco* on the ground that the complaint did not state a claim within the jurisdiction of the United States district court;

   c. The motion for a more definite statement?

2. Was the State B state court correct in its ruling on the motion to dismiss in *Jones v. Salco* on the ground that the prior judgment was a bar?

Question 20

Paul, a citizen of the State of Calvada, purchased a box of breakfast cereal produced by Krispy at a grocery store in Calvada. As part of a promotional campaign by Krispy, there was a certificate in the box which stated that by sending "the certificate and one dollar to Glassco, A Street, Central City, State of Black, USA," the sender would receive by return mail six cocktail glasses. Paul sent in the certificate and one dollar and thereafter received the glasses. While he was washing them for the first time, one shattered in his hand, cutting the tendons and permanently injuring Paul.

Paul sued Glassco for $100,000 in a Calvada state court, basing jurisdiction on a Calvada statute giving its courts jurisdiction over "any person who commits a tortious act in this state with respect to any cause of action arising out of such act." The statute further provided that in such cases, process could be served on a foreign corporation by mailing a copy of the summons and complaint by registered mail, return receipt requested, to the corporation at its "place of business outside of the state." Glassco was incorporated in and had its principal place of business in State White.

Copies of the summons and complaint were mailed by registered mail, return receipt requested, addressed to "Glassco, A Street, Central City, State of Black, USA" and were returned with the notation "not accepted by addressee."

After the statutory time for appearance had expired, the default of Glassco was entered and the case heard as a default matter. Other than medical testimony, the only evidence received was Paul's testimony concerning the manner in which he obtained the glasses and the fact that while he was carefully washing one glass it shattered in his hand. Judgment was in Paul's favor for $25,000.

1. Is the Calvada verdict a valid judgment? Discuss.

2. Assuming it is a valid judgment, may Glassco nevertheless have it set aside and, if so, on what grounds? Discuss.

3. Assuming the judgment is set aside, and a new trial is held, is Paul likely to prevail if the only evidence offered by him is the same as that presented at the hearing at which the default judgment was rendered? Discuss.

Question 21

Peter is a citizen of State Red. Stanford James is a citizen of State White. On August 20, 1990, in State White, Peter was injured when the car he was driving collided with a car owned and driven by Stanford James. The applicable statute of limitations in both States Red and White is two years.

On August 16, 1992, Peter filed suit in the U.S. district court for State Red to recover for personal injuries he received in the collision. The complaint set forth the correct date and place of the collision, but erroneously named the defendant as James Stanford.

On August 30, 1992, while Stanford James was in State Red at the invitation of Peter to discuss the settlement of Peter's claim, he was personally served with the summons and complaint. Thereafter the following occurred:

Stanford James filed a 12(b) motion to dismiss the action, or, in the alternative, to transfer the action to the U.S. district court in State White on the ground of *forum non conveniens*. Both motions were denied.

Peter then moved to amend his complaint to name Stanford James as defendant in place of James Stanford. The motion was granted.

Stanford James then filed an answer which, among other matters, alleged that Peter's claim was barred by the statute of limitations. James then moved for judgment on the pleadings on that ground. The motion was granted.

Assuming all appropriate grounds were urged in support of and in opposition to each of the motions mentioned, was the trial court correct in its rulings on the:

1. Rule 12(b) motion? Discuss.

2. Motion to dismiss for *forum non conveniens*? Discuss.

3. Motion to amend the complaint? Discuss.

4. Motion for judgment on the pleadings? Discuss.

Question 22

While visiting Austin, Texas, Paul was arrested outside of Silley's Department Store (an exclusive men's clothing store). As he was departing, Mary Poppins, the cashier at Silleys, shouted "Stop thief!" Bill Joe Bobb, a police officer who responded to Mary's shout, tackled Paul and applied a chokehold, allegedly causing him serious, permanent injuries.

Both Poppins and Bobb are citizens of Texas. Bobb lives in Austin. Paul is a citizen of Oklahoma. Bobb owns a 5% limited partnership interest in an 8-unit apartment house in Oklahoma. The limited partnership was formed in Texas, and is operated by a general partner who is domiciled in Texas. As a limited partner, Bobb has no say in how limited partnership assets are operated. Silley's does a mail order business from its department store, and 14% of its mail order sales are to persons in Oklahoma (this represents 3% of Silley's total business). Silley's is a Texas corporation. Its principal place of business is Texas.

Question 1:

Paul sued Bobb and Silley's in the U.S. district court in Oklahoma. He claimed they committed false imprisonment and were each liable to him for $85,000. Silley's and Bobb do *not* desire to stand trial in Oklahoma. Describe their procedural alternatives. Assume the Texas and Oklahoma long-arm statutes give their courts all requisites of personal jurisdiction consistent with due process.

Assumption 1 (applicable to questions 2 and 3, only):

Assume Paul did not commence an action in Oklahoma, but moved to Nebraska, where he sued Bobb under a federal civil rights statute and for assault and battery. Assume he also sued Mary and Silley's for false arrest (a tort in Nebraska).

Question 2:

Can Paul join all of these parties in a single action? (Assume personal jurisdiction is satisfied.)

Question 3:

Would the U.S. district court in Nebraska be competent to hear Paul's claim?

Assumption 2 (applicable to questions 4, 5 and 6):

Assume that Paul commenced an action against both Bobb and the Austin, Texas Police Department (the "ATPD") in the U.S. district court in Texas. Paul's claim against the latter is that it is vicariously liable for the conduct of Bobb (which conduct violated a federal civil rights statute). The ATPD, however, construes the applicable U.S. statute as precluding vicarious liability unless the Department authorized the chokehold complained of by the plaintiff. Bobb has claimed that, pursuant to his union's contract with the ATPD, the latter entity must pay legal fees incurred by him in his defense. The ATPD, however, asserts that this obligation does not arise if the conduct is alleged to be unconstitutional.

Question 4:

How can the ATPD raise its claim that it is not vicariously liable for Bobb's conduct?

Question 5:

Can Bobb assert a claim against the ATPD in the present action (*Paul v. Bobb and the ATPD*)?

Question 6:

Numerous police departments around the country are concerned that if Paul's alleged federal claim is successful, similar actions will be pursued against them. As a consequence, they desire to intervene upon the side of the ATPD. Will they be permitted to do so?

Question 23

Pam (P), a patient injured in a nursing home fire, brought a suit for $77,000 against the home's operators (D, Inc.) in U.S. District Court in State X, where the nursing home in which P resides is located. Jurisdiction was properly based on diversity of citizenship, because even though D resides in state X, her domicile is actually in State Y. Under the law of State X, the failure of a nursing home to install smoke detectors in each patient's room is considered negligence per se. P alleged D's failure to install the device; D's answer denied all allegations in the complaint.

P promptly moved for summary judgment as to liability, attaching her own sworn affidavit stating that no smoke detector had been installed in her room. D's attorney responded with a memorandum asserting, "My client stands by its Answer in this case." The court denied the motion.

P then initiated discovery. She first served an interrogatory on D asking whether it had installed a smoke detector in P's room. The appropriate corporate official responded, "No."

P also requested D to produce for inspection its fire investigator's report, hoping that the investigator's early investigation of the since-demolished home showed no smoke detectors present. D refused to comply with the discovery request. P moved to compel production, and the court ordered D to produce the report for inspection and also held D in contempt of court for refusing the discovery request.

At trial, Mac (M), D's maintenance director, testified that smoke detectors had been installed in P's room; P's motion to disallow M's testimony as inconsistent with the interrogatory answer was denied.

Was the district court correct in its ruling:

1. On P's motion for summary judgment as to liability?

2. On P's motion to compel production of the fire investigator's report?

3. Holding D in contempt for refusing P's discovery request?

4. On P's motion to disallow M's testimony concerning the installation of a smoke detector in P's room?

Discuss.

Question 24

Borrow, a resident of State A, obtained a $12,000 car loan from Finco. Finco is incorporated and has its principal place of business in State A. When Borrow began making installment repayments against the loan, he was dismayed to learn that his required monthly payments were in an amount greater than he had expected.

Borrow brought suit against Finco in a state court in State A, asserting a claim under the federal Truth-in-Lending Act (TLA). TLA specifically requires lenders to disclose to a borrower in a consumer loan transaction the amount of the monthly loan payment. TLA further provides that a borrower whose rights under TLA have been violated may bring an action against the lender in a United States District Court, or in any other court of competent jurisdiction.

Finco filed its answer denying liability and asserting a counterclaim against Borrow under state law for recovery of the full amount owed on the loan. Finco then timely removed the suit to the United States District Court for the District of State A. In the District Court, Borrow moved to remand the action. The motion was denied.

Shortly thereafter Borrow moved to amend his complaint to: (1) add an additional defendant, Dealer, the company that had sold him the car; (2) allege that Dealer violated State A's Consumer Protection Law (CPL) by providing him erroneous information about the terms of his loan; and (3) allege that Dealer's CPL violation had resulted in $20,000 in damages. Dealer is incorporated in State A and conducts all of its business there. The District Court denied the motion to amend on the ground that the court lacked subject matter jurisdiction over Borrow's claim against Dealer.

Borrow next moved for partial summary judgment which, if granted, would preclude Finco from denying that its lending agreement violated TLA. In support of this motion, Borrow offered uncontradicted evidence that in previous lawsuits brought by other borrowers in federal court, final judgments had been entered against Finco on holdings that, under circumstances identical with those in the present lawsuit, Finco's failure to make the required loan payment disclosure violated TLA. Borrow's motion was denied.

Were the District Court's rulings correct as to:

1. Borrow's motion to remand?

2. Borrow's motion to amend his complaint?

3. Borrow's motion for partial summary judgment?

Discuss.

Question 25

On March 1 of last year, Paul, a citizen of State X, was involved in a three-car accident in State Y with Dave and Al, both of whom are State Y citizens. Wilma, Paul's wife, was a passenger in his car. Immediately after the accident, Wilma obtained signed statements from two witnesses. Later, Paul employed Len, a lawyer, to study the statements and advise him. Len made some handwritten notes on the statements and placed them in his files.

On February 15 of this year, Paul filed a complaint against Dave in the United States District Court for State Y. All allegations of the complaint and the prayer for relief are set forth below:

> 1. Plaintiff is a citizen of State X. Defendant is a citizen of State Y. The amount in controversy, exclusive of interest and costs, exceeds $75,000.

> 2. On March 1 of last year, Defendant negligently operated his automobile and collided with Plaintiff's automobile.

> 3. As a result, Plaintiff suffered personal injuries, pain of body and mind, and incurred medical expenses in the sum of $25,000.

> Wherefore, Plaintiff prays for a judgment against Defendant of $250,000.

Dave timely answered Paul's complaint as follows:

> Defendant neither admits nor denies the allegations of Plaintiff's complaint, but demands strict proof of each and every allegation.

Paul did not amend his complaint, but moved for judgment on the pleadings. Dave countered with his own motion for judgment on the pleadings. The District Court denied both motions.

On May 1 of this year, Paul successfully moved to amend his complaint, adding Al as an additional defendant. After being properly served with a copy of the amended complaint, Al moved to dismiss on the ground that the applicable one-year statute of limitations for personal injury actions had expired at the time the amendment was filed and before he had notice of Paul's action. A statute of State Y provides:

> If an action is filed within the limitations period provided by law, a new defendant added after the running of that period shall not be entitled to dismissal on the ground that the period has run, if the claim against the new defendant arises out of the same occurrence as the original claim.

In the belief that this statute was controlling, the District Court denied Al's motion.

Thereafter, Al served an interrogatory on Paul asking whether Paul took "the statements of any witnesses to the accident" and requesting the submission of "copies of any such statements." Paul asserted that the interrogatory was "objectionable on grounds of work product" and refused to provide any answer or produce any documents. Al moved for an order compelling (1) an answer to the interrogatory, and (2) the production of the requested documents. The motion was granted.

Did the court rule correctly on:

1. The motions for judgment on the pleadings?

2. Al's motion to dismiss?

3. Al's motion to compel an answer to his interrogatory and the production of documents?

Discuss.

Question 26

Dan was flying his small airplane through the dark of night from his home in State X to a resort in State Y. Before he could reach his destination, he made a forced landing on a highway in State Z and hit a truck driven by Price, a resident of State Y. The truck was demolished and Price sustained personal injuries resulting in medical expenses in excess of $75,000. Although a State Z statute requires the use of headlights after sunset, the trucks headlights were not on at the time of the accident and Dan did not see the truck.

Price sued Dan in the U.S. District Court of State Z, basing jurisdiction on diversity of citizenship. The complaint stated in relevant part, "Defendant negligently failed to operate his plane in a safe manner including, specifically, failure to use carburetor heat, causing his engine to fail and causing him to crash into plaintiff."

Dan filed an answer denying negligence on his part. Neither the complaint nor the answer made any allegations of contributory negligence or the lack thereof.

Prior to trial, Dan filed a timely motion requesting that the owner of the truck, Trucko, be made a party on the ground that Trucko is indispensable to the full and final resolution of the dispute. Trucko is incorporated in State X. Trucko conducts no business in State Z, but its trucks occasionally, though not regularly, use State Z highways on trips between State X and State Y. The court denied the motion on the grounds that it had no jurisdiction over Trucko and that, even if it had jurisdiction, service of process would be difficult.

Price moved for an examination of Dan by a physician to determine whether Dan's eyesight, hearing, and physical dexterity were adequate for piloting an airplane. Over Dan's opposition, the motion was granted.

At a pretrial conference, the court entered an order stating that the case would be tried on the issue of Dan's negligence. The issue of contributory negligence was not discussed.

At the trial, Dan introduced evidence without objection, showing that the engine failed without any known cause, that this presented a sudden emergency, and that Dan could not see Price's truck because its headlights were off.

Over Price's timely objections, the court instructed the jury that it could consider the issue of possible contributory negligence on the part of Price.

Was the court correct in:

1. Denying Dan's motion to make Trucko a party and allowing the case to go forward without the presence of Trucko?

2. Granting Price's motion for a physical examination of Dan?

3. Allowing the jury to consider the issue of contributory negligence?

Discuss.

Essay Exam Answers

Answer to Question 1

Did the court properly deny APOW's motion to dismiss?

For a complaint to be sufficient under the FRCP, it must contain: (1) a proper competency allegation, (2) a short, plain statement of the claim, and (3) a description of the relief demanded by the plaintiff. The facts indicate that subject matter jurisdiction was "properly" based on diversity of citizenship, and so it must be assumed that each member of the class suffered harm in excess of $75,000. [Note that in May, 1997, Congress raised the amount in controversy requirement from $50,000 to $75,000.] APOW ("D") probably contended that the facts described in the complaint (that emissions from the plant had injured people) are not sufficient to put it on notice of the nature of the action against it. However, the plaintiffs probably argued in rebuttal that D should have recognized that numerous possible legal theories (strict liability, nuisance, negligence and trespass) were being asserted, and so D was on proper notice. While under FRCP 10(b) each claim should be set forth in a separate count, this defect alone would not justify dismissal of the action.

D probably also argued that the damages or relief claimed by the plaintiffs is not clearly described (from the given facts, this assertion appears to be well taken). Plaintiffs probably contended in rebuttal, however, that by their prayer for "damages" they intended to recover whatever losses or injuries were proven at trial. Since a court would probably accept this interpretation, D's motion was properly denied. (*See* ELO Ch.4-V(B-F).)

Was the grant of certification proper?

For a class action to be maintained (1) there must be common questions of law or fact, and (2) the representative's claim must be typical of the class represented. D probably argued that since the plaintiffs were injured on the third day of the emissions, their claims are not representative of persons harmed on the first and second days. Also, each of the plaintiffs may have been injured to a different extent, and possibly in a different manner (if different types of emissions were involved). If so, there would be no common factual issues. However, if it is likely that the emissions were all from the same source (i.e., a malfunctioning valve), certification was probably proper. The types of claims for all three days would be identical and the question of D's liability would be common to the entire class. In such instance, the representative's claims would be typical of the class (at least until it can be established that each day's emissions were from a different source). (*See* ELO Ch.8-V(B)(1) & (C)(2).)

Was the memorandum discoverable?

The discoverability of the memo depends initially on the FRCP. If it would be discoverable under the FRCP, no conflict with state law would exist (since the state has no work product doctrine). If it would **not** be discoverable under the FRCP, then an "**Erie**" issue is presented.

Under FRCP 26(b)(3), a party may discover documents prepared in anticipation of litigation or for trial by another party or her counsel, only upon showing a substantial need for the items and that they (or their "substantial equivalent") cannot otherwise be obtained without undue hardship. Plaintiffs probably contended that the memo involved was not within this privilege because it was not prepared in anticipation of litigation (i.e., there is no indication that anyone was threatening suit against D over minor accidents at **another** company's plant). D probably argued in rebuttal that (1) the memo was created to assist D in responding to claims which would inevitably be made when similar "incidents" occurred at a D plant, (2) there was no reason why plaintiffs could not re-create the memo by doing their own research, and (3) to the extent that the memo contained the lawyer's impressions or conclusions, it would absolutely be non-discoverable. Thus, the memo probably would **not** be discoverable under the FRCP. (*See* ELO Ch.5-II(E)(7-8).)

Assuming the memo was **not** discoverable under the FRCP, plaintiffs could have contended that, under the "**Erie**" doctrine, where state substantive law conflicts with the FRCP, the latter is superseded by the former. While D could have argued that *Hanna v. Plumer*, 380 U.S. 460 (1965), held that where a provision of the FRCP was validly enacted, it is controlling when in conflict with any state rule, most authorities view *Hanna* as addressing only the situation where there is a direct conflict between two "procedural" rules. Where the state rule is properly characterized as being substantive in nature (i.e., it embodies an "important" state interest), that interest will be controlling.

Plaintiffs could contend that the state legislature has a strong desire to permit discovery of any relevant unprivileged information because it abolishes the work product rule. Thus, the FRCP provision is in conflict with a substantive rule of law (and therefore the memo should be discoverable). However, since (1) discovery has always been associated with the procedural aspects of trial, (2) there is no state enactment that expressly makes work product discoverable, and (3) plaintiffs chose to litigate in a federal court (which would normally apply the FRCP), the court's decision permitting discovery of the memorandum was probably incorrect. (*See* ELO Ch.6-III(D).)

Answer to Question 2

Was Trucker ("T") an indispensable party in the State X action?

Under FRCP 19(a), a person is indispensable where (1) complete relief cannot be given to the existing parties if he is not joined, (2) the absentee's interests will be substantially prejudiced if he is not joined, or (3) the parties already subject to the action might be exposed to inconsistent judgments or double liability if he is not joined. In this instance, complete relief can be given (i.e., Rider can obtain a judgment for the full amount of his injuries from Owner). Also, T's interests will *not* be substantially prejudiced if he is not joined (joining T could only expose him to the possibility of an adverse judgment).

Owner ("O") could contend, however, that since he and T were joint tortfeasors, he could be liable for the entire judgment if T were not joined (whereas if T were joined, and they were deemed to be joint tortfeasors, O would have a right of contribution against T). Thus, the failure to join T exposes O to excessive liability. Nevertheless, Rider ("R") could probably successfully argue in rebuttal that O would not be substantially prejudiced by the failure to join since a tortfeasor has no right to expect that the plaintiff will pursue every potentially culpable party. Finally, there would be no possibility of inconsistent judgments. Since T was adjudged *not* liable in O's lawsuit, there would appear to be no way in which T could have concurrently acted in an unreasonable manner with respect to O's passenger. Thus, T was not an indispensable party. (*See* ELO Ch.8-IV(D)(1-2).)

Was the State X court correct in granting T's motion to intervene?

Under FRCP 24(a) a party has a right to intervene when the disposition of an action may, as a practical matter, impair his interests and these interests are *not* likely to be adequately represented by the existing parties. T would probably *not* come within this standard because his interests would not appear to be affected by the *R v. O* litigation. Since R's conduct with respect to the accident was different from T's, whether R won or lost would have no effect on a possible subsequent lawsuit by T against O.

However, under FRCP 24(b), one may be permitted to intervene where there is a common question of law or fact between (1) the existing action, and (2) the claim or defense sought to be asserted by the intervenor. A trial court arguably could determine that R and T share a common claim with respect to the transaction (i.e., that O operated his vehicle in a negligent manner). Thus, the trial court's decision to permit T to intervene was probably correct. (*See* ELO Ch.8-VI(B-C).)

Was the State X court correct in permitting R to cross-claim against T?

Under FRCP 13(g), a party may assert a cross-claim against a co-party if his action arises out of the occurrence which is the subject of the original action. Since R's claim against T arises out of the collision between O and T, there is little question that the court was correct in permitting R to cross-claim against T. (*See* ELO Ch.8-X(B)(1).)

What is the effect of the federal action on R's action against O?

The federal action would have no effect on R's state court action against O, since the fact that T was not negligent vis-a-vis O would *not* imply that O had failed to act reasonably with respect to R.

What is the effect of the federal action on R's cross-claim against T?

Under *res judicata* principles, where there has been a prior, final judgment between the parties or their privies with respect to the cause of action being asserted in a subsequent lawsuit, the latter action is barred. (*See* ELO Ch.9-III(C)(1).)However, O and R do not appear to be in privity with each other. O was not R's legal representative (sometimes called "procedural privy"), nor was there any type of legal relationship between O and R (sometimes called "substantive privy"). Thus, the prior federal lawsuit would probably have no effect upon R's cross-complaint against T.

What is the effect of the federal action upon T's claim against O in the federal district court?

Under FRCP 13(a), one must assert a counterclaim which he has against the opposing party if it (1) arises out of the occurrence which is the basis of the latter's claim against the former, and (2) there is no need for the presence of third parties over whom the court cannot acquire jurisdiction. If this is not done, the claim is barred. Since (1) T's claim for personal injury damages arose out of the collision between O and T (which was the basis for the former's state court action against the latter), and (2) R's presence was not necessary to T's claim against O, T will probably be barred from suing O now. (*See* ELO Ch.9-II(D)(3).)

What is the effect of the federal action upon O's counter-claim against T?

Under the *res judicata* principles described above, O's counterclaim against T for personal injuries would be merged into the earlier federal court decision that T had no liability to O.

Answer to Question 3

The motion to dismiss based upon subject matter and personal jurisdiction:

For a U.S. district court to be competent, there must be diversity of citizenship (no plaintiff and no defendant may be citizens of the same state) and the amount in controversy must exceed $75,000. [Note that in May, 1997, Congress raised the amount in controversy requirement from $50,000 to $75,000.] Seler ("S") could respond that the amount in controversy alleged by Byer ("B") is only $37,500. However, B could contend that even though the majority view is that the controversy must be worth "in excess of $75,000" to the *plaintiff,* some district courts have held that the jurisdictional amount is satisfied when the benefit or cost to *either party* could exceed $75,000. This approach amply serves the Congressional policy of keeping petty cases out of the courts. Since there is the possibility that the $85,000 figure is *not* a mistake, B could prevail on this issue. (*See* ELO Ch.3-V(B-D).)

For a court to take personal jurisdiction over an out-of-state defendant: (1) there must be a long-arm statute which permits it to do so (since the facts are silent, we'll assume that State B's long-arm statute gave its courts all personal jurisdiction consistent with due process), and (2) the defendant must have sufficient minimum contacts with the forum so as not to offend traditional notions of fair play and substantial justice. B would contend that since the contract was signed in State B, S has sufficient minimum contacts with that jurisdiction. However, an isolated appearance in one state for the purpose of concluding a business transaction pertaining to property in another state is probably *not* constitutionally adequate to create personal jurisdiction. Thus, the district court erred in denying S's motion to dismiss for lack of personal jurisdiction. (*See* ELO Ch.2-I(D-E).)

S's demand for a jury trial:

Pursuant to FRCP 38(a) and the Seventh Amendment, each party is entitled to a jury trial with respect to legal issues. While reformation has traditionally been recognized as an equitable (rather than legal) claim, S could have contended that the reformation question is inextricably associated with the legal issue of whether B breached the contract by refusing to pay S $85,000 for Whiteacre. Since *Beacon Theatres, Inc. v. Westover,* 359 U.S. 500 (1959), said legal claims must be tried prior to equitable ones, S's demand for a jury trial probably should *not* have been denied. (*See* ELO Ch.7-XIII(D-E).)

Disclosure of the appraisers' identities and the appraisals:

Pursuant to FRCP 34, documents and other tangible things must be obtained by a request to produce. Since S demanded the appraisal reports within the context of interrogatories, B was not required to comply. Thus, the court ruled correctly in this instance.

B probably objected to the other information requested on the ground that it was irrelevant (appraisal reports would not necessarily indicate the price the parties agreed to) and, possibly, that it represented B's work product.

The first objection probably would *not* be successful because a party may ordinarily obtain disclosure of any information which is reasonably calculated to lead to the discovery of admissible evidence; FRCP 26(b)(1). If the appraisals were made *prior to* the commencement of the action, they would tend to show the fair market value of Whiteacre, and therefore the probable purchase price agreed upon by the parties.

If B's appraisals showed that the land was worth $85,000, it is unlikely that S would have sold it to him for $37,500. Conversely, if the land was worth $37,500, it would tend to corroborate that a mistake had been made (i.e., B probably would not have agreed to pay $85,000 for Whiteacre). If the appraisals were made *after* the litigation had commenced, they would still be admissible (to the extent they did not contain advice or suggestions to B's attorney) because S would have the right to know the nature of the evidence which B intended to present, so that he might counter it.

The second objection will *not* be successful with respect to any expert B expects to call at trial. Under FRCP 26(a)(2), an expert who may be called to testify must prepare a report containing (1) the expert's opinions and the basis for them, (2) the data considered by the expert, (3) any exhibits the expert will use, (4) the expert's qualifications, (5) the compensation he is receiving and (6) a list of other cases in which he has testified within the prior four years. Thus, while B would not have to hand over "work product" documents, B would have to provide the information requested by S concerning the identity of testifying witnesses and their opinions within 90 days of the trial, or the court would have to exclude B from using this evidence at trial; FRCP 37(c)(1).

However, B's second objection will probably succeed with respect to any appraisers B has retained in anticipation of litigation, but who will not testify in the action. The federal rules allow discovery of such experts only upon a showing of *exceptional circumstances*: FRCP 26(b)(4)(B). Since S could retain its own appraisers, the court should not have allowed S to discover the opinions of these experts.

Thus, the court ruled correctly with respect to B's objections concerning the opinion of witnesses B expected to use at trial, but was in error to the extent the order encompassed nontestifying experts. (*See* ELO Ch.5-II(C)(1), (F)(2)(a-b), & (I)(2-4).)

Evidence submitted with respect to the judgment notwithstanding the verdict ("JNOV" or "judgment as a matter of law") motion:

A jury's determination of a factual issue should not be disturbed, unless there was an insufficient evidentiary basis for it. B probably contended that the preponderance of the evidence favored him, since he had introduced expert testimony that the land was worth only $42,200. Nevertheless, based upon the demeanor of the witnesses, the jury could have believed S, while disbelieving the testimony of B and his appraiser. Additionally, the jury might have believed that even though Whiteacre was worth only $42,200, B may have exercised poor business judgment and entered into the transaction anyway. Thus, the court was probably *not* correct in granting B's JNOV.

Procedural arguments:

Pursuant to FRCP 50(b), a party seeking a JNOV (now called "judgment as a matter of law") *must* have made a motion for a directed verdict at the close of all evidence. Since the facts do not indicate that such a motion was made, S should have contended that the JNOV was not properly granted.

Answer to Question 4

Motion to quash:

For a court to exercise personal jurisdiction over an out-of-state defendant, the latter must have sufficient minimum contacts with the forum so as not to offend traditional notions of fair play and substantial justice. There seems to be little question that Daw ("D") did ***not*** have sufficient minimum contacts with State X, since (1) the accident did not occur in that state, (2) D owns no property there, and (3) D only visited the jurisdiction for a short period of time.

However, Paul ("P") might contend that by filing an answer which defended the case on its merits after the objection to personal jurisdiction was overruled, D had waived his right to dispute this matter. While a few courts hold that when one defends on the merits she has waived the right to contest jurisdiction, in this instance we are ***not*** concerned with D's right to appeal (but rather with the correctness of the trial court's ruling). Therefore, it appears the State X court was ***not*** correct in denying D's motion to quash. (*See* ELO Ch.2-I(D) & VII(B)(1).)

Default judgment against D:

Whether the State X court was correct in granting a default judgment depends upon the resolution of two issues: (1) Whether D properly refused to answer the interrogatory; and (2) if he should have answered, whether a default judgment was an excessive sanction.

Was D's conversation with the investigator and his wife privileged?

D probably contended the conversation was not admissible because "confidential" communications to one's spouse and to one's attorney are ordinarily privileged. P probably asserted that (1) the statement to his wife was not confidential, since it was made in front of the investigator, (2) the statement to the investigator was not confidential because it was made in front of his wife, and (3) the investigator was not D's attorney. However, D should have been able to successfully argue in rebuttal that both conversations were "confidential" since (1) the statements were made in front of persons who D reasonably believed would retain his statements in confidence, and (2) the attorney-client privilege ordinarily extends to "essential" personnel of the attorney, such as the investigator. (*See* ELO Ch.5-II(D).)

Assuming the statement was not privileged, is summary judgment an appropriate sanction?

Under FRCP 37(b)(2)(C), if a party refuses to obey a court order after being directed to do so, the court may make such order as is "just" (including the right to render a default judgment against the disobedient party). However, it could be contended by D that the order was not "just" in this instance, since the failure by D to respond to this inquiry didn't materially hinder the ability of P to present his case. Also, even if D had advised his wife and the investigator that he was at fault, he might have been incorrect (not being an attorney, he would not be capable of making this determination, even if he believed he could). Thus, regardless of how damaging D's statements might appear, they would not necessarily be dispositive of the case; and the court probably should *not* have rendered a default judgment. (*See* ELO Ch.5-IV(D)(2)(c).)

How should the district court rule?

P's summary judgment:

Under usual *res judicata* principles, a plaintiff must assert all possible causes of action arising from a particular transaction or occurrence against a defendant in the initial action. Any claims not asserted are thereafter barred. Such claims are considered "merged" into the original judgment. Since the property claim and subsequent personal injury action by P arise from precisely the same facts (the car collision), P's summary judgment ("s.j.") motion should be denied.

However, there are a few jurisdictions which still adhere to a "claim" view of *res judicata*, and therefore perceive personal injuries and property damages as separate "actions." *Res judicata* would not bar P's complaint in these states.

P could alternatively assert issue preclusion. Under collateral estoppel principles, where an issue was actually litigated by a party in a prior case, the determination of that issue is binding upon him in subsequent litigation. However, since the issue of D's negligence was never "actually litigated" (i.e., P was granted a default judgment in the context of sanctions), collateral estoppel would *not* be applicable. Thus, P's s.j. motion should be denied. (*See* ELO Ch.9-II(B)(2)(a-b) & III(B)(2).)

P's motion for s.j. on D's counterclaim:

D's counterclaim ("ccl.") would, in most states, be characterized as "compulsory" since it arose from the same transaction or occurrence which is being asserted as the basis of liability by P. Under the FRCP, if a compulsory ccl. is not asserted in the first instance, it is deemed "forfeited".

However, under *Erie*, a federal district court might be obliged to refer to State X's rule of law with respect to compulsory counterclaims. Assuming State X's rule with respect to ccl's was identical to the FRCP, P's summary judgment motion on D's ccl. would be successful. If X had a contrary rule, however, the federal court must decide if State X's ccl. rule was primarily "substantive" (i.e., the state rule embodies an "important" or "substantial" state interest) or "procedural" in nature. If the necessity of asserting counterclaims is deemed "procedural" in nature, then the FRCP would be controlling, *Hanna v. Plumer*, 380 U.S. 460 (1965). However, since rules of law pertaining to compulsory counterclaims probably represent an **important** state interest (i.e., establishing when someone will, or will not, forfeit a claim); a State X rule of law with respect to ccl.'s which was contrary to the FRCP would probably be controlling.

D's s.j. on P's complaint:

For the reasons described in P's summary judgment, D's motion for s.j. on P's complaint should be granted (i.e., P's personal injury claim against D was probably merged into the initial judgment obtained by P). (*See* ELO Ch.6-III(D) & II(D)(3).)

Answer to Question 5

May State C assert personal jurisdiction over Macco ("M")?

We'll assume that (1) the lawsuit was properly filed and served, and (2) the State C court is competent to hear this matter.

Paula ("P") could initially contend that M is "physically present" in the jurisdiction by reason of (1) the relatively large amount of business which it does in the state through direct sales, and (2) the fact that it maintains an office in State C. M could contend in rebuttal, however, that language in *Shaffer v. Heitner*, 433 U.S. 186 (1977), suggests that all assertions of personal jurisdiction must be tested by the "minimal contacts" standard articulated in *International Shoe* (i.e., the defendant must have sufficient contacts with the forum state so as not to offend traditional notions of fair play and substantial justice). Since the *Shaffer* language would probably be followed, it must be determined if M has sufficient contacts with State C as *not* to contravene due process.

Three factors are generally considered in determining if it is "fair" to cause a defendant to stand trial in a particular state: (1) whether she has purposefully availed herself of the benefits of the forum, (2) whether the action is related to her contacts with that the forum, and (3) whether it was (or should have been) reasonably foreseeable to the defendant that she might be haled into court in that state. P could contend that the first and third factors are satisfied in that (1) Doctor ("D") maintained an office and did a substantial volume of business in State C, and (2) M should have recognized that if one of its machines was defective, D would be drawn into litigation in any jurisdiction in which its machines were sold. M would argue that since its activities in State C are totally unrelated to P's claim, the exercise of personal jurisdiction over M in these circumstances is probably constitutional. (*See* ELO Ch.2-III(C-D), III(G) & V(B)(7).)

Effect of Worker ("W")'s prior lawsuit on P's action against M:

Under *res judicata* principles, where there has been a final, valid judgment on the merits between the parties (or their privies) with respect to the cause of action which is being asserted in a subsequent lawsuit, the latter action is barred. Since M (1) was not a party to the earlier lawsuit, and (2) is not, in any manner, in privy with Hospital ("H"), P should have no difficulty in asserting her wrongful death action against M (despite W's prior unsuccessful suit against H).

Since M and H are not in privy and no specific finding was made with respect to the defectiveness of the machine, issue preclusion (collateral estoppel) would *not* be available to M. (*See* ELO Ch.9-I(A-B).)

Effect of W's prior lawsuit upon P's action against Doctor:

Res judicata would **not** be applicable, since D was not a defendant in the earlier lawsuit, nor was he in privity with Hospital ("H"). In fact, there was a specific finding that D was not H's agent.

The concept of mutuality prohibits assertion of collateral estoppel against a party that could not have asserted collateral estoppel against the party now asserting it. Here, D might attempt to assert collateral estoppel if this jurisdiction does not require mutuality.

Under collateral estoppel, where a particular issue has been actually litigated in a prior action, a court may preclude it from being relitigated where that issue was essential to the outcome of the earlier case. D could contend that (1) P should be deemed to be in privity with W, since — as the administrator of his estate — she is his successor-in-interest, and (2) the issue of D's alleged negligence was actually litigated.

P could argue that (1) the issue of D's negligence was not essential to the earlier case (i.e., a finding that D was not H's agent would have exonerated the latter entity from liability), and (2) her claim is different (i.e., she is seeking to recover for the damages she sustained as a consequence of W's death (rather than for his injuries, for which recovery was sought in the first action). However, D could respond that (1) where there has been a specific finding on an issue, some courts do not require the issue to have been crucial to the actual outcome of the case, and (2) the threshold issue of whether D failed to act reasonably under the circumstances would be identical in both lawsuits (i.e., P cannot recover for damages resulting from W's death, if D had been negligent).

Since (1) P's action is essentially identical to that asserted by W, and (2) the question of D's negligence was actually litigated in the initial action by a party who should be deemed to be in privity with P, a court would probably rule that the earlier finding of D's lack of negligence is binding on P. (*See* ELO Ch.9-III(B-C).)

Answer to Question 6

Did the court err in granting Dave ("D")'s motion to dismiss?

Under FRCP 15(c), a claim contained in an amendment relates back to the original pleading, whenever that claim arose out of the occurrence set forth in the original document. FRCP 15(a) states that leave to amend shall be given "when justice so requires." Since only a month had passed since the complaint was filed, there appears to have been no prejudice to D in making him defend Paul ("P")'s personal injury claim as part of the lawsuit. Thus, granting D's motion probably was an error, unless the "*Erie*" doctrine dictates a different result.

P could contend that under *Hanna v. Plumer*, 380 U.S. 460 (1965), where a state rule is in conflict with an FRCP provision, the latter is automatically controlling. Under this proposition, the personal injury claim would avoid the State Y statute of limitations (i.e., the personal injury claim would relate back to the complaint, which was filed two weeks prior to the expiration date for such actions).

However, D could make two arguments in rebuttal. First, in *Walker v. Armco Steel Corp.*, 446 U.S. 740 (1980), the Supreme Court indicated that in determining if an FRCP provision and a state substantive rule were in direct conflict, the intent of the former must be examined. In that case, the Court held that FRCP 3 was not intended to supersede the method of computing whether the state statute of limitations had expired. The court stated that an action is commenced by filing a complaint. Thus, there was no conflict between FRCP 3 and the state rule which required actual service on the defendant to toll the statute of limitations. Therefore, the state rule was controlling, because it was substantive in nature. Since the FRCP states only that an amendment relates back to the original document (rather than specifically declaring that this language supersedes an otherwise applicable state statute of limitation), D would assert that the two provisions are not in conflict and the state rule should be controlling.

Second, even if a direct conflict were found to exist, FRCP 15(c) should be deemed to be unconstitutional as applied in this instance, since it would directly affect a state substantive right (i.e., to extinguish a claim which has become relatively stale).

In *Walker v. Armco Steel Corp.*, the U.S. Supreme Court expressed a strong preference for (1) giving effect to state rules which are "substantive" in nature, and (2) avoiding a result which would be different if the action had been commenced in a state court. Thus, the U.S. district court correctly concluded that the "relation back" doctrine in FRCP 15(c) does not apply to toll the State Y statute of limitations. (*See* ELO Ch.4-IX(D) & 6-III(D)(8-9).)

Did the court err in dismissing D's third party complaint?

Insco ("I") has asserted three independent grounds for its contention that the district court should dismiss the third party complaint against it.

(a) Lack of authorization under the FRCP: This assertion should not have prevailed, since FRCP 14 specifically authorizes third-party claims.

(b) Lack of competency: Since D and Insco ("I") are both citizens of State Y, I's argument was probably that the U.S. district court was not competent to hear the impleader because diversity subject matter jurisdiction requires that no plaintiff and no defendant be citizens of the same state. However, impleader falls within the court's supplemental jurisdiction. Thus, dismissing D's complaint on this basis would probably be erroneous.

(c) Lack of substantive claim: I's argument appears to be that D, in fact, has no right of recovery against it, since the policy in question was fraudulently obtained. However, FRCP 14(a) permits an impleader claim whenever the impleaded party "may" be liable to the third-party plaintiff (i.e., the impleading party). Since whether the policy was wrongfully obtained or not appears to be a factual issue (to be decided at trial), dismissal of D's third-party complaint was probably improper. (*See* ELO Ch.8-IX(A) & IX(E)(2).)

Admission of Wit's testimony:

Pre-trial orders pursuant to FRCP 16(e) ordinarily describe matters which the parties have agreed upon with respect to the conduct of the trial. Such matters can be modified at trial only to prevent "manifest injustice." Even though P might have been aware of Wit, he would have no reason to prepare to cross-examine him as a consequence of D's failure to list Wit in the pre-trial order. Since (1) there is no indication that D had just discovered Wit, and (2) there was the possibility that Wit's testimony could tip the evidence in favor of D, the district court probably erred in permitting Wit to testify. (*See* ELO Ch.5-VI(A)(2).)

Answer to Question 7

T's Motion to Dismiss

(a) Lack of subject matter jurisdiction: Where subject matter jurisdiction is based on diversity, the complaint must allege that no plaintiff and no defendant are "citizens" of the same state. Truco ("T")'s contention that the complaint should be dismissed because of a lack of subject matter jurisdiction was probably based upon the fact that Pat ("P") has only asserted that she was a "resident" of State White. Thus, P could have resided in State White and yet have been a citizen of State Red.

However, P could have responded that the proof introduced at trial showed that she was citizen of State White. If T did not object to such evidence, it may be deemed to have impliedly consented to the litigation of that issue. In that event, the issue in question is deemed to have been raised by the pleadings; FRCP 15(b). Since T probably recognized that P intended to state that she was domiciled in (rather than a "resident" of) State White, P's complaint would probably be deemed to have been amended to conform to the evidence that she was a citizen of State White.

The fact that P was a citizen of State Red at the time the action arose is irrelevant because subject matter jurisdiction is determined at the time the complaint is filed. Since P had apparently made a bona fide re-location to State White before the action was commenced, diversity existed.

In summary, T's lack of subject matter jurisdiction defense was properly rejected. (*See* ELO Ch.3-III(E-F) & 4-X(B)(2).)

(b) Failure to join Dan ("D"): Under FRCP 19(a), a person should be joined if (1) in his absence complete relief cannot be accorded among those already parties and, (2) disposition of the action in his absence may (a) impede or impair his ability to protect his interest in the subject matter of the action, or (b) leave any of the parties subject to a substantial risk of incurring multiple liability. D satisfies none of these requirements because (1) complete relief can be accorded to P (i.e., she can recover the full amount of her injuries from T), and (2) T is not subject to multiple liability if a judgment is obtained against it, since (a) a party who may be vicariously liable for the conduct of another person should always recognize that a plaintiff need *not* join every possible potential defendant, and (b) T would be potentially liable for P's entire judgment, even if D were joined (they would be *joint* and *several* tortfeasors).

Additionally, a defendant may seek to join an allegedly necessary party; FRCP 21. Thus, P's failure to name D would not have precluded *T* from attempting to bring D into the action as an additional defendant. Since D is a citizen of State

Red, there would appear to be no personal jurisdiction problem in T's having D joined in the action.

In summary, rejection of T's contention that the action should be dismissed because of the failure to join D was proper.(*See* ELO Ch.8-IV(D).)

T's motion for a directed verdict ("judgment as a matter of law"):

T would next contend that since (1) it and P had stipulated in a pre-trial order that "…T would be liable to P if D was an employee of T," and (2) it was proven that D was not employed by T, a directed verdict was appropriate. P could make two arguments in rebuttal. First, P and T only agreed that T would be liable if D were T's employee, not that there could be no other grounds on which T's liability to P could be established. Thus, liability could be predicated on the State Red statute which enforces liability on the owner of the vehicle who gave the driver causing the accident permission to use his car.

Secondly, a pre-trial order may be modified to "…prevent manifest injustice;" FRCP 16(e). (*See* ELO Ch.5-VI(A)(2).) It would arguably be unjust to permit T to avoid liability simply because P had inadvertently alleged an incorrect basis for recovery — especially since T was in a superior position to know that D was not its employee. However, T could respond that (1) a reasonable construction of the language in question would lead T to have assumed that liability could be premised only upon a finding that D was T's employee, and (2) there is no "manifest injustice" in holding P to a pre-trial order into which she had voluntarily entered; especially when the stipulation in question probably induced T to refrain from contesting the admission of evidence which tended to show that D was driving the car with T's permission (since it would have been extraneous to T's potential liability). Under these circumstances, the stipulation, as interpreted by T, should probably be enforced.

P's motion to amend her complaint:

Assuming the stipulation was not deemed dispositive, P would argue that (as mentioned above) where an issue is actually "tried", the pleadings are deemed to conform to such evidence; FRP 15(b). However, T could contend that the question of whether D drove the vehicle involved in the collision with T's permission was not "tried", since T had no reason to contest the introduction of this evidence because it was irrelevant to whether D was T's employee. Where evidence is objected to as being at variance with the pleadings, a court may nevertheless allow the pleadings to be amended at trial where "…the merits of the action will be subserved thereby." FRCP 15(b). P could alternatively contend that justice is served by permitting it to add a claim which T knew (or should have known) from the commencement of the action was a possible basis of recovery by P. However, T could probably successfully contend in rebuttal that an injustice would result by permitting such a post-trial amendment because, in light of the pre-trial stipulation, it had no reason to rebut P's evidence bearing upon whether T permitted D to drive the vehicle which injured P. (*See* ELO Ch.4-X(B).)

Assuming, however, the court did grant P's motion to amend her complaint, T would next argue that "*Erie*" principles prevent the "relation back" of this theory to the date when the lawsuit was commenced, and therefore it is barred by the State Red statute of limitations.

Answer to Question 8

Does State White have personal jurisdiction over Albert?

A traditional basis for personal jurisdiction has been service of process upon the defendant when he was physically present in the forum; *Pennoyer v. Neff*. Nonetheless, the Supreme Court has held that the mere presence of a nonresident in the forum state is sufficient for the forum state to assert personal jurisdiction over him as long as service is made on the person while he is in the forum state; *Burnham v. Superior Court*, 495 U.S. 604 (1990). Albert's lack of other contacts with State White are irrelevant, so long as he was served in State White. Thus, State White may assert personal jurisdiction over Albert. (*See* ELO Ch.2-II(A).)

Does State White have personal jurisdiction over Par?

We'll assume that the State White legislature has enacted a long-arm statute which gives its courts all personal jurisdiction consistent with due process. Thus, there are no statutory interpretation issues.

Francis will argue that Par has sufficient contacts with State White since Par's clubs are distributed into the stream of commerce, and therefore Par should have foreseen being haled into court in every state. Also, through Albert, Par's clubs are endorsed throughout the United States. Par will, of course, contend that it has no direct contact with State White, and the fact that Albert (Par's agent) was in State White when the incident occurred is not sufficient. However, Francis should prevail. (*See* ELO Ch.2-III(G).)

Was Par validly served?

Service of process, even if in conformity with the applicable state law, must comport with due process (i.e., give such notice as is reasonably calculated under the circumstances to apprise the defendant of the action). Par might contend that service of process for it upon Albert, a non-officer, is not constitutionally adequate. However, since Par's president was also personally served, Francis should prevail on this issue. (*See* ELO Ch.2-VI(C)(3-5).)

Removal to the U.S. district court in State Red:

For Albert and Par to remove Francis' case to the U.S. district court in State Red, they would have to (1) initially remove the case to the U.S. district court in State White, since the applicable federal statute requires that an action be removed to the U.S. district court which encompasses the state court in which the litigation is pending, and (2) then make a *forum non conveniens* ("FNC") motion to transfer the case to the appropriate U.S. district court in State Red.

Removal is ordinarily proper where (1) no defendant is a citizen of the state in which a diversity action had been commenced, and (2) all of the defendants concur in seeking removal. However, this procedure is unavailable where federal subject matter jurisdiction is not satisfied. Thus, Francis could initially contend that diversity does not exist since he and Par are citizens of State Green. This assertion is premised upon the argument that a corporation is a citizen of the state in which it has its principal place of business. Since Par's major manufacturing facility is in State Green, under a "center of gravity" or "muscle" approach to determining "principal place of business," Par would be a citizen of that state thus destroying diversity.

The defendants would argue in rebuttal that a "nerve center" approach to determining Par's principal place of business should be applied, and since the important decision-making is done in State Red, Par is a citizen of that jurisdiction only. Although a division of authority exists on this point, the better view is probably that asserted by the defendants. Thus, removal would *not* be possible. (*See* ELO Ch.3-III(J)(1).)

Assuming that Par is a citizen of State Red only, the next issue is whether the defendants' FNC motion should be granted.

On motion of any party, an action in the U.S. district court may be transferred to any other U.S. district court where the case could have originally been commenced, if the "convenience of the parties and witnesses" and "…the interest of justice" so require. State Red is a more convenient forum for the defendants. Otherwise, however, State Red bears little relationship to the action (i.e., the incident occurred in State White and the golf club in question was probably manufactured in State Green). Thus, the defendants' FNC motion will probably *not* be successful. (*See* ELO Ch.2-VIII(E)(10)(a-c).)

What use may Robert, Par and Albert make of the judgment?

(a) Assuming that Francis was successful, may Robert assert collateral estoppel against Par and Albert?

Under the collateral estoppel ("CE") doctrine, where an issue which was essential to the outcome of a case was actually litigated in a prior lawsuit, re-litigation of that issue by the defendant in a subsequent case is precluded. The likelihood that CE can be asserted offensively by a different plaintiff in a subsequent lawsuit depends upon whether (1) the "mutuality" rule (i.e., if the defendant could not use CE, the plaintiff cannot either) has been abandoned, and (2) it would be unfair to permit issue preclusion. Robert will contend that issue preclusion on the questions of negligence and strict liability is appropriate, since the defendants have already litigated these issues and inconsistent judicial results could otherwise occur. Par, however, could argue in rebuttal that Robert "hung back" in the initial litigation; and is now trying to benefit from it. Robert would probably prevail if the mutuality rule is not followed in this jurisdiction.

(b) Assuming that Par and Albert were successful, could they assert CE against Robert?

CE may not be asserted defensively against a party who was not in privity with the earlier plaintiff. To permit issue preclusion in these circumstances would deprive the plaintiff of his day in court, and thereby violate due process. (*See* ELO Ch.9-III(C)(2) & III(D)(1-5).)

Answer to Question 9

Did the U.S. District Court in State A have personal jurisdiction over Devco ("D")?

Pete ("P") could assert that personal jurisdiction over D was permissible for two separate, independent reasons.

First, P could contend that D is "present" in State A by reason of the fact that its agent (Bull) is domiciled in that jurisdiction. A corporation may be found to be "present" within a jurisdiction when it (or its agent) is doing business within the forum on a regular, consistent basis. However, it is unlikely that the mere presence of an agent who is *not* engaged in corporate business within the state would suffice; *Riverside and Dan River Cotton Mills v. Menefee*, 237 U.S. 189 (1915).

Second, P could contend that personal jurisdiction can be asserted over D pursuant to the State A statute which extends to corporations "doing business within" the state. P's argument would be that D's advertising within State A (which in fact induced P to purchase the stock) should constitute "doing business" for purposes of the statute. D could contend in rebuttal, however, that (1) "doing business within" the state should be construed as requiring some form of tangible presence (rather than a mere advertisement which was contained in a paper newspaper published in a different state), and (2) even if D's conduct was within the statute, the assertion of personal jurisdiction under these circumstances would be violative of due process (i.e., mere advertisements would *not* constitute sufficient minimal contacts with State A as to avoid offending traditional notions of fair play and substantial justice).

As to the latter point, P could argue that "minimum contacts" are satisfied because D should have reasonably foreseen being haled into court in State A (i.e., D presumably knew that the newspaper in question was distributed in State A and the stock certificate was probably sent directly to P at his home address). D, of course, would contend that since (1) the sale was made through its agent's office in State B and, (2) the ad was purchased in that jurisdiction (where the newspaper is published), personal jurisdiction is lacking. Since the transaction was initiated in State B, D probably was not "doing business within" the jurisdiction under the long-arm statute, and D probably did not have sufficient minimum contacts with State A to satisfy due process. Thus, the U.S. district court should not have exercised personal jurisdiction over D.

Finally, the court's assertion that it could exercise personal jurisdiction to the extent permitted by due process is incorrect. Since there is no federal long-arm statute generally pertaining to diversity suits, the U.S. district court would be obliged to "borrow" (i.e., conform its assertion of personal jurisdiction to) State A's long-arm statute. As noted above, however, it is unlikely that even the "minimum contacts" standard required by the Fifth Amendment is met under these facts. (*See* ELO Ch.2-III(C-E) & IV(D)(2).)

Did the U.S. district court in State A have subject matter jurisdiction over the action against Bull?

For a U.S. district court to be competent based upon diversity, (1) no plaintiff and no defendant may be citizen of the same state, and (2) the amount in controversy must exceed $75,000, exclusive of interest and attorney's fees. It is assumed that the latter requirement is satisfied. The former criterion, however, would not be met if Bull is joined as a party-defendant. Individuals are considered citizens of the state in which they are domiciled (i.e., presently live and intend to remain). Although Bull works in State B, for diversity purposes he is a citizen of State A. Thus, the U.S. district court would not have subject matter jurisdiction over the claim against Bull. (*See* ELO Ch.8-IV(C)(2)(a).)

Assuming the U.S. district court had subject matter jurisdiction over P's claim against Bull, was it correct in ordering the latter to be joined as a party-defendant?

Under FRCP 20(a), all persons may be joined in one action as defendants if (1) there is asserted against them jointly, severally or in the alternative, any right to relief arising out of the same transaction or occurrence, and (2) any question of law or fact is common to all of the defendants.

The facts are unclear about the claim against Bull. If his purported liability is basically vicarious in nature (i.e., he is responsible because he was D's agent or somehow republished the allegedly false matter by tendering additional literature), the test described in the preceding sentence would be met because Bull could assert all issues which D might raise in an action by P directly against the latter entity.

However, if the basis of Bull's purported liability is an unauthorized statement he made to P, then the "common question of law or fact" element might *not* be satisfied. However, since Bull's potential liability to P is probably predicated — to at least some extent — upon his agency relationship with D, joinder was properly permitted (excluding, of course, the fact that Bull's joinder would destroy diversity). (*See* ELO Ch.8-IV(B)(1-6).)

Did the district court err in striking Pete's demand for a jury trial?

Where a "common law" claim is brought in a federal district court, either party normally has a right to a jury trial, whether state law permits a jury trial or not; FRCP 38. A "common law" claim is one which courts of law recognized prior to the adoption of the Seventh Amendment in 1791. However, there appears to be a division of authority as to whether a case can be so exceedingly complex that the Fifth Amendment right to due process can be deemed to override the Seventh

Amendment right to a jury trial. *In re Japanese Electronic Products Litigation*, 631 F.2d 1069 (3rd Cir. 1980) suggests that, in rare instances, a denial of a jury trial is appropriate. The Ninth Circuit, however, has refused to recognize a "complex case" exception to the Seventh Amendment; *In re U.S. Financial Securities Litigation*; 609 F.2d 411 (9th Cir. 1979).

In any event, this case does not appear to constitute a situation where denying the normal right to a jury trial would be appropriate, since laypersons should be able to determine if (1) the statements contained in the advertisement and promotional brochures were incorrect, and (2) D knew, or should have known, that those statements were (a) false, or (b) made without adequate knowledge as to their truth or falsity. Since P has asserted only common law fraud (rather than a federal securities violation) and such actions were recognized at "common law," the court erred in striking P's demand for a jury trial. (*See* ELO Ch.7-XIII(I)(1).)

Answer to Question 10

Valvo ("V")'s objection to Peter ("P")'s failure to join Mity ("M") as a defendant:

The joinder of a party is necessary where (1) complete relief cannot be granted to those already parties in her absence, (2) disposition of the case in her absence will impede or impair an interest which she has in the matter, *or* (3) persons already parties to the action will, in her absence, be subject to substantial risk of multiple liability. If any of these factors is satisfied, the non-litigant should be made a party if (a) she is subject to service of process, and (b) the court will not be deprived of subject matter jurisdiction if the party is joined.

In this instance, none of the elements is satisfied. P can obtain complete relief (i.e., a judgment for the full amount of his injuries) against V. M's interest in the subject matter of the action will not be impaired (i.e., any judgment against V will not have a collateral effect upon M, since this doctrine cannot be utilized offensively against a party who is unrelated to the initial defendant).

V will not be exposed to double multiple liability since (1) it would retain the right to pursue an indemnity action against M if P were successful against it, and (2) in any event, a tortfeasor cannot complain about a plaintiff's decision to abstain from suing all possible joint tortfeasors. Thus, any objection by V that P must be joined would be incorrect.

It should be noted, however, that joinder of M probably could be permitted by the court (assuming personal jurisdiction could be obtained over M) since (1) the right to relief asserted against V and M arises out of the same occurrence (the explosion), and (2) there is a common question of fact (whether V and M received notice that the valve would malfunction, and whether the valve was defective or negligently manufactured); FRCP 20(a). Joinder of M would not destroy subject matter jurisdiction since P is a citizen of State C.

Thus, assuming personal jurisdiction could be obtained over M (discussed below), it should probably be joined upon a proper motion by V; FRCP 21. (*See* ELO Ch.8-IV(B)(1-2) & IV(C)(2)(a).)

May V bring M into the case as a defendant?

V could bring M into the case as a defendant (assuming personal jurisdiction over the latter was satisfied) by means of a third-party complaint (sometimes called "impleader"); FRCP 14(a). This procedural device is appropriate where the third-party defendant (the impleaded party) may be liable to the third-party plaintiff (the impleading party) for all or part of the plaintiff's judgment against the latter. Subject matter jurisdiction would not be a problem (even though V and M are each citizens of State A), since impleader actions fall within the court's supplemental jurisdiction. (*See* ELO Ch.8-IX(E)(2).)

Joinder of parties (P and Q v. V and M):

Parties may be joined, as either plaintiffs or defendants, if (1) the claim asserted (or defended against) by them, jointly, severally or in the alternative, arises out of the same transaction or occurrence, and (2) there is a common question of law or fact; FRCP 20(a). These requisites appear to be satisfied in this instance since (1) both claims arise from the same occurrence (the explosion), and (2) there are common questions of fact (i.e., whether the valve "collar" was defectively or negligently made, whether the plaintiffs were advised of a possible malfunction). Thus, joinder of parties (subject to competency and personal jurisdiction questions discussed below) would be appropriate. (*See* ELO Ch.8-III(B)(2-4).)

Joinder of causes of action (P and Q v. V and M):

A party asserting a claim to relief may ordinarily join all the causes of action she has against a particular defendant; FRCP 18(a). Since the plaintiffs would probably be asserting negligence, products liability and breach of the implied warranty of merchantability against V and M, joinder of claims is appropriate.

Personal jurisdiction over the defendants:

Since this appears to be a diversity action, the U.S. district court would utilize (i.e., "borrow") the long-arm statute of State C, the forum in which it is located. It is assumed that the State C long-arm statute affords its courts all personal jurisdiction consistent with due process (and thereby avoids any possible statutory interpretation problems). It is also assumed that neither defendant was physically present within State C when service of process was effectuated. Service was not made upon an officer who was within the state, and neither corporation maintains a permanent office in State C from which business is solicited.

The assertion of personal jurisdiction over the defendants would still have to satisfy due process (i.e., the defendants must have such minimum contacts with the forum as not to offend traditional notions of fair play and substantial justice). In determining if this standard is satisfied, the courts ordinarily consider (1) the extent to which the defendant has purposefully availed itself of the benefits of the forum, (2) whether the defendants should have reasonably foreseen being haled into court in that state, and (3) the impact which the defendant's conduct has made within the state.

The facts are silent as to how the machinery which exploded came to be located in State C. If the sale was made directly to P and Q by V, then V would arguably foresee being haled into court in State C. In such instance, V should have been aware that if any component of the machine was defective, that defect would likely become manifest in State C. However, if V knew the machines were sold only in states other than C, there is a substantial likelihood that personal jurisdiction would be lacking; *World-Wide Volkswagen Corp. v. Woodson*, 444

U.S. 286 (1980). Similarly, personal jurisdiction could probably not be obtained over M unless it was cognizant that its valves were integrated into machinery which was sold in State C. (*See* ELO Ch.2-III(G).)

Subject matter jurisdiction over the parties:

For diversity subject matter jurisdiction to exist, (1) no defendant and no plaintiff may be citizens of the same state, and (2) the amount in controversy must exceed $75,000.

Since Q and V are citizens of State B (a corporation is a citizen of the states in which it is incorporated and has its principal place of business), a U.S. district court would *not* be competent to hear this matter. The fact that Q moved to State B subsequent to commencing the action is irrelevant for purposes of determining diversity (assuming the relocation was bona fide). (*See* ELO Ch.3-III(E) & III(J).)

Must P plead a lack of contributory negligence ("CN")?

U.S. district courts usually adhere to the FRCP where the Rules contain a provision which is on point; *Hanna v. Plumer*, 380 U.S. 460 (1965). Under FRCP 8(c), CN must be set forth as an affirmative defense. Thus, P would not be required to plead that he was not contributorily negligent.

Does P have the burden of persuasion on the issue of CN?

Where a matter is not dealt with directly in the FRCP, and it pertains to a substantive aspect of the case (the burden of proof on an issue would arguably constitute a substantive issue, since it goes to establishing a claim or defense), state law will ordinarily be followed. Whether the federal judge will apply the law of State A (where the action has been commenced) or State C (where the cause of action allegedly arose) depends upon State A law. If State A applies its own law, it should be adhered to by the federal judge. However, if a State A court would (under its conflict-of-law rules) apply the law of State C, the federal judge should also apply the law of State C.

Answer to Question 11

Bigbucks ("BB") v. Palladium Corporation ("PC")

(a) Subject matter jurisdiction: The PC could successfully contend that diversity subject matter jurisdiction was lacking in the initial lawsuit since (1) PC and BB are citizens of New York, and (2) the amount in controversy is not "in excess" of $75,000. While BB could contend that the PC waived this defect by filing an answer which failed to question the district court's competency, a lack of subject matter jurisdiction can be raised at any time; FRCP 12(h)(3). Thus, the judgment obtained by BB against the PC is void and unenforceable.

(b) Personal jurisdiction, service and venue: Even if Massachusetts has a long-arm statute which gives its courts all personal jurisdiction consistent with due process, the PC could assert that it has no contacts with that state. Also, the PC could contend that notice was not properly given, since FRCP 4(h)(1) requires that service on a corporation ordinarily be made by delivering a copy of the summons and complaint to "…an officer, managing or general agent." Since a secretary to such a party is not within the provision, proper service was *not* effectuated. However, PC waived these defects by failing to raise them in its initial response to BB's complaint; FRCP 12(h)(1). Finally, venue does properly lie in Massachusetts. Venue is appropriate in a diversity action in a judicial district in which (1) any defendant resides, if all defendants reside in the same State, (2) a substantial part of the events or omissions on which the claim is based occurred or a substantial part of the property is located, or (if there is no jurisdiction where the suit may otherwise be brought), (3) any defendant is subject to personal jurisdiction. 28 U.S.C. § 1391(a). There is no defendants' residence venue because there is no single state in which all defendants reside. There is no district in which a substantial part of the events occurred because the events were scattered over many states. Since Don was subject to personal jurisdiction in Massachusetts by virtue of his presence there, venue properly lies in the District of Massachusetts.

(c) Forum non conveniens ("FNC") motion: Any party may make a FNC motion to transfer an action in U.S. district court to a different U.S. district court, provided the case could have been commenced in the latter court. However, venue is proper in a diversity action in a judicial district in which (1) any defendant resides, if all defendants reside in the same State, (2) a substantial part of the events or omissions on which the claim is based occurred or a substantial part of the property is located, or (if there is no jurisdiction where the suit may otherwise be brought) (3) any defendant is subject to personal jurisdiction. 28 U.S.C. § 1391(a). The action may be transferred to California because PC is subject to personal jurisdiction there as a resident of that State. The FNC motion was improperly denied. (*See* ELO Ch.2-VIII(E) and 3-II(B).)

BB v. Don Pickles ("D")

(a) Personal jurisdiction: BB could contend that it obtained personal jurisdiction over D, since the latter was served within Massachusetts; *Pennoyer v. Neff.* However, there is dicta in *Shaffer v. Heitner*, 433 U.S. 186 (1977), that **all** assertions of personal jurisdiction must meet the "minimum contacts" standard articulated in *International Shoe* (i.e., the defendant must have sufficient minimum contacts with the forum so as **not** to offend traditional notions of fair play and substantial justice). Nevertheless, the Court has held that service in the forum state establishes personal jurisdiction over the defendant no matter how brief the defendant's presence in the state; *Burnham v. Superior Court*, 495 U.S. 604 (1990). (*See* ELO Ch.2-II(A).)

(b) Venue and waiver: Even if D prevailed on the issue of personal jurisdiction discussed immediately above and could have successfully objected to venue (see discussion of venue under *BB v. PC*), these objections were waived by his failure to raise them in his initial response to BB's complaint; FRCP 12(h)(1).

D v. Merv ("M")

Since BB was not seeking monetary damages from D, D's action against M was presumably for the lost income which D would have derived from appearing at the Palladium.

(a) Subject matter jurisdiction: M could have initially contended that since D and he are both citizens of Illinois, diversity was lacking. However, ancillary jurisdiction is ordinarily permitted in impleader situations. Since D's action against M is an indemnity-type claim (i.e., M would probably be viewed as having greater culpability than D, since D only naively listened to M's advice), (1) a third-party complaint was proper, and (2) the impleader action could not be dismissed for lack of subject matter jurisdiction.

(b) Service of process: Next, M could have argued that service of process should be quashed because he was "lured" into the jurisdiction (i.e., he entered Massachusetts in response to D's telephone call and D had a process server waiting at the airport). While D could argue that the thought of serving D at the airport occurred **after** the telephone conversation and there was nothing dishonest about his statements (i.e., D intended to seek another agent if BB's action against him was not dismissed), the court probably should have ruled in favor of M on this issue.

(c) Personal jurisdiction: M could argue that his temporary physical presence did not establish sufficient minimum contacts with the forum state for it to assert personal jurisdiction over him. D could counter that since M was served in Massachusetts the district court in that state could constitutionally assert personal jurisdiction over M (see discussion of jurisdiction under *BB v. D*).

Thus, the court should not grant M's motion to dismiss D's lawsuit, unless the court felt M's presence when served was involuntary. (*See* ELO Ch.8-IX(E)(2) & VII(E).)

PC v. M

(a) Subject matter jurisdiction: Since PC is a citizen of New York and possibly California (if Massachusetts follows the "muscle approach" to determine the principal place of business of a corporation) and M is a resident of Illinois, diversity subject matter jurisdiction exists over this claim. However, since PC is asserting an indemnification-type claim against M (M is arguably more culpable than PC, because the latter entity would have had no reason to believe that D was already under contract with another person), the third party action would fall under the court's supplemental jurisdiction.

(b) Service of process: Service of process was properly effected. A copy of the summons and complaint was delivered to M's office and received and acknowledged by M's secretary, who is presumably an authorized agent to receive service of process. FRCP 4(e)(2). Since this apparently did not occur, service by another means was required (unless Massachusetts law permits service by mail; FRCP 4(e)(1)). If Massachusetts does permit service of process in this manner, however, M could probably successfully raise a due process objection (i.e., permitting service by mail without any initial attempt at personal delivery of the summons and complaint is arguably *not* reasonably calculated to inform the defendant of the lawsuit).

(c) Personal jurisdiction and venue: Once a court gains jurisdiction over a party in a litigation it continues during the entire litigation. Assuming M's receipt of service in Massachusetts gave the district court there personal jurisdiction over M, it retains jurisdiction over M for the remainder of the litigation. Since venue was proper between the original parties, venue is proper for the third party claim.

(d) Determination of BB's right to an injunction: Under FRCP 38(a) and the Seventh Amendment, there is an absolute right to a jury trial with respect to legal claims in federal courts. In *Beacon Theaters, Inc. v. Westover*, 359 U.S. 500 (1959), the Supreme Court held that in a federal court, legal claims *must* be tried prior to equitable ones, in order to preserve a party's right to a jury trial. Since BB's right to injunctive relief would be premised upon the "legal" question of whether or not D was in breach of his contract with BB, the judge incorrectly determined the equitable issue first. Under the Supremacy Clause of the U.S. Constitution, any state rule which is inconsistent with the Supreme Court's interpretation of the Seventh Amendment as applied to federal court cases will be superseded. Thus, the fact that Massachusetts law permits resolution of equitable issues first is irrelevant. (*See* ELO Ch. 2-IV(C), 7-XIII(E) & 8-IX(E).)

D's defense of minority:

Amendments to pleadings are permissible at trial if the court determines that (1) "…the merits of the action will be subserved" thereby, **and** (2) the objecting party fails to satisfy the court that the admission of such evidence will prejudice her defense on the merits; FRCP 15(b). Although D could have contended that this standard is satisfied because BB could not have defended against this assertion in any event (i.e., either D is under the age of majority, or he is not), the court could have decided that D's making this assertion near the end of the litigation was unfair. Thus, the court's decision was probably correct.

Answer to Question 12

Ped ("P")'s motion to remand:

Removal to a U.S. district court when no federal question is involved is proper where (1) no defendant is a citizen of the state(s) in which the action has been commenced, and (2) "diversity" subject matter jurisdiction requirements are satisfied.

P could have contended that removal to the U.S. district court was improper on two grounds: (1) Health ("H") is a citizen of State A (a corporation is a citizen of the states in which it is incorporated and has its principal place of business), since that is where H's business is conducted (and therefore one of the defendants is a citizen of the state in which the action was commenced), and (2) "diversity" is lacking because P and H are both citizens of State A (diversity requires that no plaintiff and no defendant be citizens of the same state). Thus, federal court subject matter jurisdiction does not exist. If, however, the board of directors of H ordinarily met in State H, **and** State A follows a "nerve center" approach in determining a corporation's principal place of business (i.e., a corporation's principal place of business is deemed to be located where the central decision-making takes place), H would be a citizen of State H only, and removal would have been proper.

However, since (1) the day-to-day corporate decisions are presumably made at the hospital in State A, and (2) State A is where H's entire business operations are conducted, State A would probably be deemed to be H's place of business for "citizenship" purposes. Thus, remand back to the state court was proper. (*See* ELO Ch.3-VII(A) & III(J)(1).)

H's demurrer:

In some states, defendants can be joined only if their liability to the plaintiff arises out of the same "transaction or occurrence." Thus, H would contend that joinder of D and H was not proper since two distinct occurrences were involved: (1) the traffic accident involving P and D, and (2) the treatment which P subsequently received at H's hospital.

In determining if claims arise from the same "transaction or occurrences," state courts typically apply one of two standards: (1) whether the events which serve as the basis for each claim are "logically related," **or** (2) whether "common evidence" would be introduced in trials regarding each claim. Either test appears to be met in this instance.

The claims are "logically related" in that H's liability should be diminished to the extent it can be shown P's injuries in the traffic accident are distinguishable from those which he allegedly sustained at the hospital. Also, an initial tortfeasor is ordinarily liable for additional injuries caused to the plaintiff by medical personnel acting in a negligent manner, unless the latter's conduct can be characterized as "reckless" (in which case, the initial tortfeasor is *not* responsible for the subsequent enhancement of the plaintiff's injuries). Since a determination of each defendant's conduct is pertinent to deciding the extent of liability properly allocated between them, the claims are probably "logically related." The "common evidence" test would also be satisfied for the reasons described above (i.e., evidence as to P's initial injuries and the conduct of H's medical personnel would be pertinent in an action against either D or H for purposes of determining each party's precise liability to P).

Finally, it should be mentioned that a few jurisdictions follow the FRCP. Under the applicable rule, claims against multiple defendants can be joined as long as (1) they arose out of the same transaction or occurrence, and (2) there is at least one common issue of law or fact; FRCP 20(a). Since this provision has been liberally construed, it would probably be concluded that (1) P's claims against both D and H "arose" from the same occurrence (i.e., the traffic accident), and (2) there are common questions of fact (i.e., the extent to which each defendant's conduct caused injury to P, and whether H's personnel performed their duties in a reckless or merely negligent, manner).

Thus, joinder of claims was proper, and H's demurrer was properly denied. (*See* ELO Ch.8-IV(B)(2-4).)

P's request for admissions:

In many states, requests for an admission of a legal conclusion are *not* permissible. However, requests for admissions relating to facts or the application of law to facts (e.g., leaving a rake on a sidewalk is negligent) are ordinarily proper. In states which follow the FRCP, a party may request admissions pertaining to (1) statements or opinions of fact, or (2) the application of law to facts; FRCP 36(a). P's request is probably improper because it basically asks H and D to admit all of the elements of P's cause of action (which apparently is negligence). As such, it is requesting admission of a purely legal conclusion. Thus, the court properly sustained the objections to P's request for admissions.

D's motion for a new trial:

Misconduct by jurors is an established ground for granting a mistrial. Quotient verdicts (i.e., where the verdict is determined by dividing a particular sum by the number of jurors) are usually viewed as improper, since the figure does not represent the collective decision of the jury as to the actual damages sustained by a plaintiff. The verdict is arguably subject to this defect because the amount of P's damages was determined by adding the differing opinions as to liability and dividing by the total number of jurors.

In rebuttal, however, P could have made two arguments. First, some jurisdictions (including the federal courts) do not permit evidence of jury deliberations (except to show the possible influence of external factors upon the jurors). If this were such a jurisdiction, the affidavits could not be considered in the determination of whether a new trial should be granted. Second, the use of a quotient verdict as a **starting point** for discussing the amount of a judgment which should be rendered is not improper. Since the jury agreed on the $43,652.89 amount after that figure was derived from the quotient method, P could probably successfully argue that the verdict was proper (despite the occurrences described in the affidavits).

Assuming evidence of jury deliberations is admissible, D might also have contended that the total lack of discussion on the substantive issues was improper because **immediately** after entering the jury room, a vote of liability was taken and returned against the defendants. However, P could have argued that since the jury members presumably understood the legal issues under consideration, their verdict of liability evidenced a determination by each juror that P had successfully satisfied the burden of proof on the *prima facie* elements of his action.

In summary, the court's refusal to order a new trial (on any aspect of the case) was probably correct. (*See* ELO Ch.7-VI(F).)

Answer to Question 13

Was Dod ("D") an indispensable party?

A person should be joined if, in her absence, (1) complete relief cannot be accorded to the existing parties, (2) disposition of the case will impair her ability to protect an interest which she has in the action, or (3) disposition of the action without her could result in an existing party's being exposed to multiple liability.

Cozy Nook ("CN") could contend that D is an indispensable party since (1) he has an interest in the action (the apartment D now occupies could be jeopardized), since Abel ("A") seeks to lease the dwelling now rented by D, and (2) CN would be exposed to multiple liability since a verdict in favor of A would oblige CN to dispossess D, thereby exposing CN to an action by the latter for breach of the lease agreement.

However, A could argue in rebuttal that D's interest would not necessarily be affected by A's action because (1) A has alternatively sought a similar apartment in the building, and (2) even if no similar apartment were available, A could probably be adequately compensated by monetary damages (the rental differential between the initial apartment and the one in which A is now living, as well as any moving expenses attendant upon the relocation).

Additionally, CN is not exposed to the risk of multiple liability for the same obligation, since it knew (or should have known) that its conduct toward A could result in liability by a subsequent tenant if A subsequently asserted his legal rights. Therefore, it appears that D's joinder (which probably would not be possible since D does not appear to have any contacts with State White) is not necessary. Thus, D could not be characterized as an indispensable party and the court should overrule CN's motion to dismiss on this basis. (*See* ELO Ch.8-IV(D)(2-5).)

Did the court lack personal jurisdiction over CN?

A traditional basis of obtaining personal jurisdiction over an out-of-state defendant is service of process within the forum. Thus, A would contend that since CN's president was personally served within State White, personal jurisdiction over that entity was obtained.

CN could, however, make two arguments in rebuttal. First, there is language in *Shaffer v. Heitner*, 433 U.S. 186 (1977), which indicates all assertions of personal jurisdiction over an out-of-state defendant must be tested by the "minimum contacts" standard set forth in *International Shoe*. The defendant must have such minimum contacts with the forum as to not offend traditional notions of fair play and substantial justice. Assuming this view were adhered to by State White courts, CN could contend that a single account within a jurisdiction which is unrelated to the plaintiff's action does not constitute an adequate basis for making it stand trial within State White. Although A could argue that by maintaining the account, CN is availing itself of the protection of State White's banking laws, CN is likely to prevail on this question. (*See* ELO Ch.2-III(A)(2).)

Was service of process on CN's president proper?

CN could alternatively contend that, even if physical presence within the jurisdiction is still a valid means of obtaining personal jurisdiction over an out-of-state defendant, the service of process upon CN's president should be quashed. CN's argument would be that since its President was responding to a legal proceeding (the attachment hearing) when he was served with process, the court should exercise its discretion to grant immunity from service of process in this instance.

A, however, could argue that this theory has ordinarily been applied where the defendant had voluntarily chosen to assist in a forum-related proceeding (i.e., been a witness (1) to a legislative hearing, or (2) at *another's* trial). It has **not** traditionally been extended to situations where the defendant was in the jurisdiction to protect his personal interests (i.e., to release CN's bank account from A's attachment). Nevertheless, an enlightened court would probably rule in favor of CN. To hold otherwise would almost always result in a defendant's being required to stand trial in any state in which he had an asset. This outcome would frustrate the Supreme Court's effort in *Shaffer v. Heitner*, 433 U.S. 186 (1977), to make the assertion of *quasi-in-rem* jurisdiction roughly equivalent to *in personam* jurisdiction.(*See* ELO Ch.2-V(C)(7).)

Is State White an inconvenient forum?

In its discretion, a court may decline to exercise jurisdiction. Factors considered in making this determination are: access to proof; ability to secure attendance of key witnesses; the forum's relationship to the matter; and the potential necessity of viewing the premises.

CN could contend that since (1) the action arose in State Red, (2) D is domiciled in State Red, and (3) CN is a State Red corporation, dismissal is proper. A could then re-institute the action in State Red.

However, A could argue in rebuttal that (1) the presentation of evidence would not be significantly impaired by conducting the trial in State White (i.e., the matter will primarily involve the oral testimony of A and CN's representatives; the mere fact that D subsequently rented the apartment desired by A does not make D's testimony essential), and (2) State White has an interest in affording its citizens a convenient forum. Thus, dismissal is unlikely. (*See* ELO Ch.2-VIII(D).)

Is CN entitled to a jury trial?

In *Dice v. Akron, Canton & Youngstown Railroad Company*, 342 U.S. 359 (1952), the Supreme Court held that a state procedural rule (which did not permit a jury trial with respect to the particular issue under scrutiny) is overridden where it conflicts with a federal statute which allowed a jury trial on the claim in question. The court reasoned that where a procedural aspect is embodied in a U.S. statute which creates a federal cause of action and is important to the successful assertion of that claim, it must be observed by a state court. The only difference between the *Dice* case and the present situation is that in the latter the right to a jury trial has been judicially (as opposed to legislatively) created. However, since an interpretation of federal law by the U.S. Supreme Court is binding upon a state court, CN's demand for a jury trial should be granted (regardless of any contrary local procedure). (*See* ELO Ch.6-IV(C).)

Answer to Question 14

Was dismissal because of lack of subject matter jurisdiction correct?

Federal district courts are competent to hear diversity actions where no plaintiff and no defendant are citizens of the same state and the amount in controversy exceeds $75,000, exclusive of interest and costs. Since there is no question that Don ("D") and Tinselware ("T") are citizens of different states, whether the court's dismissal was proper or not will turn on whether D's damages were in excess of $75,000.

T could contend that since D expended exactly $75,000 to purchase the widgets, the "in excess of" $75,000 requirement was not satisfied. However, since D intended to resell the widgets, he is entitled to recover consequential damages, including lost profits, his damages meet the monetary requirement for diversity. Thus, assuming there was no "legal certainty" that D's claim would not exceed $75,000, dismissal for lack of competency was not correct. (*See* ELO Ch.3-V(A-D).)

Did the court lack personal jurisdiction over T?

U.S. district courts "borrow" the long-arm statute of the state in which they are located. Since the facts do not describe the California long-arm statute, it is assumed that the courts of that state have been legislatively authorized to assert all personal jurisdiction is consistent with due process.

Nevertheless, personal jurisdiction could not be exercised over T unless due process is also satisfied (i.e., T had such minimum contacts with California as not to offend traditional notions of fair play and substantial justice). T could contend that since (1) it does no business in California, (2) the contract was made in Arizona, and (3) the items in question were delivered to D in Arizona, it would not be constitutionally permissible to require it to defend the action in California.

D will argue that T (1) initiated the transaction by calling him in California, and (2) T knew that any defects in the items would not be discovered until D had returned to California. Thus, T should have reasonably foreseen being haled into court in California.

However, because only a commercial (as opposed to a personal injury) loss is being asserted by D, the court was probably correct in dismissing the action against T for lack of personal jurisdiction. (*See* ELO Ch.2-III(F).)

Was the court correct in dismissing the action because of lack of proper service?

Under the FRCP, service may be made upon a corporation by delivering a copy of the summons and complaint to an officer, managing or general agent. Since

Maureen appears to hold none of these titles (she is an employee), service of process by this manner would be improper.

However, under FRCP 4(h)(1), a summons and complaint may be served in accordance with the law of the state in which the U.S. District Court is located.

Since California has a statute which permits service of process upon a corporation by mailing, the issue is whether the application of this statute is constitutionally valid. Due process requires that a defendant be given such notice as is reasonably calculated under the circumstances to apprise him of the lawsuit.

While D might argue that service by mailing to the President of a corporation is proper, this assertion would probably fail. This is the correct result because pieces of mail sent to a corporation are rarely received directly by the individual addressee. Thus, there would be a significant possibility that the document could be received by an employee who is unhappy with management or might not understand the importance of legal papers. As a consequence, the summons and complaint could intentionally or inadvertently be discarded (without ever reaching the hands of the proper person). Thus, dismissal for improper service was probably correct. (*See* ELO Ch.2-IV(C)(2) & VI(A)(1).)

Could the court have transferred the action to the U.S. district court in Nevada?

When a *forum non conveniens* motion is appropriate, a U.S. district court may dismiss the matter or transfer it to any other federal district court in which the action might have originally been commenced. Where subject matter jurisdiction is based on diversity, venue is proper in a judicial district in which (1) any defendant resides, if all defendants reside in the same State, (2) a substantial part of the events or omissions on which the claim is based occurred or a substantial part of the property is located, or (if there is no jurisdiction where the suit may otherwise be brought) (3) any defendant is subject to personal jurisdiction. 28 U.S.C. § 1391(a). Since Nevada meets none of these criteria, the court could ***not*** have transferred the action to the U.S. District Court in that state. (*See* ELO Ch.2-VIII(E)(1).)

Was the dismissal of D's action against Maureen correct?

D's action against Maureen is not an amendment to an existing lawsuit (the initial case having already been dismissed). Thus, dismissal of D's complaint against Maureen was proper if the applicable statute of limitations had expired.

Answer to Question 15

Is the U.S. district court competent?

For diversity purposes, a corporation is deemed to be a citizen of the states in which it is incorporated or has its principal place of business. Although Defendant ("D") is incorporated in Massachusetts, the facts are unclear as to its principal place of business. If the district court in California adheres to a "muscle approach" in determining this question, D could contend that there is a lack of diversity, since its main booking terminal (which presumably is the place at which orders for Defendant's services are accepted, and therefore Defendant's revenues produced) is in Arizona — the same state of which Pete ("P") is a citizen. (The domicile of the class representative of a class is controlling for diversity purposes.)

P, however, could make two arguments in rebuttal. First, if the California district court adheres to a "nerve center" approach, D's principal place of business would be where its corporate decision-making takes place. Second, the booking terminal should be viewed merely as a place where tickets for D's flights are recorded. The "business" is actually done where orders are given to a travel agency or where D's ticket personnel are stationed. Although more information is needed (i.e., whether the U.S. district court in California adheres to a "nerve center" or "muscle" approach), it will be assumed that most reservations for D's flights are *initiated* outside of Arizona. Thus, Arizona is probably not D's principal place of business (even if a "muscle approach" were followed), and the U.S. district court is competent.

Additionally, it should be mentioned that in a class action based on diversity, the claim of *each member* of the class must exceed $75,000. Thus, any passenger who did not suffer injuries and losses in excess of $75,000 would have to be dropped from the class (the facts indicate that only "minor" injuries were suffered by the persons on the plane). However, since mental distress could have been suffered (in addition to physical injuries), an allegation that the jurisdictional amount is satisfied for each member of the class would probably be accepted by the court (i.e., it could *not* be determined to a "legal certainty" that a verdict exceeding $75,000 would not be rendered for each member of the class). (*See* ELO Ch.3-III(J)(1) & V(E)(2)(c).)

Is a class action maintainable?

For a class action to be maintainable, four requisites must be met: (1) the class is so numerous that joinder of all members is impracticable, (2) there are questions of law or fact common to the class, (3) the claims of the representative are typical of the class she seeks to represent, and (4) the representative is capable of fairly and adequately protecting the interests of the class. Assuming these conditions are satisfied, P is apparently asserting an FRCP 23(b)(3) class action (i.e., common questions of law or fact predominate and a class action is superior to any other method of adjudication).

D could contend that (1) the class is not sufficiently numerous (only 40 persons, even assuming that each member of the class has a claim in excess of $75,000), and (2) since each passenger's injuries are different, common questions of fact do not predominate.

While 40 is not a large number, joinder of claims is probably impracticable since the plaintiffs are from various states, and therefore many members of the class could assert venue objections. Additionally, the objective of judicial economy is realized by combining 40 potential lawsuits into one action. Finally, any plaintiffs who did not desire to be a part of the class would have a right to opt out of the group; FRCP 23(c)(2). Thus, a "numerosity" objection by D should be overcome.

Finally, while each plaintiff's injuries are different in type and extent, common questions of law or fact probably still predominate since the initial question of D's liability to the group for the accident is common to the entire class. Thus, a class action is probably appropriate. (*See* ELO Ch.8-V(C)(1-3) & V(F).)

Is venue proper?

A diversity action may be brought in a judicial district in which (1) any defendant resides, if all defendants reside in the same State, (2) a substantial part of the events or omissions on which the claim is based occurred or a substantial part of the property is located, or (if there is no jurisdiction where the suit may otherwise be brought) (3) any defendant is subject to personal jurisdiction. 28 U.S.C. § 1391(a). Venue is proper in California. The majority of the defendant's flights originate and land there, and therefore this in-state systematic and continuous activity will subject the defendant to personal jurisdiction in California. D should prevail on this question. (*See* ELO Ch.2.-VIII(E)(1).)

Should the action be transferred to Massachusetts?

On motion of any party, an action pending in a U.S. district court may be transferred to any other U.S. district court where the case could have originally been commenced, if the "convenience of the parties and witnesses" and "…the interest of justice" so require. (*See* ELO Ch.2-VIII(E)(10).) Since the accident occurred in Massachusetts (when the aircraft was taking off from Boston), the action could have been commenced in that state. While a plaintiff's choice of forum is not easily disturbed, it is likely that all non-party witnesses reside in Massachusetts and medical records pertaining to the victims are located in that jurisdiction (presumably, the victims were treated at the airport or taken to hospitals in the Boston area). Thus, D's *forum non conveniens* motion will probably be granted.

Can the Donald Company ("DC") be impleaded by D?

A third-party claim (sometimes referred to as "impleader") is appropriate where the complainant has a indemnity-type claim against the third-party defendant (the party being impleaded); FRCP 14. DC could contend that impleader is improper because (1) the evidence of engine malfunction is "non-conclusive," (2) D and DC are citizens of the same state (and thus, subject matter jurisdiction is lacking), (3) personal jurisdiction is lacking, and (4) venue is improper.

D could respond that (1) it is only necessary that the third-party claimant "may" have an indemnity-type claim against the third-party defendant (there need not be a strong likelihood that liability will actually be established at trial), (2) ancillary jurisdiction is ordinarily applied in impleader situations to preclude competency requisites, (3) since DC presumably knew that (a) its engines were ordinarily integrated in D's aircraft, and (b) D's airplanes often flew into and out of Massachusetts, DC should have reasonably foreseen being haled into court in that state (and thus, the "minimum contacts" necessary to satisfy due process are met), and (4) since DC has flights out of Massachusetts, it probably could be deemed to "reside" in that state for purposes of venue. Thus, D's attempt to implead DC should be successful. (*See* ELO Ch.8-IX(A-E).)

Answer to Question 16

Paul ("P")'s motion for leave to file his first amended complaint.

(a) Would an amendment to P's complaint be permitted under the FRCP?
Under FRCP 15(a), a party may amend his pleading any time before a responsive pleading is served. If a responsive pleading has been served, a pleading may be amended with leave of court (which "…shall be freely given when justice so requires"); FRCP 15(a). The facts are unclear as to whether or not Doe ("D") answered P's initial complaint prior to July 1. If no answer had been served, then P would have had an absolute right to file his first amended complaint.

Even if D had filed an answer, no prejudice (i.e., inability to locate an important witness) appears to result to D by permitting P to amend his complaint for the purpose of attempting to recover for the fracture of his other leg. Thus, P's first amended complaint would be proper under the FRCP. (*See* ELO Ch.4-IX(B-C).)

(b) Is the amendment barred by the Erie doctrine? P could have contended that the statute of limitations is not applicable to the initial amendment, since recovery for the fracture of his other leg does not constitute a *new* cause of action. The amendment seeks merely to reflect an additional injury which P sustained as a consequence of the occurrence for which the suit was originally brought. D, of course, would have argued that the fracture to P's other leg constituted a new cause of action. However, P probably should have prevailed on this question. Thus, the court's refusal to allow Paul to file the first amended complaint was erroneous.

P's motion for leave to file his second amended complaint:
As noted above, leave to amend a pleading may be granted prior to trial whenever "…justice so requires…" Since the alleged rescission occurred on February 20, 1990, P's request for leave to file a second amended complaint (presumably made within 30 days of D's answer, which was filed on July 25, 1990) would still be within the one-year statute of limitations.

It should be noted that D's claim that P had executed a release of all claims held by the latter against D would probably constitute an affirmative defense. Since P is asserting that the purported release was invalid, it was probably unnecessary for him to amend his complaint a second time. This is because statements in a pleading to which no response is required (such as an affirmative defense) are taken to be denied; FRCP 8(c),(d).

D's application for an order for a medical examination and copies of medical reports.

(a) The medical examination: When the physical condition of a party is in controversy, the court may order the individual to submit to an examination by

a physician for good cause shown; FRCP 35. The notice of examination should specify the scope of the examination and the person or persons by whom it is to be made.

Since P is seeking to recover for personal injuries suffered as a consequence of D's allegedly negligent driving, D would probably be entitled to conduct a physical examination of P. Without such an examination, it would be virtually impossible to contradict evidence introduced by D to prove the extent of the injuries he suffered. Thus, the court's order for the medical examination was proper.

(b) Copies of all medical and hospital records: A party may ordinarily discover any non-privileged matter relevant to the pending action; FRCP 26(b)(1). The fact that the information sought to be obtained would be inadmissible at trial is **not** a basis for a successful objection, if such data appears to be reasonably calculated to lead to the discovery of admissible evidence.

P could contend, however, that (1) pursuant to FRCP 34(a), he could only be required to produce the documents in question for the purpose of permitting D to copy them (P, would not be obliged to make the copies), (2) P's hospital records are within the physician-client privilege, and (3) while medical and hospital records since the date of the accident might be pertinent, P's medical history one year prior to the accident is not relevant.

With respect to P's second argument, D could contend that the physician-patient privilege is ordinarily not extended to situations where the party involved has placed his own physical condition in issue (which P has done in this instance by claiming damages for injuries sustained as a consequence of the accident).

P's third objection could probably also be overcome because P's pre-accident physical condition is pertinent for purposes of verifying that the injuries for which P is demanding damages were not extant at the time the accident occurred. However, there does not appear to be a satisfactory rebuttal to P's initial contention (i.e., that he is only obliged to permit D to copy the medical and hospital reports). However, even if the court did rule improperly in requiring P to furnish copies of his medical records to D, this determination would probably constitute "harmless error." The question of who should bear the expense and inconvenience of copying particular items is probably not so "…inconsistent with substantial justice" as to constitute a basis for granting a new trial; FRCP 61. (*See* ELO Ch.5-III(H-I).)

D's motion for a separate trial without a jury with respect to the issues raised by the second amended complaint:

The Seventh Amendment assures litigants in a federal court the right to have all "legal" claims determined by a jury; FRCP 38(a). In *Beacon Theatres, Inc. v. Westover*, 359 U.S. 500 (1959), the U.S. Supreme Court held that where an issue of fact is common to both a legal and equitable claim, trial of the legal issues by a jury should precede determination of the equitable claims by the judge (except, possibly, where the party asserting an equitable claim would be irreparably harmed by the delay necessarily inherent in a full hearing on the legal issues).

D's action for rescission (while traditionally viewed as an "equitable" claim) embodies the "legal" issue of whether the release was fraudulently obtained. (In *Dairy Queen v. Wood*, 369 U.S. 469 (1962), the U.S. Supreme Court held that the nature of a claim is not determined by the label attached to it in the pleadings.) Thus, even if it were proper to try the rescission issue before the question of D's possible liability for the accident (i.e., if P's release was valid, it would be unnecessary to determine D's alleged liability and P's damages), P would probably still be entitled to have the jury determine the fraud issue. If the fraud allegation is resolved in favor of P, the court would then decide the strictly equitable question of whether it should exercise its discretionary power to negate the release.

Thus, D's motion should ***not*** have been granted. (*See* ELO Ch.7-XIII(D-G).)

Answer to Question 17

Zonco ("Z")'s motion to dismiss for failure to join Smith

A person who is subject to service of process and whose joinder will not deprive the court of subject matter jurisdiction must ordinarily be joined as a party to the action if (1) in her absence complete relief cannot be accorded to the existing parties, (2) disposition of the case in her absence may impede her ability to protect an interest relating to the subject matter of the action, *or* (3) her absence may subject a party to a substantial risk of incurring multiple liability for a single obligation; FRCP 19(a).

First, complete relief can be afforded to Paul ("P"), since he could obtain a judgment against Z for the full amount of his injuries. Second, Smith ("S")'s interest in the action will not be impaired by his absence (in fact, his presence in the litigation could only result in liability to him).

Finally, Z is not exposed to multiple liability because (1) it probably can assert an indemnity action against S for any judgment obtained by P, and (2) the risk of a judgment being recovered entirely from one of the tortfeasors is always a possibility when two or more parties are jointly and *severally* liable for the plaintiff's injuries.

Thus, the court correctly denied Z's motion to dismiss for failure to join S. (*See* ELO Ch.8-IV(D).)

P's notice to produce:

A party may obtain discovery of documents prepared for litigation or trial (1) for another party, or (2) by or for that party's representative (including her insurer), only upon a showing that substantial need for such materials exists and they are otherwise unobtainable without undue hardship; FRCP 26(b)(3).

Since the co-worker's statement was made to Z's insurer, Z could contend that it is within the work-product privilege. However, P could argue that there is a "substantial need" for the co-worker's statement since it was (presumably) given relatively soon after the accident, and would therefore be the most reliable version of the incident. While Z could depose the co-worker and arguably obtain the same information, since the co-worker would probably be a hostile witness (i.e., the co-worker is employed by Z, and might therefore be reluctant to make any comments which could adversely affect her employer in the litigation), the co-worker's statements to Z's insurance adjuster (which were not made to an adversarial party) are arguably not otherwise discoverable. Nevertheless, the trial court was probably correct in sustaining Z's refusal to produce the statement without at least an initial attempt by P to take the co-worker's deposition. (*See* ELO Ch.5-II(E)(7).)

P's summary judgment ("SJ") motion:

A summary judgment should be granted when there is no genuine issue as to any material fact and the moving party is entitled to prevail as a matter of law; FRCP 56(c).

P could contend that where an affidavit based upon personal knowledge establishes the material facts of a controversy, the adverse party must respond by a similar affidavit which disputes the facts asserted in the earlier one. Since Z did not contest the statements which S made in his deposition (i.e., that brake failure was the cause of the collision with P), P's SJ motion should arguably have been granted on the issue of liability.

However, Z could have argued that (1) depositions cannot be filed (even though under oath) by themselves (rather, they should be supplemented by an affidavit), (2) the fact that the brakes on Z's truck failed would not establish that Z had been negligent (i.e., it is at least possible that Z had the brakes examined by an independent automotive agency only a day before the alleged accident, or had otherwise used reasonable care to maintain its trucks), and (3) even if Smith's deposition established that the brakes on the truck had not been properly maintained by Z, P would still have to establish that (i) S was acting within the "course and scope" of Z's business, or (ii) that Z was otherwise aware that S might utilize its truck, for Z to be vicariously liable. Thus, P's SJ motion was properly denied. (*See* ELO Ch.7-IV(D).)

Z's motion for a judgment notwithstanding the verdict ("JNOV"), now called "judgment as a matter of law":

A JNOV (which results in the entry of judgment for the party who lost the trial) is proper where there is no legally sufficient basis for the determination reached by the jury. Z could have contended that while there was uncontradicted testimony that S was employed by Z and that P had suffered personal injury as a consequence of Smith's conduct, there apparently was no proof that P was acting within the course and scope of his employment (or at least with Z's knowledge). Thus, even if S was responsible for the accident, P failed to introduce any proof that Z was vicariously liable for S's conduct. However, if the accident occurred during regular business hours, it is possible that the jury could have inferred that S was employed by Z, and was acting within the scope of his employment at the time of the accident. Thus, the court properly denied Z's motion for a JNOV. (*See* ELO Ch.7-XI(A)(1).)

P's motion for a new trial:

A federal court may grant a new trial if the verdict (1) is against the clear weight of the evidence, or (2) will result in a miscarriage of justice, even though there may be substantial evidence which would prevent a directed verdict from being granted. The trial judge's determination that $85,000 does not adequately represent the pain and suffering would probably not be reversible. This is because the judge had the opportunity to personally observe the witness' testimony and evidence. However, granting a new trial unless the defendant agreed to raise the damage award was improper, since *additur* (a judicial order for a new trial unless the defendant consents to higher damages) has been found to be a violation of the Seventh Amendment for federal trial purposes; *Dimick v. Schiedt*, 293 U.S. 474 (1935). Thus, the trial court probably could grant a new trial solely on the issue of damages, but could not condition it upon Z's agreement to pay P an enhanced verdict. (*See* ELO Ch.7-IX(B) & IX(H)(2).)

Answer to Question 18

Dumbo's motion to Dismiss

(a) Personal jurisdiction: Paul ("P") could contend that personal jurisdiction exists because Dumbo ("D") is physically present within the jurisdiction via its warehouse and (presumably) attendant employees. D could contend in rebuttal, however, that there is language in *Shaffer v. Heitner*, 433 U.S. 186 (1977), which suggests that all assertions of personal jurisdiction must satisfy the "minimum contacts" standard articulated by the U.S. Supreme Court in *International Shoe*.

However, even if this interpretation of the *Shaffer v. Heitner* decision were followed by the federal courts in Ohio, P could nevertheless argue that the "minimum contacts" test is met in this instance because D has purposefully availed itself of the benefits of the forum by (1) maintaining a business establishment and having permanent employees in the state, and (2) doing 5% of its business within the jurisdiction. Additionally, since P was a citizen of Ohio, it should have been "reasonably foreseeable" to D that it might be haled into court in Ohio if a dispute pertaining to performance of the agreement arose.

D, of course, would contend in rebuttal that (1) 5% is a relatively small proportion of its overall business operations (especially if its income is derived in a somewhat even manner from all the states), and (2) if the contract had been accepted in Pennsylvania, the latter jurisdiction would be the appropriate one in which to litigate questions pertaining to its performance. The "minimum contacts" standard is probably satisfied, and the court's decision on this question was proper. (*See* ELO Ch.2-III(F) & V(C)(7-9).)

(b) Service of process: Pursuant to FRCP 4(h)(1), service of process may be accomplished in accordance with the law of the state in which the U.S. district court is located. Thus, service of process was, in effect, accomplished in compliance with the FRCP. Also, since process was personally served upon each member of D's board of directors, it would probably be deemed constitutional (i.e., reasonably calculated to inform the defendant of the lawsuit against it). Thus, the court correctly denied D's motion to dismiss upon this ground. (*See* ELO Ch.2-IV(C)(2).)

(c) Failure to state a claim upon which relief could be granted: Under FRCP 12(b), a motion to dismiss for failure to state a claim upon which relief can be granted is treated as a summary judgment motion when additional documents (here, the Points and Authorities) are appended. A summary judgment motion should be granted when there is no genuine issue as to any material fact; FRCP 56(c). Although the Points and Authorities submitted by P indicates that common law copyright has not been extended to video games, the district court could have determined that the U.S. Supreme Court would (if confronted with

this issue) apply the copyright law to this relatively new form of entertainment. Thus, the court's decision was probably correct. (*See* ELO Ch.7-IV(D).)

Is the default judgment valid?

A party may move for a default judgment after the expiration of 20 days from service of a summary judgment motion upon an adverse party if the party has not replied; FRCP 56(a). Since D's counterclaim was made upon P's attorney on February 23, D could contend that the 20-day period expired on March 14 (when the entry of default was made). However, P could respond that under FRCP 6(a), the day of the default "…from which the designated period of time begins to run shall not be included" in the computation of the 20-day period. Thus, if March 14 is excluded from the 20-day period, the entry of default was one day premature (and therefore void).

D could argue in rebuttal that even if the entry of default was one day early, this fact is inconsequential since (1) P did not file an answer by March 15 (the 20th day), and (2) the default judgment was not entered until March 16. However, given the usual judicial reluctance to grant default judgments, it is likely that P would prevail on this question.

Was the amount of the default judgment proper?

A default judgment cannot be entered by the clerk of the court unless the plaintiff's claim is for a sum which can be made certain by computation. In other cases, the moving party must apply to the court for a default judgment, and at least three days notice must be given to the defaulting party (if he has appeared in the action); FRCP 55(b).

While the amount paid to Susan would constitute a "sum certain", the $10,000 portion of the judgment reflecting the materials delivered to P would not (i.e., this amount would have to be "proved up" by P). Thus, a default judgment against P, only in the amount of $80,000, should have been entered.

D's motion for judgment on the pleadings:

D's assertion that P admitted the allegations of its affirmative defense by not responding to them is incorrect. Under the FRCP, averments in an affirmative defense are deemed to be denied if no responsive pleading is made; FRCP 8(d). (*See* ELO Ch.4-VII(B)(1).)

D's assertion that *res judicata* principles preclude a successful action by P would probably be successful. In a majority of jurisdictions, P would be precluded from re-litigating the breach of contract action inherent in D's judgment. However, if, as discussed above, the purported default judgment is probably invalid, D's motion for judgment on the pleadings should not be granted.

Should P's motion to set aside the default judgment be granted?

Pursuant to FRCP 60(b), a judgment may be set aside where it is the result of a mistake, inadvertence or excusable neglect.

Although P's attorney could assert that the summer clerk's accidental misplacement of D's responsive pleading comes within this standard, D would probably prevail on this issue. P's attorney should have entered the date to respond on her calendar prior to giving the document to the summer clerk. However, since (as discussed above) the default judgment is probably invalid because it was prematurely filed, no valid judgment against P exists.

Answer to Question 19

The FRCP 12(b) motion to dismiss the case:

Since U.S. district courts "borrow" the long-arm statute of the state in which they are located, it is assumed that the State B legislature has enacted a law which gives its courts all personal jurisdiction consistent with due process.

Salco ("S")'s FRCP 12(b) motion probably asserted that it does not have the "minimum contacts" with State B necessary to satisfy due process (i.e., S does not have sufficient minimum contacts with the forum as to avoid offending traditional notions of fair play and substantial justice). S would contend that it has not availed itself of the benefits of the forum because (1) it employs no agents or salespersons within State B, (2) its advertising is purchased in magazines published outside State B, and (3) the amount of business done with citizens of State B ($75,000) is relatively small.

Poe ("P") could argue in rebuttal, however, that S should have reasonably foreseen being haled into the forum because it was aware (via its employees who received the orders and sent the items) that numerous persons from State B were purchasing its clocks.

Although a close question, S's motion to dismiss the case for lack of personal jurisdiction probably should have been granted.

S could have also asserted that the notice which it received was constitutionally defective (i.e., not reasonably calculated under the circumstances to give it notice of the action against it). (The fact that service of process was made in accordance with State B law presents no problem, since the FRCP specifically authorizes service of process in conformity with the laws of the state in which the U.S. district court is sitting.) S probably contended that service by mail (even a registered mailing) in the first instance is impermissible where the summons and complaint could probably have been personally served upon the defendant (i.e., presumably, the names and addresses of S's officers or directors could have easily been obtained from the State A corporate records). Registered mailing is always fraught with the possibility that someone could sign for the item and yet (not appreciating the legal significance of the document contained inside) fail to read it or deliver it to the appropriate person.

However, P could argue that the president of a corporation is likely to appreciate the potential importance of registered mail.

Although a close question, P would probably prevail on this issue. However, as discussed above, since personal jurisdiction was probably lacking, S's FRCP 12(b) motion to dismiss should have been granted. (*See* ELO Ch.2-III(F-G) & VI(C).)

The motion to remand the case back to the state court:

An action cannot be removed to a U.S. district court unless federal subject matter jurisdiction exists. S's motion to remand was probably based upon the assertion that P (and each member of the class) did not possess a claim against it in "excess of" $75,000. In *Zahn v. International Paper Co.*, 414 U.S. 291 (1973), the U.S. Supreme Court held that the claims of the class may *not* be aggregated for the purpose of satisfying the amount in controversy requirement for "diversity" subject matter jurisdiction.

P could contend in rebuttal that if the $25,000,000 in punitive damages were distributed amongst each of the members of the plaintiff class, the claims of each person would exceed $75,000. P would also point out that the "amount in controversy" requisite should be considered satisfied, unless the court determines "to a legal certainty" that the damages sought by the plaintiff could not be recovered. Nevertheless, because punitive damages are relatively speculative, a U.S. district court would probably *not* allocate a *pro rata* amount of the total damages demanded by the plaintiff to each member of the class in determining if the "in excess of $75,000" element was met.

Thus, the motion to remand was improperly denied. (*See* ELO Ch.3-V(E)(2)(c) & 8-V(I)(1).)

The motion for a more definite statement:

If a complaint is so vague or ambiguous that the defendant cannot reasonably be required to frame a responsive pleading, he may move for a more definite statement; FRCP 12(e). S could have contended that since allegations of fraud must be stated with particularity (FRCP 9(b)), its motion for a more definite statement is appropriate. P's complaint apparently alleged only that the clocks were purchased as a consequence of S's misrepresentations, without any description of the allegedly fraudulent statements. While P could contend in rebuttal that the exact wording upon which the complaint is predicated could be developed during discovery, the court's denial of S's motion for a more definite statement was probably improper. (*See* ELO Ch.4-V(D).)

Was Jones ("J") barred from suing S?

If, as discussed above, subject matter jurisdiction was lacking because each class member's claim did not exceed $75,000, the district court judgment would be invalid. It would therefore not be binding upon J (a void judgment may always be collaterally attacked by a non-party to the original action; FRCP 60(b)(4)).

Assuming, however, that subject matter jurisdiction did exist, more facts would have to be ascertained to determine if J's claim was barred or not. Under FRCP 23(b)(3) actions, each member of the class must be given notice and an opportunity to "opt out" of the action if she desires to do so; FRCP 23(c)(2).

Assuming J received adequate notice of the action, his claim would be barred. If adequate notice had not been received by J, his present action against S could be maintained. (*See* ELO Ch.8-V(G-H).)

Answer to Question 20

A default judgment is valid when it is statutorily and constitutionally sound. We'll assume that the Calvada state court is competent to hear the matter upon which Paul ("P") sued Glassco ("G") for $100,000.

Did P comply with the statutory requirements of the Calvada long-arm statute?

G could contend that the Calvada long-arm statute does not apply to it because: (1) it is not a "person," and (2) since the defective manufacture of the glasses occurred in State White, the cause of action did not arise out of "a tortious act" in Calvada. P would argue in rebuttal that: (1) a corporation should be deemed a "person," since it is an independent legal entity and the word "natural" would have been inserted before the word "person" by the legislators if they had intended the statute to pertain only to individuals, and (2) the action arose when P was injured, and that "act" occurred in Calvada. P should prevail on these issues.

Can the Calvada court constitutionally exercise personal jurisdiction over G?

To give personal jurisdiction over an out-of-state defendant, she must have sufficient "minimum contacts" with the forum state as not to offend traditional notions of substantial justice and fair play. G would argue that since (1) it does no business in Calvada (the offer was made and accepted in State Black, where the Certificates are received and orders filled by G's employees), and (2) at $1.00 per set, G is not really, "selling" the glasses (apparently, Krispy is paying the major portion of the cost because $1.00 would probably not even cover the expense of mailing and handling), it should not be required to undertake a trial in Calvada.

P would contend in rebuttal, however, that since G (1) knew that the cereal certificate would be distributed throughout the country, and (2) had received the order from Calvada, it should have foreseen the possibility of being haled into court in Calvada. P should prevail. (*See* ELO Ch.2-III(G).)

Was there statutory compliance with the notice (i.e., service of process) statute of Calvada?

A default judgment is not valid if service was not accomplished in conformity with the applicable statute and in a constitutionally valid manner. G would argue that the statutory words "its place of business" should be construed to mean its "principal place of business," since the word "its" suggests a single place, and therefore only the primary place of business would suffice. While P would contend in rebuttal that "its place of business" means the place where the plaintiff conducted his business with the corporation, G should prevail on this issue. Therefore, the judgment should be overturned.

Assuming, however, there was compliance with the Calvada notice statute, is the statute constitutionally valid?

Notice must be "reasonably calculated" under the circumstances to apprise the defendant of the action. G would contend that mailing a registered or certified letter to a corporation should not suffice, since relatively low level personnel in a mailroom could either (1) lose a certified letter, or (2) (if unhappy with management) deliberately misplace such an item.

P could argue in rebuttal that a registered or certified mailing should suffice, since people ordinarily recognize that important documents come by such means. Therefore, there is little likelihood that documents mailed in this manner would *not* come to the attention of the proper persons. It should be noted, however, that under the FRCP, delivery of a summons and complaint by mail is not valid unless the recipient explicitly acknowledges receipt. G would probably prevail on this issue also. (*See* ELO Ch.2-VI(C)(2-5).)

If the judgment is valid, should it be overturned?

An otherwise valid default judgment may be overturned (1) for good cause, or (2) where there has been justifiable mistake, inadvertence or excusable neglect on the part of the defendant; FRCP 55(c).

G would contend that there has been mistake and inadvertence by reason of the fact that employees at the distribution plant justifiably refused to accept the certified mailing because they probably felt they lacked authority to accept a registered mailing and the letter would be re-mailed to G's main office if service was refused. While P will contend in rebuttal that it is not justifiable to refuse a certified mailing simply because the receiver is uncertain as to his authority to accept it, G would probably prevail on this point too.

Is Paul likely to prevail on the same evidence?

G could also contend that there was insufficient evidence for the finding it liable, since P failed to show that G was negligent in the manufacture of the glasses. However, P could argue that under the theories of products liability — breach of the implied warranty of merchantability or negligence (via use of the *res ipsa loquitor* doctrine) — there was adequate evidence to prove the default judgment. It is unclear, however, as to how the jury determined that P's damages were $25,000. Without proof of medical bills or lost income, there was arguably insufficient proof for this aspect of the judgment. While P could contend that a jury could infer that he suffered pain and suffering in the amount of $25,000, more evidence would probably have to be introduced to sustain this aspect of the judgment.

Answer to Question 21

The FRCP 12(b) motion to quash:

It is assumed that P claimed damages in excess of $75,000.

Although service within a jurisdiction has been a traditional basis for obtaining personal jurisdiction over an out-of-state citizen, James ("J") could have made two objections within the context of his FRCP 12 motion to dismiss Peter ("P")'s action. First, where a defendant is "lured" into a jurisdiction (usually on a false premise), a court, in its discretion, may ordinarily quash the service of process; FRCP 12(b)(5).

Second, there is language in *Shaffer v. Heitner*, 433 U.S. 186 (1977), which suggests that all assertions of personal jurisdiction must be tested by "minimum contacts." Since J is a citizen of State White and the accident occurred in that jurisdiction, there is no indication from the facts that J had any contacts (whatsoever) with State Red.

P could contend that (assuming it was the fact), merely because he "invited" J into State White to discuss his claim, he did not promise that service of process would not be made. If J was concerned about being served in State Red, he could have (1) refused P's offer, or (2) required P to stipulate in advance that no attempt to serve him would be made. P could also assert that the Supreme Court has held that even after *Shaffer* service of process within a forum is still a valid means of obtaining personal jurisdiction over an individual; *Burnham v. Superior Court*, 495 U.S. 604 (1990). Thus, the court's ruling was probably proper. (*See* ELO Ch.2-VII(E) & V(C)(7-9).)

J's forum non conveniens ("FNC") motion:

An action commenced in a U.S. district court may be transferred to another federal court in a different judicial district if (1) the action could have been commenced in the latter district court, and (2) the "…convenience of the parties and witnesses…" would be accommodated by the transfer. Since P's action is based upon diversity, it could have been initiated in State Red (the jurisdiction in which the defendant resides). (*See* ELO Ch.2-VIII(E)(10).) J could argue that State White is the more appropriate forum because (1) any witnesses to the accident are presumably domiciled there, and (2) any hospital or medical records would presumably be found in that state. It is unclear from the facts how far apart States Red and White are located. However, if it is a significant distance, J would probably prevail on this question (despite the fact that a "…plaintiff's choice of forum should rarely be disturbed," *Gulf Oil v. Gilbert*, 330 U.S. 501 (1947)).

P's motion to amend his complaint:

Under the FRCP, a party may amend her pleading at any time before a "responsive" pleading has been served. FRCP 15(a). Since FRCP 12(b) and FNC motions are not pleadings to which a response must be filed, J was entitled to amend his complaint as of right. (*See* ELO Ch.4-IX(B)(1).)

J's motion for a judgment on the pleadings:

J apparently contended that since the amendment (which correctly stated J's name) was not made until the applicable statute of limitations had expired, he was entitled to a judgment on the pleadings. P could point out that the FRCP provides that an amendment *changing the party* relates back to the date of the original pleading if within the 120 day period for service of the summons and complaint the party named in the amended pleading (1) has received such notice of the action that it will not be prejudiced in defending itself and (2) knew (or should have known) that, but for the mistaken identity, the action would have been brought against him. FRCP 15(c).

While the two conditions appear to be satisfied, it is unclear whether P amended his complaint within 120 days of filing the original complaint. If not, P could argue that he is not attempting to *change* or *add* a party. Rather, he simply desires to correctly state the name of the person he is already suing. P is more likely to prevail on this issue since J (1) has apparently not suffered prejudice by the delay in effectuating the name change, and (2) in effect, has waived any objection by responding to P's action (via the FRCP 12(b) and FNC motions, as well as his answer).

Since there is no FRCP provision precluding the correction of a party's name, the amendment would probably relate back to P's original complaint (and therefore be within the statute of limitations).

The facts are silent as to whether there is a State Red rule of law which specifically precludes relation back for statute of limitations purposes in a situation such as that posed by the present case. If there were such rule, J would argue that it is substantive in nature, and therefore (under *Erie* principles) would be controlling. P could contend in rebuttal that a statute of limitations rule is procedural in nature (and therefore federal procedural law is determinative). However, the Supreme Court has indicated that the computation of time for purposes of deciding when a cause of action can no longer be asserted is a substantive rule; *Walker v. Armco Steel Corp.*, 446 U.S. 740 (1980). Since a similar rationale could be applied to the change of a party's identity, J would probably prevail on this issue.

However, in the absence of any State Red rule of law specifically stating that a name change may not relate back to the original pleading, (as indicated above) P should prevail. (*See* ELO Ch.4-IX(D)(4).)

Answer to Question 22

Question 1:

The defendants could appear in the U.S. district court in Oklahoma and make an FRCP 12(b)(2) motion to dismiss the action. To yield personal jurisdiction over an out-of-state citizen, he must have sufficient "minimum contacts" with the forum as to not offend traditional notions of fair play and substantial justice. In determining if this standard is satisfied, a court will ordinarily weigh (1) the extent to which the defendant has availed him of the benefits of the forum, (2) whether the defendant could reasonably foresee being haled into court in that state, and (3) the relationship between the wrong allegedly committed by the defendant and its impact within the forum. Although Paul ("P") would contend that (1) Bobb ("B') availed himself of the forum by having an interest in a limited partnership which had an asset within the state, and (2) Silley's ("S") should have foreseen being haled into Oklahoma since 3% of its business was attributable to that jurisdiction, he probably will *not* be successful. As a limited partner, B has no authority or active role in the operation of the apartment house in Oklahoma. Additionally, since (1) S's sales in Oklahoma were (a) a small proportion of its overall business, and (b) of the mail order variety, and (2) the mail order purchases have no relationship to P's alleged injury, it is also unlikely that personal jurisdiction over S would be found.

Alternatively, S could fail to appear in Oklahoma, and then collaterally attack the default judgment when P attempted to enforce it in Texas. If the situs of B's limited partnership interest is Texas, B could adopt a similar strategy. However, if B's limited partnership interest can be attached or seized in Oklahoma (i.e., 5% of the net proceeds derived from the apartment house could be seized in that state), B would have to appear in the district court in Oklahoma. If he did not, P would be able to satisfy a default judgment from B's partnership proceeds.

If B and S did appear in Oklahoma, and their FRCP 12(b) motion was unsuccessful, they could make a *forum non conveniens* ("FNC") motion to transfer the action to the judicial district of the U.S. district court which encompasses Austin, Texas. Venue for a diversity action would be satisfied because the cause of action arose in that judicial district. In support of this motion, the defendants could argue that all witnesses to the incident probably live in that area. However, since relatively few potential witnesses are probably involved, it is unlikely that an FNC motion would be successful. (*See* ELO Ch.2-III(C-E), VII(D), VIII(D-E).)

Question 2:

Joinder of claims against multiple defendants is permissible where (1) the claims asserted against them arise out of the same transaction or occurrence, and (2) there is common question of law or fact; FRCP 20(a). Most federal courts adhere to the view that claims arise from the same occurrence if they are "logically related." Since all of P's claims arise from the incident which occurred outside S's store, the initial condition is probably satisfied. As to the second condition, a factual issue which must be resolved in both actions would be whether P had actually taken something from S. If he had, then B's conduct may have been privileged (assuming he had not used excessive force) and the arrest would not have been "false." Thus, the claims could probably be joined. (*See* ELO Ch.8-IV(B)(2-3).)

Question 3:

The court would appear to be competent since (1) the claim against B is predicated upon a federal statute (i.e., a federal claim), and (2) there is diversity between P and Mary ("M"), and between P and S. With respect to the latter action, it is assumed that P is claiming damages in excess of $75,000. Finally, the assault and battery claim against B could be supported by both (a) supplemental jurisdiction, and (b) diversity (assuming the alleged damages exceed $75,000).

Question 4:

The ATPD could make an FRCP 12(b)(6) motion (i.e., that P failed to state a claim upon which relief could be granted). If the ATPD attached a Points and Authorities and/or an affidavit from its chief-of-police (asserting that it had never authorized the specific conduct in question), its FRCP 12(b) motion, would be treated as a motion for summary judgment; FRCP 12(b). If this motion failed, the ATPD could file an answer alleging that it did not authorize the particular conduct in question (i.e., B's applying the chokehold upon P), and then move for a judgment on the pleadings; FRCP 12(c).

Question 5:

B could assert a cross-claim against the ATPD if his action against that entity is deemed to arise out of the occurrence which is the subject of P's claim. The ATPD could contend that no logical relationship between the two claims exists because (1) P's injury arose out of a physical act (the chokehold), and (2) B's action arises from a written agreement.

However, B could argue in rebuttal that (1) the ATPD's liability to him, if any, arises from his conduct vis-a-vis P, and (2) FRCP 13(g) specifically states that a cross-claim may include an action for indemnification. Thus, B's claim against the ATPD would probably be allowed by the district court.

The facts that (1) B and the ATPD are citizens of the same jurisdiction, and (2) the amount involved is unstated, are not relevant since ancillary jurisdiction exists with respect to cross-claims. (*See* ELO Ch.8-X(B-C).)

Question 6:

A person may intervene as of right into a federal case where (1) she has an interest in the subject matter of the action, (2) the action may impair her ability to protect that interest, **and** (3) her interest is not adequately represented by an existing party; FRCP 24(a). P could probably contend that there is no right to intervene because (1) a decision by a U.S. district court in Texas would not be binding upon federal courts outside of that district, and (2) there is (presumably) no reason to believe that the ATPD's counsel would not adequately assert its contention that no federal claim exists. The potential intervenors could argue in rebuttal that if B prevailed, and the decision was affirmed on appeal, (1) a precedent would be set in that circuit, and (2) the ruling could have a persuasive effect on other district courts in the nation.

Additionally, since P is claiming only $85,000, the ATPD may not have retained the best counsel available to defend this matter. Nevertheless, a court would probably hold that the other police departments could **not** intervene as of right.

Intervention is permissible where the applicants wish to assert a claim or defense similar to that alleged by an existing party; FRCP 24(b). While permissive intervention will not be granted where the applicant's presence would serve no useful purpose (i.e., the ATPD could effectively argue against B's conduct being interpreted as a federal claim), the court, in its discretion, could allow intervention in these circumstances. Since the intervenors would merely be submitting a brief in opposition to the legal aspects of P's claim (i.e., that the conduct in question constituted a federal claim), intervention would not have a disruptive impact upon the case. (*See* ELO Ch.8-VI(B-C).)

Answer to Question 23

1.   Was the court correct in denying P's motion for summary judgment ("SJ")?

When a summary judgment motion is supported by an affidavit based upon personal knowledge and which describes facts which are admissible into evidence at trial, the adverse party may **not** rest upon the allegations contained in his pleadings. The latter must respond with affidavits or statements made under oath during discovery; FRCP 56(e). Thus, P probably contended that, because D's attorney failed to respond with a statement made under oath, SJ upon the question of liability was appropriate.

However, while the failure to install a smoke detector in a patient's room constitutes **negligence per se**, it does **not** establish liability. It establishes only that one element of negligence (i.e., the defendant failed to have acted reasonably) is present. In this case, D might still be able to successfully contend that causation is absent (i.e., even with a functioning smoke detector, P would have suffered exactly the same injuries).

Thus, the court was correct in denying P's SJ motion.

2.   Was the court correct in ordering D to produce the fire investigator's report?

A party may ordinarily obtain discovery of documents prepared by another party in anticipation of litigation or trial only upon a showing that the former (1) has a substantial need for the item, and (2) is unable, without undue hardship, to obtain the equivalent by other means; FRCP 26(b)(3). P probably argued that (1) there is a substantial need for the report, since it greatly assists in establishing an important fact (i.e., P's room did not have a smoke detector in it) which D has denied, and (2) this fact can no longer be verified by P, since the home has been demolished.

D might have contended in rebuttal that the appropriate corporate officer had already admitted in an interrogatory that there was no smoke detector in P's room. Therefore, there was no substantial need for the report. However, the court was probably correct in ordering D to produce this item since a statement made in an interrogatory may be contradicted by that party at trial (as occurred in this case).

3.   Was the court correct in holding D in contempt for refusing P's discovery request?

When a party does not furnish information sought to be discovered, the party seeking discovery must ordinarily seek an FRCP 37(a) order compelling discovery. If such an order is obtained **and** the discoveree **persists** in his refusal, the court may order a variety of sanctions (including holding the disobedient party in contempt); FRCP 37(b). However, since the court in this instance held D in contempt *at the same time* that it issued the Rule 37(a) order compelling production of the inspection, the contempt ruling was probably improper.

4. Was the court correct in denying P's motion to disallow M's testimony?

There is no rule which precludes testimony simply because it is inconsistent with an answer to an interrogatory. The statement made in the interrogatory may be used (1) to impeach M, and (2) as substantive evidence against D (under the FRE the corporate official's response is *not* hearsay; FRE 801(d)(2). The court, therefore, was correct in denying P's motion.

Answer to Question 24

1. Borrow's ("B") motion to remand

When the plaintiff's complaint is premised upon a federal claim, the defendant (regardless of citizenship) can have the action removed to the federal district court which encompasses the place where the action is pending. Since B's claim is based upon a federal statute (the TLA), Finco ("F") was entitled to have the action removed to the applicable U.S. District Court.

If a federal judge subsequently concludes that removal does not satisfy the applicable statutory requirements, the case must be remanded back to the state court. Additionally, the judge may, in his discretion, remand the case back to state court if there is also a pendent state claim and it is likely that the federal claim will be dismissed before trial. Since neither of these circumstances are present, the court correctly denied B's motion to remand.

2. B's motion to amend his complaint

Dealer ("D") probably contended that, since (1) it is a citizen of State A (where it is incorporated and conducts all of its business), and (2) B is a resident of State A, diversity subject matter jurisdiction is *not* satisfied for the state law claim which B is asserting against him. Additionally, only $20,000 in damages is being asserted (far short of the necessary jurisdictional amount of "in excess of" $75,000). Thus, the federal court had to deny the motion.

However, under *supplemental party jurisdiction* principles, where a valid federal claim has been asserted, a federal court may hear a claim against a party over whom it would otherwise *not* have subject matter jurisdiction, if that claim is *transactionally related* to the underlying federal claim. D could contend that the claims are *not transactionally related*, since B is contending that D provided B with erroneous information while the claim against F asserts complete failure to disclose required data. However, since both of B's claims pertain to the circumstances surrounding his signing of the papers with regard to his vehicle purchase, it is likely that the "transactionally related" requirement is satisfied.

Thus, the court incorrectly ruled that it lacked subject matter jurisdiction over B's action against D.

3. B's motion for partial summary judgment

Summary judgment is proper when there is no "genuine issue of material fact" with respect to one or more aspects of the lawsuit.

B is apparently contending that, under collateral estoppel principles, where the identical issue was actually litigated in a prior lawsuit by the party, a court may preclude re-litigation of that issue in a subsequent proceeding, thereby finding in favor of B on the issue of TLA violation.

B's argument is not likely to succeed for two reasons. First, there is a question as to whether this jurisdiction recognizes the "mutuality rule." If it does, issue preclusion is not available to B, since F could not have utilized this doctrine against B.

Second, even assuming the "mutuality rule" is *not* applicable, issue preclusion is inappropriate. The fact that F had, on prior occasions with completely different parties, failed to disclose required information does not warrant application of collateral estoppel. Those transactions were entirely independent of the factual issues in this case. Therefore, withholding information in one, or even several, instances does not prove F behaved similarly in dealing with B.

Thus, the court should deny B's partial summary judgment motion.

Answer to Question 25

1. Motions for judgment on the pleadings

A motion for judgment on the pleadings challenges only the sufficiency of the adversary's pleadings (i.e., it does not assert defects which do **not** appear on the face of the pleadings). In federal court, a complaint need only adequately inform the defendant of the nature of the action against him/her and state the relief requested.

Dave ("D") might have argued that the complaint (1) failed to describe the basis of his negligent conduct (i.e., it merely stated he was "negligent" as a legal conclusion), and (2) prayed for an amount ($250,000) far in excess of Paul ("P")'s alleged injuries (i.e., $25,000). However, P probably successfully asserted in rebuttal that (1) it should have been obvious to D that P was contending that the former had not operated his vehicle in a reasonable manner, and (2) the mere fact that the prayer did not coincide with the injuries set forth in the body of the document does not cause a complaint to fail (damages must always be proven).

An answer must effectively deny the plaintiff's allegations for those assertions to be put into issue. Failure to adequately deny allegations contained in a complaint constitutes an admission of those assertions. However, damages are always deemed to be in issue (even if **not** adequately denied); FRCP 9(d). Since D's answer does not unequivocally "deny" the assertions contained in P's complaint, P probably argued that D, in effect, admitted them (except for damages). D could have argued that, since his answer stated that he did not "admit" the assertions contained in P's complaint, he impliedly denied them. This argument would probably fail, however, since D's answer stated that the allegations in P's complaint were not denied. Thus, the District Court should have granted P's motion for a judgment on the pleadings (exclusive of his prayer for damages).

2. Al's motion to dismiss

Under the FRCP, an amendment changing the party against whom an action is being asserted relates back to the date of the original pleading, if (1) the claim arose out of the occurrence set forth in the initial pleading, (2) the defendant knew (or should have known) that, but for a mistake pertaining to the identity of the proper party, the action would have been brought against him/her, **and** (3) the claim is asserted within the applicable statute of limitation period; FRCP 15(c).

While the statute speaks in terms of changing a pre-existing party, it has been deemed to apply to attempts by a plaintiff to **add** a new party to the case; *Anderson v. Papillon*, 445 F.2d 841 (5th Cir. 1971). Since (1) Al was unaware of P's action against D, and (2) the statute of limitation would have run against Al in the absence of the relation-back doctrine, the court improperly denied Al's motion to dismiss P's complaint against him.

P could have contended, however, that State Y's relation-back statute should apply under *Erie* principles: when a state substantive rule and the FRCP are in direct conflict, the former should control. While Al could have asserted in rebuttal that the State Y statute is procedural (rather than substantive) in nature, and therefore the FRCP should be determinative, this contention would probably **not** be successful. Statute of limitation rules have ordinarily been deemed to be important, substantive rights. Thus, assuming Al is not prejudiced in his defense by being added as a defendant at this time (in which event, there would be a violation of his due process rights to a fair trial), P can add Al to the lawsuit. (There is no question that the action against Al arose from the same occurrence that gave rise to P's claim against D.)

3. Al's motion to compel an answer to his interrogatory and the production of documents

A party may obtain relevant papers which were prepared in anticipation of litigation by (or for) another party, or his/her representative, only upon a showing that the party seeking discovery (1) has a substantial need for them, and (2) is otherwise unable to obtain those materials without undue hardship; FRCP 26(b)(3). The "work product" privilege, however, prevents discovery of opinions, legal theories or mental impressions of another party's attorney.

P might have asserted that Al's demand does not meet the requirements of FRCP 26(b)(3) because (1) Wilma was acting pursuant to his direction when she obtained the statements from the two witnesses, and (2) Al could obtain this information by directly questioning those persons. If that is true, then the information was obtained in anticipation of litigation and Al can easily obtain that information. The statements, therefore, are not discoverable. However, there was no indication that Wilma was acting pursuant to P's instructions or under his direction. Second, there is a substantial need for this information because, even if Al's attorney questioned those witnesses directly, there is no other means of determining if their answers were consistent. Thus, P should be required to answer Al's interrogatory. (Interestingly, P could have possibly answered D's interrogatory in the negative, since Wilma, rather than P, took the statements in question.)

If, however, the notes that P's attorney made on these statements contain legal theories, impressions or conclusions, they are protected by the work product privilege. Al can obtain these statements, but Len's notes must be somehow deleted.

Answer to Question 26

1. *Was the denial of Dan (D)'s motion to make Trucko (T) a party proper?*

A person must be joined as a party where the failure to do so: (1) will result in the inability of the court to grant complete relief to persons who are already parties, (2) may impair that person's ability to protect an interest relating to the subject matter of the action, or (3) leaves any party to the action subject to a substantial risk of incurring liability or inconsistent obligations. If such a person is not subject to service of process, or if his joinder will deprive the court of subject matter jurisdiction, the case will ordinarily be dismissed.

Price can contend that T is not a necessary party. Complete relief can be given to Price (i.e., he can obtain a judgment for the full amount of his injuries against D).

Additionally, D's interests are not prejudiced by the absence of T. Even assuming D could show Price's truck lacked lights, T's absence as a defendant would **not** preclude D from offering evidence of this fact in his defense (i.e., to show there was no causal relationship between D's conduct and P's injuries). If D offered such evidence and prevailed, the determination of this issue would not preclude T from relitigating this question if Price subsequently sued T.

Thus, the court was correct in denying D's motion to join T.

However, the court's statement that it had no personal jurisdiction over T is probably incorrect. Assuming State Z has a long-arm statute which applies to T, the "minimum contacts" test is likely to be satisfied by the fact that Price's injury arose from T's conduct within the jurisdiction. Finally, it's difficult to know what the court intended by its statement that "service of process would be difficult." If personal jurisdiction can be exercised over T, effectuating service is usually a relatively facile matter.

Thus, the court probably ruled correctly, but for the wrong reasons.

2. *Was the order approving an examination of D's physical capabilities proper?*

Under FRCP 35, upon a showing of good cause, the court may order a physical examination of a party where his condition is in controversy. D can argue that, since Price has alleged that the accident was caused by the former's failure to use carburetor heat, D's physical condition is **not** in controversy. Price can respond that, while the lack of carburetor heat may have caused D to land the plane, a pilot possessing ordinary physical attributes would have nevertheless been able to avoid the accident.

The court's decision was probably incorrect. It should have awaited discovery by Price of evidence which tended to show that D's physical impairment contributed, in some manner, to the accident. Once this was established, Price's FRCP 35 motion would be proper.

3.   Was the court's instruction to the jury that it could consider evidence of Price's contributory negligence proper?

Affirmative defenses must ordinarily be specifically pleaded by a defendant; FRCP 8(c). However, when issues not raised by the pleadings are litigated at trial, those issues are treated as if alleged in the pleadings; FRCP 15(b). Since D introduced evidence at the trial showing that Price's truck lacked lights without objection by the latter party, the pleadings are deemed to be amended to contain an assertion of Price's contributory negligence.

Thus, the court's instruction permitting the jury to consider Price's possible contributory negligence was proper.

Multiple-Choice Questions

1. Paul, a State District Attorney, files a complaint in the proper U.S. district court seeking to enjoin a pro-communist rally. He alleges the rally is being held without a license, in violation of a state statute. Paul asserts federal question jurisdiction by alleging that the defendants have publicly claimed immunity for such rallies on First Amendment grounds.

    Denton, the group leader, files an FRCP 12(b)(1) motion to dismiss for lack of subject matter jurisdiction. He alternatively claims immunity from prosecution under the First Amendment as an affirmative defense.

    Denton's motion should be:

    (A) Granted, because there is no subject matter jurisdiction.
    (B) Granted, because Denton has asserted a First Amendment defense.
    (C) Denied, because there is "federal question" subject matter jurisdiction.
    (D) Denied, because Paul's claim involves the U.S. Constitution.

2. Paula and Pete were hit by a truck driven by an employee of the D Corporation. The accident occurred in California, where Paula and Pete were living at that time. D's headquarters are in Florida, but its principal place of business is in Michigan. It is incorporated in Delaware. After the accident, Paula and Pete moved to Miami, Florida, where they planned to retire.

    After moving, they contacted a lawyer who filed suit against D in the appropriate U.S. district court where Paula and Pete lived, alleging diversity jurisdiction. The suit alleged that each plaintiff had suffered personal injuries in excess of $75,000. D moved to dismiss the case for lack of subject matter jurisdiction.

    D's motion should be:

    (A) Granted, because the plaintiffs were citizens of California when they were injured.
    (B) Granted, because D's headquarters are in Florida.
    (C) Denied, because diversity subject matter jurisdiction exists.
    (D) Denied, because D is a citizen of Delaware only.

3. P files suit in the U.S. district court in Nevada alleging a federal claim (i.e., racial discrimination against him occurring in Texas). The defendant is a citizen of California, and all of the witnesses live in Texas. P lives in Nevada. The defendant moves to change the venue to California, or alternatively, to Texas. Which of the following is correct?

(A) The action may only be transferred to California.

(B) The action may be transferred to California or Texas.

(C) The action must be dismissed, since it was commenced in an improper forum.

(D) It is discretionary with the court whether to retain the action or transfer it to California or Texas.

4. Priscilla filed suit against Derek for recovery of a shipment of cargo lost at sea. The suit was filed in a court of general jurisdiction in State A. Derek was personally served at his home in State B. He has no contacts with State A. Derek made a general appearance in the State A court and filed a demurrer to the complaint. The demurrer was overruled and the case proceeded to trial, where Priscilla prevailed.

You may assume that Priscilla's claim is in admiralty, which is within the exclusive jurisdiction of the federal courts. On appeal, Derek asserted (1) lack of personal jurisdiction; and (2) lack of subject matter jurisdiction. Derek should:

(A) Prevail on both (1) and (2).

(B) Prevail on (1) only.

(C) Prevail on (2) only.

(D) Lose on both (1) and (2).

5. Plaintiff, a citizen of State A, filed suit against Defendant in a State A court, alleging a claim based upon a federal statute. Defendant, also a citizen of State A, filed a petition for removal to the federal court which encompasses the judicial district in which the state court is located.

Should the action be removed?

(A) No, because the action could not have originally been brought in the U.S. district court to which removal has been requested.

(B) Yes, because Plaintiff's action arises under a U.S. Statute.

(C) Yes, because state courts, even those of general jurisdiction, do not have subject matter jurisdiction over federal claims.

(D) No, because Defendant is a citizen of State A.

6. Acme became involved in a labor dispute with the Steamroller's Union (the entity which ordinarily supplied workers for Acme's plant). Acme brought an action against Steamroller's Union ("Union") in the appropriate U.S. district court, claiming $75,000 in damages as a consequence of Union's conduct in harassing and intimidating non-union workers in violation of the National Labor Relations Act and applicable state law.

Acme is an Indiana corporation and Union (an unincorporated association) has members who are domiciled in every state, except New York and New Jersey. Union answered by denying Acme's allegations and filing a $15,000 counterclaim (which asserted that Acme had deliberately made false accusations about Union to the local papers for the purpose of obtaining favorable press coverage).

If Union moves to dismiss for lack of subject matter jurisdiction, it should:

(A) Prevail, because there is no diversity.
(B) Prevail, because Acme has not claimed monetary damages in excess of $75,000.
(C) Lose, because subject matter jurisdiction is satisfied.
(D) Lose, because a state claim has been asserted in a federal court.

7. Bank is a Missouri Corporation. Bank has a savings account in the name of one of its customers, Harvey Hunt, who was domiciled in California. Harvey recently died. In his will, Harvey left the entire account (in the specific amount of $7,000) to his nephew Sam, a citizen of Texas. On the same day that Sam showed up to claim the money, Jay appeared at Bank and presented a notarized agreement signed by Harvey assigning the entire bank account to Jay. Jay is a citizen of New York.

Bank filed a statutory interpleader action in the U.S. district court for the judicial district of California in which it is located. Which of the following statements is correct?

(A) The case should be dismissed because the citizenship of Sam will be imputed to Harvey. Thus, diversity of citizenship will be lacking.
(B) Although there is complete diversity between adverse parties, the case lacks the necessary amount in controversy. Thus, it should be dismissed for lack of subject matter jurisdiction.
(C) The case would be subject to a motion to dismiss under Rule 12(b)(3) because venue in a statutory interpleader action would be proper only in a district where one of the claimants resides.
(D) Both A and B.

8. In a state court of general jurisdiction, Pete sued the Big Time Corporation for personal injuries he received in an auto collision with a truck driven by a Big Time truck driver. Doris was the President of Big Time when the accident occurred. Pete personally served Big Time Corporation by handing the summons and complaint to Doris the day before she retired. In the excitement of her retirement, Doris neglected to deliver the papers to anyone else at Big Time. A default was entered against Big Time.

Other than service upon Doris, Big Time never received notice of the pending lawsuit prior to the entry of a default judgment. Big Time now moves to quash service of process. You may assume that applicable state law pertaining to service of process is identical to the Federal Rules of Civil Procedure. Which of the following statements is probably correct?

(A) Service should be quashed because Big Time Corporation did not receive actual notice of the pending lawsuit.

(B) Service should be quashed because Doris was not an officer of Big Time at the time an answer was due.

(C) Service should be quashed because the summons and complaint was served by Pete.

(D) Big Time's motion should be denied.

9. Plaintiff, a citizen of California, sues The Bank of Nevada ("Bank") in the U.S. district court for the District of Nevada. Bank has its only place of business in Nevada. Plaintiff seeks an order directing Bank to deliver the proceeds of a savings account in the amount of $80,000 to her. She alleges an agreement between her and Krooke, also a California citizen, whereby they each deposited an equal amount of money in the account, to be held solely in the name of Krooke. She further alleges that Krooke has asked Bank to split the account equally and to deliver a passbook to her, but that Bank refused to do this.

The Bank answers by alleging that it refused to make the transfer because Krooke claims that Plaintiff assigned her interest in the account to him as repayment for a loan. Bank makes a motion to dismiss for failure to join Krooke as a party. At a hearing on this issue, the court orders joinder of Krooke and then dismisses for lack of complete diversity. Which of the following statements is correct?

I.   Plaintiff will not be barred from refiling the action in a state court since the dismissal on the grounds provided in FRCP 12(b)(7) does *not* constitute an adjudication on the merits.

II. The court should not have required the joinder of Krooke because it destroyed diversity.

III. The court should not have dismissed the action because it has pendent jurisdiction over Plaintiff's claim against Krooke.

IV. The court should not have dismissed the action because there was diversity between Plaintiff and Bank.

(A) I only.

(B) II only.

(C) I and IV.

(D) II and III.

10. P, a citizen of Idaho, brings a multimillion dollar diversity action for wrongful death in the proper U.S. district court against his wife's employer, D Construction Company, a Washington corporation. He alleges that D negligently allowed scaffolding to collapse while his wife was walking beneath it. D impleads T, the manufacturer of the scaffolding, alleging that it would have a right to indemnity from T as a consequence of the latter's negligent manufacture of the equipment. T is an Idaho corporation.

P was granted leave to file an amended complaint alleging negligent manufacture against T. Thereafter, T moved to dismiss P's action against it for lack of subject matter jurisdiction. Which of the following statements is correct?

(A) The motion should be denied because of the pendent jurisdiction doctrine.

(B) The motion should be denied because of the ancillary jurisdiction doctrine.

(C) The motion should be granted because diversity is lacking.

(D) The motion should be granted because there is diversity between P and D.

11. P, a citizen of California, filed an action in the U.S. district court in Los Angeles against D, a Texas corporation, and Z, a New York corporation, alleging that (1) they were engaged in a conspiracy to fix prices in violation of the Sherman Act, 15 U.S.C. Section l, and (2) that his actual damages from the conduct of the defendants was $73,000.

P further alleged in a second cause of action that D is wrongfully withholding $1,000 which P paid to D as a deposit for a computer which was not delivered. Which of the following statements is correct?

(A) The action should be dismissed by the district court since the value of the aggregated claims does not meet the amount in controversy requirement.

(B) The district court may exercise pendent jurisdiction over the second cause of action only if it arises from a common nucleus of operative facts with the first cause of action.

(C) The federal court has subject matter jurisdiction because there is complete diversity of citizenship between all plaintiffs and defendants.

(D) None of the above.

12. P brings an action against D in a state court of general jurisdiction in California. P is a citizen of California. D is a citizen of New York. P alleges that D has infringed upon a patent recently granted to P by the U.S. Patent and Trademark Office. P seeks $75,000 in damages and an injunction barring D from further acts of infringement. Patent infringement matters are within the exclusive jurisdiction of the federal courts.

    D is personally served with a copy of the summons and complaint when his airplane lands in Los Angeles International Airport on a brief stopover. The flight was bound for Hawaii. D fails to answer the complaint and P obtains a default judgment. P then seeks to enforce the judgment in a New York state court.

    Which of the following statements is correct?

    (A) The Court in California did not have subject matter jurisdiction over the action. Thus, P's judgment is not entitled to Full Faith and Credit from a New York court.

    (B) Even if *Shaffer v. Heitner* does not alter the traditional rule that service of process within a state is a valid means of obtaining personal jurisdiction over a defendant, the California state court never obtained personal jurisdiction over D since he does not reside in California. Thus, the judgment is not entitled to Full Faith and Credit from a New York Court.

    (C) By failing to appear, D waived his right to object to subject matter and personal jurisdiction.

    (D) None of the above.

13. P, a citizen of Arizona, was injured in an automobile accident in New Mexico. The driver of the other vehicle was D, a citizen of Texas. New Mexico is a comparative negligence state and the law of New Mexico would apply to this action. P knows that D's damages are $46,000. P brings her action in the only U.S. district court in Arizona, alleging in good faith that she has incurred damages in the total amount of $75,000. Which of the following statements is correct?

    I.   Venue is not proper.
    II. The federal court lacks subject mater jurisdiction because the claim does not meet the amount in controversy requirement.
    III. The federal court has subject matter jurisdiction because the parties are diverse and P's claim satisfies the amount in controversy requirement.

    (A) I only.
    (B) II only.

(C) III only.

(D) I and II.

14. Packer, a New York citizen, purchased a mountain- side home in Lake Tahoe, Nevada, from Denton. Packer asked Denton if Denton was sure that the land on which the home is situated was geologically sound. Denton (aware that there was a major fault under the home) nevertheless responded to Packer's question in a positive manner. Two months after Packer occupied the house, it collapsed. Packer brings an action for fraud against Denton in the appropriate U.S. district court. The complaint alleges that "Denton fraudulently induced Plaintiff to enter into the purchase agreement for the house and land." Denton moved for a more definite statement under FRCP 12(e). Which of the following statements is correct?

(A) The motion should be granted, since the FRCP requires that circumstances constituting fraud must be stated with particularity.

(B) The motion should be denied, since the FRCP requires only that the pleader give a short, plain statement of the claim for relief.

(C) The motion should be denied if the complaint is adequate under Nevada law.

(D) None of the above.

15. D, a Michigan corporation, sells its automobiles through independent dealers. D's principal place of business is Detroit. All dealers have dealership agreements which they executed with D at the time they were appointed to be dealers. Their agreements entitle them to sell in their areas cars manufactured by D. This year, D has produced a new sports car — which is a radical departure from its previous automobiles. D decides that it will not sell this car to its existing dealers, but instead will enter into agreements with new dealers to handle the new sports car line. Twelve dealers in California jointly file actions for breach of contract and an injunction against D in the appropriate U.S. district court. D moves to sever the actions. Which of the following statements is correct?

(A) The motion should be granted, since the plaintiffs are all citizens of the same state.

(B) The motion should be denied, because plaintiffs are compelled to join their actions if their claims arise out of the same transaction or series of transactions.

(C) The motion should be granted, if (a) the court finds that the claims arise out of the same transaction or series of transactions, and (b) there are common issues of law and fact to all of the claims.

(D) None of the above.

16. North America Insurance Company ("NAIC"), an Illinois corporation with its principal place of business in New York, is sued by five of its policyholders in a class action. The complaint alleges that NAIC overcharged them and 2,000 other persons in their states for automobile insurance. The class seeks a refund of the overcharges.

The plaintiffs in the action are Adams ("A"), a citizen of Arizona; Baron ("B"), a student domiciled in Arizona, but attending law school in California; Collins ("C"), a citizen of Colorado; Dante ("D"), a citizen of Delaware; and, Ellwood ("E"), a citizen of Florida. The amounts of the overcharges claimed by the named plaintiffs are: A, $85,000; B, $30,000; C, $75,000; D, $39,000; and E, $84,000. Which of the following statements is correct?

(A) The federal court lacks subject matter jurisdiction over the action since the diversity requirement is not met.

(B) The federal court must dismiss the action because the claim of each of the representatives fails to meet the amount in controversy requirement.

(C) The federal court has subject matter jurisdiction, since the aggregate claims of the class representatives meet the amount in controversy requirement.

(D) None of the above.

17. P, a citizen of New York, brings an action against D, in the U.S. district court in New York (the judicial district in which P lives). D is a citizen of Michigan. P alleges $90,000 in damages based on an alleged breach of contract by D to manufacture equipment for P's restaurants.

Subsequently, D brings an action against P for $80,000 in a New York court of general jurisdiction for personal injuries suffered by D when he slipped on a banana peel while at P's restaurant in New York three weeks before the parties were initially introduced. P seeks to remove the state court action to the New York U.S. district court. Which of the following statements is correct?

I.   D's action may **not** be removed.

II. Assuming the state court action meets applicable subject matter jurisdiction requirements, it could be removed to the appropriate U.S. district court in New York.

III. D was **not** required to assert his action in the original federal court litigation initiated by P, since it did not arise out of the same transaction or occurrence as P's action.

(A) I only.

(B) II only.

(C) II and III.

(D) III only.

18. Abel, a Colorado citizen, is injured when her car is hit by Chance, also a Colorado citizen. Chance is a minor who was served drinks illegally at a bar located in Wyoming owned by Baker, a Wyoming citizen. Abel brings an action in the only U.S. district court in Colorado against Baker, alleging negligence and breach of a statutory duty.

Thirty days after answering, Baker files a motion seeking leave to file a third-party claim (i.e., an impleader action) against Chance, based entirely upon Chance's unpaid bar bill, and failure to pay for a used car which Baker had sold to Chance. Which of the following statements is correct?

I. The motion will be denied because Baker's claim does not assert that Chance may be liable to Baker on all or part of Abel's claim.

II. If the court finds that Baker may properly implead Chance, Chance will probably be allowed to assert *any* claim he has against Baker.

III. Chance cannot be made a party to the action by Baker because that would destroy diversity subject matter jurisdiction.

(A) I only.

(B) II only.

(C) I and III.

(D) I and II.

19. Paul, a citizen of Ohio, was involved in a three-car auto collision with Peter and Mary. Paul sued Peter and Mary in the only U.S. district court in Maine. The defendants were citizens of Maine. Paul's action against each defendant was for personal injuries in the amount of $70,000 and property damage in the amount of $9,000. Which of the following statements is correct?

I. Paul might be permitted to assert a $1,000 breach of contract action against Mary.

II. Peter might be permitted to assert a $12,000 breach of contract action against Mary.

III. Paul's action should be dismissed because no single claim satisfies the "amount in controversy" requirement.

(A) I only.

(B) II only.

(C) I and II.

(D) I and III.

20. Railroad Corporation brings a class action in the U.S. district court for the Eastern District of Ohio against the members of the United Railroad Fireman's Union ("Union"). The class action complaint names four officers of Union as class representatives.

Railroad is a Pennsylvania corporation, which has its principal place of business in New York. Union is an unincorporated association which has its headquarters in Ohio, where the major portion of its administrative work is performed. All of the officers of Union are citizens of Pennsylvania. The membership of Union includes railroad employees who reside in Michigan, Pennsylvania and Ohio.

The action asserts that members of Union destroyed railroad property in Pennsylvania during a strike. Which of the following statements is correct?

  I.   Venue is proper only in Ohio, assuming Union has sufficient contacts there to satisfy personal jurisdiction.
 II.   The action cannot be brought in a U.S. district court, unless it is based on a federal claim.
III.   Since this is an action involving an unincorporated labor organization, it is outside the subject matter jurisdiction of federal courts.

  (A) I only.
  (B) II only.
  (C) III only.
  (D) I and II.

21. John owns Riverdale, a palatial residence. Bill owns the adjoining residence. One day Matt, Bill's butler, started a fire on Bill's estate to burn some excess rubbish. Unfortunately, the fire got out of control, and burned down John's residence. It also caused considerable damage to the rest of Riverdale. John sustained some injuries and was hospitalized for ten days. John files an action against Bill, in which he seeks damages in excess of $300,000 for property loss caused by the fire. If John obtains a judgment against Bill, which of the following statements is correct?

  (A) Bill cannot sue Matt.
  (B) Any action by John against Matt is barred.
  (C) The judgment against Bill would not be binding upon Matt in a subsequent lawsuit by John against Matt.
  (D) John's claim against Bill for personal injuries is not barred by normal *res judicata* principles because that action was not litigated in the *John v. Bill* lawsuit.

22. Acme became involved in a labor dispute with the Steamroller's Union, the entity which ordinarily supplied workers for Acme's plant. Acme commenced an action against Steamroller's Union ("Union") in the appropriate U.S. district court, claiming $90,000 in damages as a consequence of Union's conduct in harassing and intimidating non-union workers in violation of the National Labor Relations Act and applicable state law.

Acme is an Indiana corporation, and Union (an unincorporated association) has members domiciled in every state, except New York and New Jersey. Union answered by denying Acme's allegations and filing a $80,000 counterclaim (which asserted that Acme deliberately made false accusations about Union to the local papers for the purpose of obtaining favorable press coverage). If Acme moves to dismiss Union's counterclaim for lack of subject matter jurisdiction, it should:

(A) Lose, if Union's counterclaim is mandatory in nature.
(B) Prevail, if Union's counterclaim is permissive in nature.
(C) Prevail, since Acme has asserted a state cause of action.
(D) Lose, because diversity does not exist.

Questions 23-25 are based upon the following facts:

Paul was injured while operating a drill press manufactured by Manco. Paul properly commenced an action against Manco in the appropriate U.S. district court. Prior to trial, Paul sought discovery of a report which had been made to Manco by Brown, a claims investigator for Manco. Brown had inspected the machine and investigated the circumstances of the accident immediately thereafter. The machine was subsequently destroyed in a fire and Brown has retired (leaving no forwarding address).

In selecting the jury, the judge conducted the *voir dire*, but refused Manco's request that the judge ask the members of the jury panel whether any of them were prejudiced against corporations. A verdict was returned in favor of Paul for $75,000. Manco moved for a new trial.

The trial judge agreed to grant a new trial, unless Paul accepted a reduction in the verdict from $75,000 to $25,000. Paul agreed to the reduction under protest. Paul then appealed. He asserted as error the trial court's order granting a new trial unless he accepted a reduction in the verdict from $75,000 to $25,000.

23. Paul's request for Brown's report should be:

(A) Granted, because tangible items prepared in anticipation of litigation or trial are not discoverable.

(B) Granted, even if prepared in anticipation of litigation or trial, provided Paul can show that there is a substantial need for the information and he is otherwise unable to obtain it without undue hardship.

(C) Denied, because it was apparently prepared at Manco's request (rather than at the instigation of Manco's attorney).

(D) Denied, if Manco procured the report at the suggestion of its legal counsel.

24. The trial judge's refusal to comply with Manco's request at the *voir dire* was:

(A) Correct, because the question was irrelevant to the issues of the case.

(B) Correct, because Manco could have exercised a peremptory challenge against the potential juror.

(C) Erroneous, because prejudice against a party is a proper subject for inquiry at *voir dire*.

(D) Erroneous, because when the trial judge conducts the *voir dire*, he must ask any questions requested by counsel.

25. Paul's appeal from the order of remittitur should be:

(A) Successful, since the court's order violated Paul's Seventh Amendment right to a trial by jury upon the issue of damages.

(B) Successful, unless the trial court abused its discretion in ordering a new trial if Paul had not agreed to the lessened sum.

(C) Unsuccessful, because Paul elected to accept the remittitur.

(D) Unsuccessful, because the Seventh Amendment does not apply to damage issues.

Questions 26-28 are based upon the following facts:

Ten college students in State X filed a class action in U.S. district court. The complaint requested that five specifically named state officials, the defendants, be enjoined from enforcing the state's flag desecration statute which was alleged to be unconstitutional. The class that the plaintiffs sought to represent was all college students in State X. The defendants filed motions requesting that:

(1) The complaint be dismissed on the grounds that the court lacked subject matter jurisdiction; and

(2) The court deny certification of the class.

26. The defendants' motion to dismiss for lack of subject matter jurisdiction should be:

(A) Denied, because a First Amendment claim is involved.

(B) Denied, only if there is diversity of citizenship between the plaintiffs (representatives), and the defendants, and the amount claimed by each member of the plaintiff class satisfies the "amount in controversy" requirement.

(C) Granted, because no specific assertion has been made that each plaintiff has suffered damages in excess of $75,000.

(D) Granted, if any member of the plaintiff class and any defendant are citizens of the same state.

27. The defendants' strongest argument to deny certification of the plaintiff class would probably be that:

(A) The "numerosity" element is absent.

(B) The plaintiffs have failed to allege that each member of the prospective class will suffer damages in excess of $75,000.

(C) The representatives do not adequately represent the interests of the entire class.

(D) It would be impossible to individually notify each member of the proposed class by mail.

28. If the court refused to certify the class, which of the following would be true?

(A) The plaintiffs could immediately appeal the court's decision.

(B) The plaintiffs could not appeal immediately, but would be obliged to try the action on the merits as a non-class action.

(C) The plaintiffs would waive any right to appeal if they elected to first try the case on its merits.

(D) The court would be obliged to dismiss the case.

Questions 29-31 are based upon the following facts:

Arnold and Bates, citizens of State Z, are plaintiffs in an action brought in the United States district court in State X against Manco, a State Y corporation, and Storeco, a State X corporation. Manco's office and plant are located in State Y. At no time has Manco had an office or sales staff in State X. Storeco's sole place of business is in State X.

The complaint alleges that each of the plaintiffs sustained serious personal injuries when a blade broke on an electric lawn mower while the equipment was being demonstrated by a clerk in Storeco's store in State X. Each plaintiff requested damages in the sum of $80,000. The mower had been manufactured by Manco and shipped to Roe in State Z. Roe had a contract with Manco to act as exclusive distributor of Manco products in eleven states, including X and Z.

Process was served personally on the president of Manco at Manco's office in State Y and on the president of Storeco at its office in State X. Thereafter, the following occurred:

(1) Manco moved to dismiss the action on the ground that the court had no jurisdiction over it;

(2) Storeco filed a counterclaim against Arnold for $72,000 alleged to be due for merchandise previously sold to Arnold; and

(3) Manco filed a cross-claim against Storeco for $12,000 alleged to be due for merchandise previously sold by Manco to Storeco.

29. The U.S. district court can assert ***personal*** jurisdiction over Manco:

(A) If State X has an appropriate long-arm statute and the assertion of personal jurisdiction would comport with due process.

(B) If the assertion of personal jurisdiction would comport with due process. There is nationwide service of process in actions commenced in federal court.

(C) If the amount in controversy exceeds $75,000, exclusive of interest and costs.

(D) If process was served upon Manco in accordance with both federal and State X law.

30. A motion to strike Storeco's counterclaim should be:

(A) Dismissed, because there is supplemental jurisdiction.

(B) Dismissed, because Arnold has implicitly consented to personal jurisdiction by commencing an action in State X.

(C) Granted, because the amount owed to Storeco is only $72,000.

(D) Granted, because Storeco's counterclaim is compulsory.

31. A motion to strike Manco's cross-claim against Storeco should be:

(A) Granted, because the cross-claim is unrelated to the plaintiff's action.

(B) Granted, because there is no supplemental jurisdiction with respect to this action.

(C) Denied, if the court believes that Manco's action will not confuse or divert the jury with respect to the original claim.

(D) Denied, because there is diversity subject matter jurisdiction with respect to Manco's cross-claim against Storeco.

32. You may assume that this jurisdiction has abandoned the "mutuality rule" pertaining to collateral estoppel.

Paul is the executor of the estate of Carol. Paul files an action on behalf of the estate in the applicable state court against Doris (Carol's nurse) alleging that Doris converted Carol's money. Although Doris was authorized to deposit funds into Carol's account at the local bank ("Bank"), Paul claims that Doris also withdrew funds for her own use. At trial, the jury found that Carol had made an *inter vivos* gift to Doris of the money in question.

Thereafter, Paul commenced an action against Bank in the applicable U.S. district court, alleging that the withdrawals by Doris were not authorized by Carol, and therefore Bank had breached its contractual relationship with Carol. Which of the following statements is correct?

(A) There will be no collateral estoppel from the first case because that action was not commenced in a federal court.

(B) Bank should be able to use the factual determination in favor of Doris in the first case as a shield to the claims of Paul in the second action.

(C) Since Carol and Bank are in privity, Paul will be bound by the issues determined in the first case.

(D) None of the above.

33. On behalf of herself and the 92 specific students in her class, P brought an FRCP 23(b)(2) class action against D, claiming that D had arbitrarily assigned final grades in a law school course by drawing names and numbers from two different hats.

P sought declaratory relief and an injunction, forcing the teacher to withdraw the original grades and submit a new set based upon actually having read the students' papers. While P was a citizen of State Z, all of her classmates and D were citizens of State Y. The suit was filed in a U.S. district court in State Y, which entered judgment for D after the jury found that P had failed to prove that D did not read the exams. The judgment was affirmed on appeal.

Thereafter, X, one of the students in the class who had received a grade of 65, brought an action against D in a State Z court, seeking $76,000 in damages for D's alleged failure to actually read X's exam, as a result of which X received his lowest grade in law school. Which of the following statements is correct?

(A) The judgment rendered in the first action is entitled to Full Faith and Credit in the present suit, even if the U.S. district court lacked subject matter jurisdiction.

(B) The U.S. district court lacked subject matter jurisdiction because members of the plaintiff class and D were citizens of the same state (State Y).

(C) Assuming the federal court had subject matter jurisdiction, D can preclude X from seeking to prove that D failed to read the exams, even though X's action seeks to recover monetary damages (rather than injunctive relief).

(D) None of the above.

34. P and D had an automobile accident in State X. P, a citizen of State Y, sued D, a citizen of State X, in a State Y court of general jurisdiction. D had recently inherited some vacant land in State Y. D was also personally served with process at his home in State X. Assuming *Hess v. Pawloski*, 274 U.S. 352 (1927) is no longer "good law," which of the following statements is correct?

I.   If State Y has a typical non-resident motorist statute, there is an adequate basis for obtaining personal jurisdiction over D.

II. Even in the absence of a long-arm statute, most courts would probably hold that D's inheritance of property in State Y, coupled with notice of the suit by personal service, is sufficient for the exercise of personal jurisdiction over D in State Y.

(A) I only.

(B) II only.

(C) I and II.

(D) Neither I nor II.

35. P, who had been employed by D, was fired when D learned that P, who was unmarried, was living with Q. P and Q sued D in the appropriate U.S. district court. P sought $58,000 for breach of their employment contract, $10,000 for violation of a federal civil rights statute, and $9,000 for damages which D had caused to P's car after P loaned it to D earlier that year. Q claimed $12,000 in damages as a result of P's wrongful termination, since she is now obliged to pay their entire apartment rental by herself. Prior to his discharge, P contributed one-half of the rental amount.

P and Q are both citizens of State X. D is a citizen of State Y. Which of the following statements is correct?

(A) The Federal Rules of Civil Procedure do **not** allow all the claims of P and Q to be joined together in a single action.

(B) A U.S. district court would have subject matter jurisdiction over Q's claim.

(C) If P failed to assert the claim for damages to his car in this action, it would be barred.

(D) None of the above.

36. In a three-car collision, P's car was rear-ended by D, who was in turn rear-ended by E. P, brought an action against D in the U.S. district court in the state in which P was domiciled. P sought to recover $80,000 for damages to his Mercedes. D filed a counterclaim against P, seeking $1,152 for damages to his Volkswagen.

D also filed two claims against E, the driver behind him, one seeking $80,000 in the event that D was liable to P, and the other seeking $1,152 for the damages caused to D's Volkswagen. P and D are both citizens of State X; E is a citizen of State Y. Judgment was entered for P against D, but all the other claims were found to be without merit.

E has now filed a lawsuit against P and D in the U.S. district court in X, seeking $1 million for personal injuries suffered in the earlier auto accident. P and D have each counterclaimed, seeking $1 million for their own personal injuries, and have filed similar cross-claims against each other. Which of the following statements is correct?

(A) The court in the initial action lacked subject matter jurisdiction.

(B) Apart from any possible subject matter jurisdiction problems in the prior suit, E could have filed any claim arising out of the prior accident which he had against P.

(C) Apart from any possible subject matter jurisdiction problems in the prior suit, P and D may not assert their claims against each other in the present action.

(D) All of the above.

37. P brings an action against D, E and F, asserting (1) infringement of copyright, and (2) breach of contract. Copyright actions are exclusively within the subject matter jurisdiction of federal courts.

All of the claims arose from the defendants' having produced a television show based upon a script that P had written for them. P seeks to recover $80,000 from each of the defendants. All of the parties are citizens of California. Which of the following statements is correct?

(A) If this action is filed in a California state court, the defendants could have it removed to federal court.

(B) If this action is filed in federal court, dismissal for lack of subject matter jurisdiction would be required.

(C) If this case goes to trial in a state court, and judgment is entered against P, P will have waived any lack of subject matter jurisdiction by failing to assert it before or during trial.

(D) None of the above.

38. P, the publisher of a magazine, announced that D was the winner of a $5,000 prize for the best poem of the month. However, before P awarded the prize to D, P received a letter from E. E claimed he had written the poem and D's entry was stolen from him or F, E's agent.

P, a citizen of State X, brought a statutory interpleader action in the appropriate U.S. district court against D and E, seeking a declaratory judgment as to which of them was entitled to the prize money. D is a citizen of State Y, and E is a citizen of State X. Which of the following statements is correct?

(A) The federal court lacks subject matter jurisdiction over this action.

(B) E may file a third party claim based upon negligence against his agent, F, a citizen of State X, seeking $5,000 from F in the event the prize money is awarded to D.

(C) Venue is proper in either State X or Y.

(D) None of the above.

39. Plaintiff, a citizen of Arizona, sued Defendant, a citizen of Washington state, in the U.S. district court in Arizona for breach of contract seeking $78,000 in damages. Defendant answered by denying that a contract was formed.

Plaintiff and Defendant stipulated that the jury would consist of eight persons. Trial was held, and seven jurors voted in favor of Plaintiff. One juror voted for Defendant. The jurors then deliberated on the amount of damages and rendered a verdict in favor of Plaintiff for $18,500. Defendant appealed the ruling. On which of the following grounds would Defendant be most likely to prevail on appeal?

(A) The ruling was defective because it was rendered by less than twelve jurors.

(B) The ruling was defective because it was based on a non-unanimous vote.

(C) The court did not have subject matter jurisdiction because the verdict did not exceed $75,000.

(D) The court lacked personal jurisdiction.

40. An automobile accident occurred in State Y involving P, Q and a vehicle driven by an employee of D. The car in which P and Q were riding was a Ferrari which they had purchased together for $79,000 (P contributing $40,000 towards the purchase price, and Q the remaining $39,000). The car was destroyed in the collision.

P and Q are citizens of State X, and D is a corporation organized under the laws of State Z, with its principal place of business in Y. It does business in all 50 states. One year after the accident, P and Q sued D to recover a total of $79,000 in damages for the loss of their car. Which of the following statements is correct?

(A) If this suit was properly commencedin a state court in State Y, D could have the action removed to a federal court.

(B) If this action was filed in the U.S. district court in State W, D could probably have the action transferred to a U.S. district court in State Y; but the federal court in State Y would have to apply the statute of limitations which the U.S. district court in State W would have applied.

(C) Subject matter jurisdiction does *not* exist because neither P nor Q had invested a sum in excess of $75,000 in the car.

(D) None of the above.

Questions 41-42 are based upon the following facts:

Phil was driving his car in San Diego, California, when he was involved in an accident with Dowd. Phil lives in San Diego. Dowd is a citizen of Alabama. The registered owner of the car Dowd was driving is Ellwood (a citizen of Kentucky). Phil filed an timely action against Dowd in the appropriate U.S. district court in California. The complaint contained a proper subject matter jurisdiction allegation.

41. The complaint alleged only that there was a collision between the cars driven by Phil and Dowd, and that Phil suffered personal injuries and property damage in the amount of $85,000. If Dowd filed a motion to dismiss for failure to state a claim upon which relief could be granted, the court would probably:

(A) Grant the motion, without leave to amend.

(B) Grant the motion, with leave to amend.

(C) Overrule the motion, since Phil's complaint fails to identify the legal theory upon which his claim is predicated.

(D) Grant the motion, but only if the applicable statute of limitations under California law had expired.

42. The complaint contained a proper subject matter jurisdiction allegation and asserted that (1) the collision was caused by Dowd's negligence in driving into the rear of Phil's car while Phil was lawfully stopped at a red light, or (2) alternatively, the collision was caused by Dowd's negligence in driving through a red light and into Phil while the latter was lawfully driving through an intersection. If Dowd filed a motion to dismiss for failure to state a cause of action upon which relief can be granted, the court would probably:

(A) Grant the motion, on grounds of inconsistency.

(B) Grant the motion, since Phil has pleaded a legal conclusion (i.e., that Dowd was negligent in his conduct).

(C) Overrule the motion, since alternative grounds for relief are permissible under the FRCP.

(D) Overrule the motion, but require Phil to strike one of the inconsistent claims.

43. P is a citizen of New York who works in New Jersey. D and E are citizens of New Jersey who work in that state. One day, D borrowed E's car, advising E that he intended to use it to pick up his sister in Trenton (the capital of New Jersey).

However, D drove to New York to take a new girlfriend to Coney Island (which is in Brooklyn, New York). Unfortunately, D became involved in a traffic accident with P while driving in New York City.

P brought an action against E in the proper U.S. district court in New York for personal injuries and property damages in the amount of $80,000. A New York statute permits an action against the owner of a motor vehicle where he loaned the car to the person who was driving it when the incident occurred. If E makes an FRCP 12(b)(2) motion to dismiss the action for lack of personal jurisdiction, he should:

(A) Prevail, since the assertion of personal jurisdiction over him would probably violate due process.

(B) Lose the motion, but the court may possibly require Phil to amend the complaint to make it more definite.

(C) Lose, because federal courts have nationwide service of process.

(D) Prevail, if the applicable statute of limitations under New York state law had expired subsequent to commencement of the suit.

44. P is incorporated in State X, but has its principal place of business in State Z. P corporation does substantial business in every state, except W. P filed an action against D Insurance Company and E. D is a corporation existing under the laws of State Y, where it has its principal place of business. D also does business in States X and Z. E, a natural person, is a citizen of Ontario, Canada.

P's claim against E arises out of a fire occurring at P's plant in State X. P's claim against D is for breach of contract, based upon D's refusal to pay P the proceeds under a fire insurance policy which P had purchased from D. Both claims are for $100,000. Which of the following statements is correct?

I.   If this action were filed in the U.S. district court for State Z, subject matter jurisdiction would exist and venue would be proper.

II. If this action was properly commenced in a State W court, the defendants could remove the action to the appropriate U.S. district court, even though the action could not have been commenced in a U.S. district court in State W.

III. P's joinder of D and E in one action is *not* proper, since P is asserting two distinct causes of action.

(A) I alone.
(B) III alone.
(C) I and II.
(D) None of the above.

45. P suffered permanent personal injuries in an auto accident with D and E. D and E were each driving separate cars. X, P's insurance company, paid P the maximum limit of $100,000 under the policy.

Having collected from her insurance company, P then brought an action against D in the proper U.S. district court, seeking $500,000 for her personal injuries. Assume the "collateral source" rule is in effect in this jurisdiction (i.e., a plaintiff's recovery in tort from a defendant is *not* diminished by any insurance or other collateral sources which reimbursed the former for all or any portion of her damages). P is a citizen of State X, and D and E are citizens of State Y. Which of the following statements is correct?

I.   D may object to P's bringing this action on the ground that the insurance company, rather than P, is the real party in interest (under the insurance agreement X is subrogated to P's right's to the extent that P's claim against D is paid by X).

II. If D contends that the accident was caused exclusively by the negligence of E, D may implead E seeking to recover $77,000 from the latter for the damages which E caused to D's car.

III. Whether or not D files a claim against E, E may intervene as of right as a defendant and file actions for her damages against both P and D.

(A) I and II only.

(B) II and III only.

(C) III only.

(D) None of the above.

46. Delbert liked to cut across Pat's land on his way to law school. Pat, however, disliked Delbert because Delbert had become somewhat arrogant since he made Law Review. When Pat asked Delbert to cease using the shortcut, he responded that his time was "extremely valuable" and therefore it was a "private necessity."

Pat instituted an action against Delbert in the appropriate U.S. district court, demanding that Delbert be enjoined from utilizing her land. You may assume that competency and jurisdictional requisites are satisfied. Although her real property had not been damaged by Delbert's constant encroachments, she also requested nominal monetary damages. Which of the following statements is correct?

(A) Delbert is entitled to a jury trial with respect to the trespass issue.

(B) Delbert is not entitled to a jury trial on the trespass claim, since the primary relief Pat is seeking is an injunction.

(C) As a consequence of the "clean-up doctrine," the court, in its discretion, may decide both the legal and equitable issues.

(D) There is no right to a jury trial because trespass was not a "suit at common law" under the Seventh Amendment.

47. P, a citizen of State X, and Q, a citizen of State Y, sued D, a citizen of State Z for breach of contract occurring in State Z. The action was filed in the U.S. district court in State Y, and D was ***improperly*** served. Upon learning of the suit, D made a successful motion to transfer the case to the U.S. district court in State Z. Which of the following statements is correct?

(A) The federal court properly transferred the action to State Z.

(B) The federal court in State Y should have dismissed the action because venue in the U.S. district court in State Y was improper.

(C) The federal court in State Y should have denied D's motion to transfer the case since he was improperly served.

(D) None of the above.

Questions 48-50 are based upon the following facts:

E, a State X corporation, designed a building for Smith, a citizen of State Y, six years ago. Part of that building collapsed last year, causing damage in excess of $80,000.

Smith filed an action against E in the U.S. district court in State X, alleging that his damages resulted from the negligent design of the building. E filed an answer denying negligence and asserting as an affirmative defense that the statute of limitations for negligence is two years.

At the time the building was being constructed, Jones, an attorney and member of E's board of directors, and who occasionally handled legal matters for E, prepared and sent the following memorandum to the president of E:

> I have been informed by Tom Withers, an architect who used to work for E, that the materials being used by the contractor, Builder Corp., in constructing the building are substandard.

Smith filed a timely motion for pre-trial production of the Jones' memorandum. The motion was denied.

Smith filed a timely motion for summary judgment, relying on an affidavit made by Withers which set forth facts consistent with Jones' memorandum. E also filed a motion for summary judgment, accompanied by an affidavit that the building had been constructed six years ago. Both motions were denied.

48. If E asserted the work product privilege in response to Smith's motion for production of Jones' memorandum:

   (A) E should prevail, because Jones was an attorney.
   (B) E should prevail, because it reflects Jones's impressions about E's potential liability.
   (C) Smith should prevail, because it is relevant to his action.
   (D) Smith should prevail, if Jones is not representing E in the present action.

49. Smith's motion for summary judgment was properly denied because:

   (A) Based upon Wither's affidavit, genuine issues of fact remain as to the negligence of E.
   (B) Wither's affidavit did not address E's affirmative defense.
   (C) Because of the reason set forth in (B), but not (A).
   (D) Because of the reasons set forth in (A) and (B).

50. E's motion for a summary judgment was:

   (A) Improperly denied, because the building was constructed six years ago.
   (B) Improperly denied, because Smith failed to file a responsive affidavit.
   (C) Properly denied, because the accident occurred only recently.
   (D) Properly denied if E has the burden of proof with respect to its statute of limitations defense.

51. P and D were involved in a car accident in Texas. P is a citizen of State X and D is a citizen of New York. The State X service of process statute is similar to FRCP 4. P sued D in a State X court of general jurisdiction. P served D by sending, via first class mail, the summons and complaint to D in New York. D received these documents, but failed to respond to them. P then obtained a default judgment. If P sought to enforce the judgment in New York:

(A) The judgment should be given Full Faith and Credit by a New York court, since D had actually received the summons and complaint.

(B) D may collaterally attack the judgment for insufficient service of process.

(C) The judgment should be given Full Faith and Credit because a default judgment is usually deemed to be "on the merits."

(D) Choices (A) and (C) are correct, but not (B).

52. P commenced an action against D in a State X court of general jurisdiction. D is a citizen of State Z and P is a citizen of State X. D owned a boat which he kept at a pier in Houston, Texas.

Pursuant to Texas law, P obtained an attachment against D's boat. When properly served with notice of the attachment, D moved to quash it. The boat is probably worth $20,000. P's action is for breach of contract and alleges damages in the amount of $15,000. Which of the following statements is correct?

(A) The attachment should be quashed if a Texas court could not constitutionally assume personal jurisdiction over D.

(B) Pre-judgment attachments are *per se* unconstitutional.

(C) If D's motion was denied, P could apply all of the proceeds from sale of the boat to his obligation.

(D) Choices (A) and (B) are correct, but not (C).

53. P, a citizen of Utah, was involved in an auto accident with D, a citizen of Minnesota. The accident occurred in Utah.

Pursuant to the applicable Utah long-arm statute, P sued D in a Utah state court of general jurisdiction for $80,000. P also named C as a defendant. C was D's insurer. Pursuant to Utah law, this type of action was permissible. C is incorporated in Delaware and has its principal place of business in Utah.

D's petition to remove the case to the applicable U.S. district court should be:

(A) Granted, because D is not a citizen of Utah.

(B) Denied, because C's principal place of business is Utah.

(C) Denied if C joins in the petition.

(D) Granted, because the amount in controversy requirement is satisfied.

54. Dr. Dumb, a citizen of State A, performed emergency surgery upon Pam, a citizen of State B, for which he charged $5,000. Pam was injured during the surgery. She filed a negligence lawsuit against Dr. Dumb in the appropriate U.S. district court in State A for $90,000. Dr. Dumb impleads Insurance Co., a corporation incorporated in State B and doing business in States A and B, for payment on his malpractice insurance policy if Pam should win her lawsuit. Which of the following causes of action may be joined?

I. A $3,000 counterclaim by Dr. Dumb against Pam for damage done when Pam, angry at the results of the operation, broke three of Dr. Dumb's office windows, if the counterclaim is deemed "permissive".

II. A claim by Pam against Insurance Co. for the non-payment of a $76,000 claim on an insurance policy she maintained with Insurance Co. when her car was stolen, if Insurance Co.'s principal place of business is in State A.

(A) I only.

(B) II only.

(C) I and II.

(D) Neither I nor II.

55. A (plaintiff) properly commenced a diversity action in the applicable U.S. district against B. A claimed that he and B had entered a valid contract, that B had repudiated the agreement, and that as a consequence A had sustained economic losses in the amount of $90,000. B answered by denying the existence of a contractual agreement.

At trial, B attempted to introduce evidence that A had made an anticipatory repudiation of the alleged agreement prior to the time that B's performance was due. If this assertion is correct, B would have an affirmative defense to A's action (even if a valid contract had been formed).

If A made a timely objection to the introduction of B's evidence pertaining to anticipatory repudiation:

(A) His objection *must* be sustained, because the evidence is outside the pleadings.

(B) The evidence may be admitted, in the discretion of the court.

(C) The objection must be sustained, because amendments to pleadings cannot be made after trial has been commenced.

(D) The evidence must be admitted, since it is relevant to B's defense. However, if it is admitted, A is entitled to a continuance to meet such evidence.

56. The State X Rules of Civil Procedure are basically equivalent to the FRCP. Paul sued Donna in a State X court, alleging that, at Donna's home, Donna hit Paul on the head with a hammer, and that Paul suffered injuries in the amount of $15,000. Donna moved to dismiss the case, but her motion was denied.

Paul then amended his complaint to add as damages the lost wages resulting from having to miss work. Donna answered by denying that she hit Paul, and, as an affirmative defense, claimed that she hit Paul because he was attacking her.

Paul then moved for summary judgment based on an affidavit signed by his cousin, Bill, stating that Paul told him Donna struck Paul out of jealousy (rather than because Paul was attacking her). Which of the following statements is correct?

(A) Donna's motion to dismiss should have been granted, since Paul did not state his legal theory.

(B) Donna's pleadings are defective because they are inconsistent, answering that she did not hit Paul and also stating as a defense the reason why she had hit Paul.

(C) Paul's amendment is permissible, even without leave of court.

(D) Paul's summary judgment motion should be granted because it was supported by an affidavit.

57. X, a citizen of Oregon, sued Y, a large Colorado corporation doing business only in Colorado. The action asserted that Y failed to provide training, support and service for a $85,000 computer system which Y had sold to X.

X sued Y in the U.S. district court in Oregon. Although the contract was accepted and signed in Colorado, there was a provision which stipulated that in the event of litigation, Y could be sued by X in Oregon. Y moved for transfer of the action to the U.S. district court in Colorado, claiming that its training, support and service personnel, who would be witnesses, are domiciled in Colorado. The Colorado damage remedies are more favorable to Y than the corresponding rules in Oregon.

Which of the following statements is correct?

(A) Transfer of the action will probably be granted.

(B) If Y's motion is granted, the law of Oregon regarding damages will be applied.

(C) The provision stipulating that Y would stand trial in Oregon is unconstitutional if Y did not have "minimum contacts" with Oregon.

(D) None of the above.

58. Daleon Motors, a Delaware corporation which has its principal place of business in Michigan, created the Daleon automobile. Approximately 3,000 of these vehicles were sold before it was discovered that the brake lining was defective. As a consequence, the car became virtually undrivable after about 500 miles. Paul, a citizen of Rhode Island, purchased a Daleon automobile in that state.

Paul commenced an FRCP 23(b)(3) class action against Daleon on behalf of all of the purchasers of automobile in the U.S. district court for Rhode Island, contending that the plaintiff class is entitled to return of the purchase price for fraud. Daleon Motors had advertised its car as being the "safest" in the world. Each Daleon car cost $77,000.

After Paul commenced the action, Daleon claimed that its offices had been broken into and its records of Daleon purchasers destroyed. Paul personally knows of two other purchasers of Daleon cars. One is a citizen of New Mexico and the other is a citizen of Delaware.

Which of the following statements is correct?

(A) Daleon could successfully make a motion to dismiss the class action, since at least one of the purchasers is a citizen of Delaware.

(B) Notice to the prospective class by publication in the major newspapers throughout the country will probably be permissible (except that mailing to the two known buyers will be required).

(C) Notice to the class may be dispensed with in light of the suspicious destruction of the names and addresses of prospective class members while such data was within Daleon's possession.

(D) None of the above.

59. P sued Amusement Co. for injuries sustained when she fell while getting off a ferris wheel at the Amusement Co.'s park. The lock holding the seat had prematurely broken open. At P's suggestion, her boyfriend immediately took pictures of the broken lock. Since the park was still open, Amusement Co. hired a locksmith to replace the lock that same afternoon. The locksmith had to completely disassemble the broken lock. P's attorney hired an expert

locksmith to prepare a report and testify at trial regarding the defective nature of the lock.

Amusement Co. moved to discover the report prepared by P's expert and the pictures taken by P's boyfriend of the broken lock. P claims both the pictures and the report are covered by the work product privilege.

Which of the following statements is correct?

(A) Amusement Co. may not view the pictures or the report.
(B) Amusement Co. may view the pictures and obtain the report.
(C) Amusement Co. may view the pictures, but not obtain the report.
(D) Amusement Co. may not view the pictures, but may obtain the report.

60. Acme is a Georgia corporation which has its principal place of business in Alabama. Polly used to live in Alabama and work at Acme's Arkansas plant. However, she was recently terminated from her employment with Acme. She consulted an attorney who advised her that her termination was wrongful under a law recently enacted by Congress. The lawyer also informed Polly that Georgia had the most liberal procedures for prosecuting this type of action.

Polly moved to Georgia, where she is now working as a waitress, and commenced an action in the appropriate state court against Acme for wrongful termination under the applicable U.S. law and a similar Georgia statute. Polly seeks $80,000 in damages. Acme filed a petition to remove the case to the U.S. district court in Georgia.

The petition should be:

(A) Denied, because Polly moved to Georgia only for the purpose of acquiring a more advantageous forum for litigation.
(B) Denied, because there is a lack of diversity.
(C) Granted, because one of her actions is a federal claim.
(D) Granted, because there is no diversity of citizenship because citizenship is determined at the time the cause of action arose.

61. Each of twenty persons who are domiciled throughout Texas, Oklahoma and Nebraska, asserted a claim of $25,000 against XYZ Corp., a Maryland corporation. Their joinder of claims is based upon the assertion that fumes from XYZ's plant in Arkansas caused them minor respiratory problems. XYZ's principal place of business is in Maryland. May the twenty persons sue XYZ Corp. in a U.S. district court?

(A) Yes, but *only* if their claim is based upon a federal statute.

(B) Yes, but *only* if the plaintiffs aggregate their claims in a class action.

(C) Yes, because diversity of citizenship exists between the entire plaintiff class and XYZ.

(D) Yes, but *only* if there is diversity of citizenship between the class representative and XYZ.

62. P was injured when he attempted to rescue X from a burning car. X and Y had collided at an intersection. P sued Y in the appropriate U.S. district court, but not X. Y claims that X's conduct was the exclusive cause of the accident which resulted in injury to P, and moves to join X in the action. Under applicable state law, if X is not named as a defendant and X and Y were joint and several tortfeasors, Y would have no right of contribution from X.

P is a citizen of Minnesota, Y is a citizen of Vermont, and X is a citizen of Minnesota. Y's motion should be:

(A) Granted, because there is a common nucleus of operative facts.

(B) Granted, because Y's contention that X was responsible for the accident may (at trial) prove to be correct.

(C) Denied, because X is not an indispensable party.

(D) Denied, because joinder of X would destroy subject matter jurisdiction.

63. Arnold borrowed $76,000 from Bill and signed a promissory note in which he promised to repay that sum, plus interest in six months. Chuck guaranteed the note, and promised to pay the sum due to Bill in the event Arnold defaulted. Arnold became delinquent under the note, and Bill sued Arnold. Arnold asserted a usury defense to Bill's claim. Which of the following statements is correct?

(A) A judgment in favor of Bill is *res judicata* as to Chuck.

(B) A judgment in favor of Bill would result in issue preclusion against Chuck as to those issues which had been fully litigated in *Bill v. Arnold*.

(C) If Arnold won on the issue of usury, Chuck could probably assert collateral estoppel in an action brought by Bill against Chuck on the guaranty.

(D) None of the above.

64. Paul loaned $77,000 to Jim. Ralph guaranteed the loan. Subsequently, Jim became delinquent in his payments. Paul sued Jim in the appropriate U.S. district court. Paul is a citizen of State X and Jim is a citizen of State Y. Ralph is a citizen of State X. Which of the following statements is correct?

(A) Ralph is an indispensable party, because Jim could otherwise be liable for the full amount of Paul's judgment.

(B) The court would probably permit Ralph to intervene on Jim's side, if Ralph chose to do so.

(C) Ralph may intervene on Jim's side as of right, since otherwise he could be precluded from raising any issues which were fully and fairly litigated in Paul's action against Jim (if Paul subsequently sued Ralph on the guarantee).

(D) None of the above.

65. Polly, a citizen of Nevada, purchased $7,000 of ABC Corporation securities from her broker, Don, also a citizen of Nevada. However, because ABC was insolvent, the securities were later shown to be worthless. Polly sued Don in the appropriate U.S. district court for violation of federal securities law. Which of the following claims or actions may be joined or occur in Polly's suit against Don?

   I. *Polly v. Don* for injuries caused when Don's car rear-ended Polly's car following a party which they had both attended.

   II. *Don v. ABC Corporation*, a Nevada corporation, if, as part of their contract the latter entity warranted its solvency to Don.

   (A) I only.
   (B) II only.
   (C) I and II.
   (D) Neither I nor II.

66. P sues D for trespass at her Los Angeles residence. The action was properly commenced in a U.S. district court. D defends by claiming that he was in New York at the time when the incident allegedly took place. D intends to call Wanda as a witness to testify that she saw him in New York on the day in question. P believes Wanda is hopelessly nearsighted and could easily have mistaken someone else for D.

   To impeach Wanda's testimony, P sends Wanda a Notice to Appear for Medical Examination before a licensed opthamologist selected by P. Which of the following statements is correct?

   (A) W must appear, but D is entitled to a copy of the opthamologist's findings.

   (B) W must appear, since her eyesight is in issue.

(C) W need not appear, because she is not a party to the action.

(D) W need not appear, because physicians making medical examinations must be selected by the judge.

67. Denny, a citizen of Texas, leased an apartment from Polly, a citizen of California, under a one-year rental agreement at $500 per month. The rental agreement states that Denny may not sublet the premises to any person of Oriental ancestry. With six months remaining on the lease, Denny sublet the apartment to an individual of Chinese ancestry.

Polly sued Denny in the appropriate U.S. district court for breach of contract, seeking to evict Denny and recover the remaining six months' rent. The complaint stated that Denny violated the terms of the rental agreement, and asserts that the clause concerning subletting does ***not*** violate the U.S. Constitution. Denny moves to dismiss the case for lack of subject matter jurisdiction.

With respect to Denny's motion:

(A) Denny will win because subject matter jurisdiction based upon a federal claim is lacking.

(B) Denny will win because subject matter jurisdiction based upon diversity is lacking.

(C) Both (A) and (B).

(D) Denny will lose.

68. Mel is an investment banker. He handles the accounts of Ms. Wine and Ms. Ball. Mel decided to invest some of their money in a new entrepreneurial enterprise he had just started. Unfortunately, things did not go well. In a period of months, all of Wine's and Ball's money was gone.

Ball sued Mel for breach of fiduciary duty. She recovered a default judgment for the full amount of her claim. Which of the following statements is correct?

(A) Ball's judgment is *res judicata* with respect to a subsequent lawsuit by Wine against Mel.

(B) Assuming the mutuality doctrine is inapplicable, a court may permit Wine to assert collateral estoppel in a subsequent lawsuit by Wine against Mel.

(C) Ball's judgment should have no effect on a subsequent lawsuit by Wine against Mel.

(D) None of the above.

69. P sues as the sole representative of a class of persons who had brought limited partnership interests in worthless oil producing property from D. P alleges that all purchasers received identical written sales materials (which contained numerous misrepresentations), and that many members of the class also received verbal "pitches" which were also fraudulent.

P commenced an FRCP 23(b)(3) class action based upon diversity subject matter jurisdiction against D in the appropriate U.S. district court. Which of the following statements is correct?

(A) If the court refuses to certify the proposed class, P may appeal the decision immediately.

(B) Assuming the class is certified, P may enter into a settlement agreement with D, as long as notice is given to all members of the class and a majority approve of the compromise.

(C) Assuming the class is certified, if P prevails in the suit he is **not** entitled to recover attorney's fees, unless a federal statute explictly provides for such an award.

(D) None of the above.

70. Art and Bob were riding in a car driven by Art, when they were suddenly rear-ended by Oscar. Art is a citizen of Illinois and Oscar is a citizen of Ohio. Art commenced a lawsuit in the appropriate U.S. district court of Ohio (where the accident had occurred), claiming $80,000 in injuries and damages as a result of the occurrence. Bob (a citizen of Ohio) seeks to intervene. However, his injuries were far less severe than those suffered by Art. Bob has been informed by his attorney that he would probably not be able to recover more than $11,000.

Bob's motion to intervene should be:

(A) Granted, because there is supplemental jurisdiction.

(B) Granted, because he is an indispensable party.

(C) Denied, because there is no subject matter jurisdiction over his claim against Oscar.

(D) Denied, unless Bob believes in good faith that his attorney's calculation of potential damages is incorrect.

71. Bill and Joe were riding in a car owned by Ellwood. Bill is a citizen of Georgia and Joe is a citizen of Arkansas. They were involved in an accident in Tennessee with Carl (a citizen of Alabama). Insurco is a Georgia corporation, which has its principal place of business in Alabama. Ellwood is a citizen of Texas. Melvin, a citizen of Alabama, who was visiting his uncle in

Tennessee when the accident occurred, was injured while extricating Bill and Joe from their vehicle.

Melvin and Carl have threatened to sue Ellwood, contending that he is vicariously liable for the alleged negligence of Joe (who was driving the car). Insurco contends that it is not liable for Joe's driving, but commences an interpleader action against Bill, Joe, Carl, Ellwood and Melvin in the U.S. district court in Alabama. The policy limit of Ellwood's insurance is $75,000. Carl and Melvin claim personal injuries in excess of that amount.

Which of the following statements is correct?

(A) The action is appropriate under "statutory" interpleader.
(B) The action is appropriate under "rule" interpleader.
(C) Under statutory or rule interpleader, the U.S. district court would be obliged to refer to the long-arm statute enacted in Tennessee to determine if personal jurisdiction could be asserted over the defendants.
(D) Interpleader is inappropriate, since Insurco is contending that it is not liable under the policy.

Questions 72-74 are based on the following facts:

Joan visited Dr. Brown. After examining her, he put some drops in her left ear. She then left. However, she continued to have difficulties with her balance. Three weeks after her visit to Dr. Brown, Joan fell and sustained serious injuries. Joan sued Dr. Brown and requested a jury trial. The action was properly commenced in a U.S. district court.

At trial, Joan testified to the foregoing, and then called Dr. Edward to the stand. He testified that, in his opinion, (1) he had examined Joan and found substantial damage to her inner ear, (2) the damage was caused by a fluid containing acid. Joan rested her case. Dr. Brown took the stand and testified that (1) Joan had been suffering from an infection which affected the inner ear, and (2) he had put some drops of perforium (an innocuous, non-acidic substance) into her ear. He further stated on cross-examination that the bottle containing perforium stood in the vicinity of a bottle containing an acidic substance. He then rested his case. In rebuttal, Joan called Dr. Edward who stated that the injury to Joan's inner ear is totally inconsistent with Dr. Brown's assertion of an infection. All sides then rested.

72. If Joan moves for judgment as a matter of law (formerly called a "directed verdict"):

  (A) Her motion should be granted because Dr. Brown admitted that the perforium bottle stood near a bottle containing an acidic substance.

  (B) Her motion should be granted, but not for the reason set forth in (A).

  (C) Her motion should be denied.

  (D) None of the above.

73. Assume that Dr. Brown (rather than Joan) moved for a directed verdict ("judgment as matter of law"), and that the motion was granted. Joan then appeals. The Court of Appeals should:

  (A) Reverse the judgment and order a new trial.

  (B) Reverse the judgment and direct that judgment be entered for Joan.

  (C) Affirm the judgment.

  (D) None of the above.

74. Assume neither party moved for a directed verdict ("judgment as matter of law"). The case goes to the jury which returns a verdict for Joan. Dr. Brown then moves for a JNOV and, in the alternative, for a new trial. The trial judge grants the motion for a JNOV, but denies the motion for a new trial. Joan then appeals the JNOV granted by the trial court. The Court of Appeals should:

  (A) Reverse the judgment, since a motion for a new trial cannot be joined with a JNOV.

  (B) Affirm the judgment.

  (C) Reverse the judgment, but order a new trial.

  (D) Reverse the judgment and reinstate the verdict for Joan.

75. X, a citizen of Kentucky, entered into a contract to sell a car to Z, also a citizen of Kentucky. However, when Z was late in tendering a prepayment, X advised Z that he was no longer bound to complete the transaction. Z unequivocally informed X that the contract was still binding. Prior to the due date for delivery of the automobile under the original agreement, X entered into a new transaction with Y, whereby X agreed to sell the vehicle to Y for a higher amount than had been agreed to by Z.

Y is a citizen of Ohio. Y was aware of the outstanding contract which X had with Z, but was assured by the former that Z's right in the automobile had been lawfully terminated. X subsequently repudiated his contract with Y, contending it was entered into under coercive circumstances. Y commenced an action against X in the appropriate U.S. district court for specific performance and breach of contract. X moved to dismiss upon the ground that Z was an indispensable party. The court will probably:

(A) Grant the motion, because Z has an interest in the vehicle.
(B) Grant the motion, because Z entered into an agreement with X for purchase of the car prior to Y.
(C) Deny the motion, because ancillary jurisdiction will permit the court to exercise subject matter jurisdiction over Z.
(D) Deny the motion, because a court, in equity and good conscience, could proceed with the action.

Questions 76-78 are based on the following facts:

Paul was a citizen of Colorado. He was an employee of Construction Company, a Colorado Corporation. Paul was killed one day when some scaffolding collapsed. The scaffolding had been provided by a subcontractor for the job, Big Builders (a U.S. corporation). Paul's wife, Mary, as the executrix of his estate, sued Construction Company. She had moved to South Dakota just prior to commencing the lawsuit. The action is brought in the only U.S. district court in Colorado on the theory that Construction Company had been negligent in failing to inspect the defective scaffolding supplied by Big Builders. Colorado law provides that a general contractor is presumed to have not inspected materials supplied to it by a subcontractor. This presumption is rebuttable. At the time of his death, Paul owed Construction Company $7,000 in advanced wages. The amount claimed by Mary is $1,000,000.

76. Which of the following statements is correct?

(A) Big Builders may intervene as of right.
(B) Construction Company can implead Big Builders, if personal jurisdiction and venue requirements are satisfied.
(C) Construction Company could assert a counterclaim for the advance in wages which it made to Paul.
(D) None of the above.

77. At the trial, Construction Company introduced evidence showing that Paul had been warned by his supervisor not to work near the scaffolding until it had been thoroughly checked, since it looked unsafe. However, Paul had disregarded the supervisor's instruction. Mary then produced a witness who testified that Paul had always objected to working close to scaffolding. If no further evidence was introduced by either side:

(A) Construction Company's motion for a directed verdict ("judgment as matter of law") would have to be granted.

(B) Construction Company's motion for a directed verdict would have to be denied.

(C) Mary's motion for a directed verdict would have to be granted.

(D) If the jury rendered a verdict for Construction Company, Mary's motion for a JNOV must be granted.

78. Assume that (1) each side introduced substantial evidence pertaining to whether Construction Company had adequately inspected the scaffolding, and (2) the case was tried by the judge. Following the trial, the judge entered findings of fact and conclusions of law. The judge found that Construction Company had adequately inspected the scaffolding, and therefore, Mary was entitled to nothing. Based upon the foregoing:

(A) The judgment must be set aside, because it is clearly erroneous.

(B) The judgment must be set aside, because it is inconsistent with the applicable presumption.

(C) The finding of fact must be set aside, because there was substantial evidence which controverted it.

(D) None of the above.

79. Paul was rear-ended by John, a 17-year old. The car that John was driving was owned by Mary. Paul is a citizen of Vermont. John and Mary (who is John's mother) are citizens of Maine. The accident occurred in Vermont. Paul sued Mary and John in the U.S. district court in Maine pursuant to a Vermont statute which made parents liable for the negligent driving of their minor children. The suit demanded $90,000 in damages. Which of the following statements is correct?

(A) Mary may assert a cross-claim against John.

(B) If Mary fails to assert a cross-claim against John, any claim by her against him will be barred.

(C) Mary may not assert a cross-claim against John.

(D) Mary may assert a counterclaim against John.

Questions 80-81 are based on the following fact situation:

Albert wrote a best selling book called "The Trials and Tribulations of a First-Year Law Student." However, he began to suspect that the publisher, Beacon House, a Virginia Corporation whose principal place of business is in that state, was not giving him an accurate accounting of his royalties.

Albert invaded a meeting of the nine-member Board of Directors of Beacon House, where he found Don (a member of the Board of Directors and the President of Beacon House). When Albert verbally accused Don of cheating him by downscaling the number of Albert's books that had actually been sold, Don grabbed Albert by the shoulders and shouted, "Shut up, you idiot!" Albert then punched Don in the face and left. Albert went to the local newspaper (called *The Star*) and advised them that he was cheated out of thousands of dollars by Don.

The Star printed a story reiterating Don's accusations, and warning writers about publishers. The story mentioned that Don was the President of Beacon House. Albert is a citizen of Arizona, Don is a citizen of Massachusetts, and *The Star* is incorporated in New York and has its principal place of business in Arizona.

80. Assume that *The Star* was sued by Beacon House for defamation in the U.S. district court in Arizona. The lawsuit alleged damages of $500,000. Which of the following statements is correct?

   (A) *The Star* cannot successfully implead Albert, because they are citizens of the same state.
   (B) Albert can intervene as of right on the side of *The Star*.
   (C) *The Star* may implead Albert on the ground that he is solely liable to Beacon House.
   (D) *The Star* probably can implead Albert.

81. Assume that (1) Beacon House sued both *The Star* and Albert in the only U.S. district court in Arizona for defamation, claiming damages in the amount of $100,000, (2) the "mutuality rule" for collateral estoppel has been abandoned in this jurisdiction, and (3) a verdict was returned in favor of Beacon House in the amount of $50,000. Which of the following statements is correct?

   (A) *The Star* could not file a cross-claim against Albert because they are citizens of the same state.
   (B) If Albert counterclaimed against Beacon House for an accounting on his royalties, he would not be entitled to a jury trial.
   (C) Don might be able to assert collateral estoppel offensively against *The Star* in a subsequent action for defamation against that entity.
   (D) Don would be barred from commencing an action against *The Star* or Albert, since he could have intervened in the present action (*Beacon House v. The Star and Albert*) without destroying diversity.

82. X left a will creating a trust for the benefit of A, B, C and D, with T as trustee. A owns 25% of the trust, B owns 25%, C owns 25%, and D owns 25%. A, B and C are citizens of California; D and the trustee are citizens of Ohio. A, B

and C sue T in the U.S. district court in Ohio, based on diversity, for distribution of the $10 million trust, claiming that the terms of the trust require immediate distribution of the res. T interprets the provisions of the trust to permit distribution only after three additional years. For tax purposes, D is content to have the trust continue for three more years.

T moves to dismiss the action for failure to join D as an indispensable party. The motion should be:

(A) Denied, because diversity is not defeated as long as any defendant is diverse from any plaintiff, and the amount in controversy exceeds $75,000.

(B) Denied, because D's interests are more consistent with T's.

(C) Granted, because there will be a lack of diversity if D is joined as a plaintiff.

(D) Granted, because D is an indispensable party.

83. Plaintiff sued Defendant in a State X court. The Federal Rules of Civil Procedure are followed in State X. Plaintiff seeks to recover for personal injuries suffered as a result of a battery inflicted upon him by Defendant. Defendant simply denied Plaintiff's allegations. Plaintiff demanded a trial by jury. Along with the forms for a general verdict, the court submitted written interrogatories to the jury. In answering these interrogatories, the jury found that: Defendant had hit Plaintiff with a vase; that Defendant intended to so hit Plaintiff; that Defendant caused Plaintiff damages as alleged in the complaint. The jury also returned a judgment against Plaintiff.

The judge then ordered a new trial. Plaintiff then filed a stipulation of voluntary dismissal, which was also signed by Defendant. Which of the following statements is correct?

(A) Plaintiff may later bring an action against Defendant on the same facts.

(B) Where the jury's answers to interrogatories conflict with a general verdict, the judge must enter a verdict in conformity with such answers.

(C) Where a jury's answer to interrogatories conflict with a general verdict, the judge must (1) enter the general verdict, or (2) order a new trial.

(D) None of the above.

84. Don, while traveling to a nearby relative's house, is injured by a vehicle negligently operated by an Acme employee who was using his car for an Acme business purpose. After initiating an action against Acme (but prior to trial), Don seeks to discover if Acme has insurance. Assuming this jurisdiction follows the FRCP, which of the following are correct regarding discovery of the insurance policy covering the Acme vehicle?

(A) If the insurance policy is not admissible at trial, the insurance policy is not discoverable.

(B) Insurance maintained by a party is never discoverable.

(C) An insured party must disclose an insurance policy if the insurer may be liable for all or part of a judgment entered against the insured.

(D) Insurance is discoverable only where it is relevant to the *prima facie* issues of the case.

85. Andy Attorney is a new associate at a prestigious downtown law firm. He is involved in a major federal securities fraud case in the local U.S. district court. Andy has noticed and taken many depositions in the case, but is now confronted with the following allegations:

I. Andy's examination of a witness was conducted in a manner designed to embarrass the deponent;

II. Andy failed to attend a deposition which he had scheduled for another party;

III. Although a party who was deposed by Andy was not represented by counsel, Andy nevertheless insisted upon carrying out the deposition; and

IV. Andy objected to almost every question asked his client at a deposition, and all answers were made subject to Andy's objections.

Which of the foregoing assertions could result in sanctions against Andy and his client?

(A) I and II.

(B) II, III, and IV.

(C) II and IV.

(D) II only.

86. Ripoff Corporation has engaged in price fixing, causing persons who purchased their stereo equipment to pay $50 per item more than required. Mark Music sues Ripoff in an appropriate United States district court for a federal anti-trust violation as representative of the class of persons who have brought Ripoff stereo equipment within the applicable statute of limitations. The class is certified under FRCP 23(b)(3).

The following notice is prepared for mailing to all class members (approximately 125,000 persons):

You are hereby notified that a class action has been brought in U.S. district court under Rule 23(b)(3) of the Federal Rules of Civil Procedure by Mr. Mark Music on behalf of all persons who have purchased Ripoff stereo equipment.

You may opt out of the class within one month of this notice. If you choose to remain in the action, you may appear through an attorney.

Which of the following is correct?

(A) If Mark is unable to pay the costs of mailing notice to all 125,000 class members, the court may, in its discretion and for good cause shown, order Ripoff to pay these costs.

(B) If a class member opts out and Ripoff prevails at trial, Ripoff can assert collateral estoppel against that individual in a subsequent lawsuit.

(C) The notice to class members is not adequate.

(D) None of the above.

87. Counselor Carlos Clark has been retained to defend WDM Corporation, an international microchip kingpin, in a federal anti-trust action commenced by Plaintiff, a corporation, in the appropriate U.S. district court. After Clark sought discovery of a large volume of documents from Plaintiff, Plaintiff advised Clark that it objected to his discovery requests on the following grounds:

I.   The documents sought are privileged;

II.   The information is factual in nature and relates to the Plaintiff's claims;

III. The documents sought were not calculated to lead to the discovery of admissible evidence; and

IV.   The evidence sought is obtainable from a less expensive source.

Which, if any, of the foregoing objections might be valid?

(A) I, III and IV.

(B) I and II.

(C) I and III.

(D) II and IV.

88. P filed an action against D corporation for material breach of contract and misrepresentation in the sale of a home located in a subdivision. An agent of D allegedly represented to P that the property was in excellent condition and ready for occupancy. Actually, P found that (1) the plumbing was defective, and (2) there were termites in the basement. Prior to filing the action, P's attorney consulted with an economist concerning P's damages. Which of the following statements is correct?

(A) The economist's opinion is discoverable.

(B) The opinion of the economist is *not* discoverable absent *exceptional circumstances.*

(C) The opinion of an expert is discoverable only if it is solicited or obtained prior to the commencement of litigation.

(D) Discovery of an expert's opinion is privileged.

89. Plaintiff sued Defendant in a State X court of general jurisdiction for injuries suffered in an auto accident in State X. Plaintiff is a citizen of State X and Defendant is a citizen of State Y. State X is a comparative negligence state. The jury finds Defendant 80% at fault, and Plaintiff 20% at fault, and rules that Defendant must pay Plaintiff $16,000 for the latter's injuries.

Since all of Defendant's assets are in State Y, Plaintiff sued Defendant on the State X judgment in a State Y court. State Y is a contributory negligence state. Assuming the State X decision is final, which of the following statements is correct?

(A) *Res judicata* precludes Plaintiff from suing on the State X judgment in State Y because the two actions involve the same parties and the same occurrence.

(B) Full Faith and Credit need not be granted to the State X judgment.

(C) The State Y court may hold a trial *de novo* because that jurisdiction does not recognize comparative negligence.

(D) State Y must grant Full Faith and Credit to the State X Court judgment, if Defendant had a full and fair opportunity to litigate on the merits.

90. A sued B, seeking personal injuries and property damage in the amount of $100,000 for B's negligence in causing a collision with a car driven by A. A lost, with the jury expressly finding that B was not negligent. C (a pedestrian walking along the street when he saw the accident) suffered back injuries when he attempted to extricate A from the latter's vehicle. C sued B, claiming B negligently caused the accident with A's car, and was therefore responsible for C's personal injuries. In the latter action, B made a motion to dismiss based upon the decision rendered in A's earlier lawsuit. The court:

(A) May grant B's motion, because it has discretion to determine if it will apply collateral estoppel principles.

(B) Must grant B's motion, because C's action is barred under *res judicata* principles.

(C) Should deny B's motion, because it may not apply collateral estoppel in the context of the facts presented.

(D) Should deny B's motion, only if the concept of mutuality of estoppel is not applied in this jurisdiction.

Questions 91-93 are based on the following facts:

Dodo is a State X partnership composed of Jim Do and Bob Do. They manufacture and lease large ovens which are used in restaurants. Dodo's only plant and business office is in State X. Three months ago, the president of Dominic's (a fashionable eating spot in State Z) made a trip to State X and leased an oven from Dodo. Dominic's is incorporated in State Z, where its restaurant is located. The stock of Dominic's is held by Carl, Fred, and Alice. The Do brothers are domiciled in State X.

Two weeks ago, Paul (an employee of Dominic's) was hurt when the "door" of the leased oven suddenly fell open on him. Paul sued both Dodo and Dominic's in the U.S. district court in State Z. Jim and Bob Do were personally served in State X. Dominic's was served pursuant to a State Z statute which permits notice of the lawsuit to be (1) left with someone of "suitable discretion" at the defendant's home or main business premises, or (2) if no such person is available, posted on the door which is most often used by the occupants of the defendant's home or main business premises. Paul's process server utilized the latter method. The president of Dominic's saw the notice and delivered the summons and service of process to the corporation's attorney.

91. To determine if subject matter jurisdiction is proper, it would be helpful to know:

   I.   The domicile of the shareholders of Dominic's.
   II. The domicile of Paul.
   III. If State Z has a long-arm statute.
   IV. The extent of Paul's injuries.

   (A) I and III.
   (B) II and IV.
   (C) III and IV.
   (D) II and III.

92. With respect to the notice given to Dominic's, which of the following statements is probably the most accurate?

   (A) Under these circumstances, it is constitutionally invalid.
   (B) It is invalid because it failed to comply with the FRCP.
   (C) It is valid because the corporation received actual notice of Paul's action.
   (D) It is valid because the FRCP authorizes service of process in accordance with the law of the state in which it is located.

93. In determining if the assertion of personal jurisdiction over Dodo is proper, which of the following factors are pertinent?

    I.   The State Z long-arm statute.

    II. Whether Dodo was aware where the leased range would be used.

    III. Whether Dodo presently does any other business in State Z (whether or not that business is unrelated to the Dominic's lease).

    IV. The physical health of Jim and Bob Do.

    (A) 1, 2 and 3.

    (B) 2, 3 and 4.

    (C) 1, 2 and 4.

    (D) 1 and 2.

Questions 94-96 are based upon the following facts:

Paul sued his employer, Acme corporation, in the proper U.S. district court in State X, claiming that (1) Dan (an Acme supervisor) had defamed him by informing the president of Acme that Dan was an ineffectual employee, and that this statement was within the scope of Dan's employment at Acme, and (2) Acme owed Dan $5,000 in unused vacation pay. As a consequence of both harms, Paul claimed damages in the aggregate amount of $80,000.

Acme responded to Paul's complaint with an FRCP 12(b) motion to dismiss Paul's complaint on the grounds that Dan was an indispensable party and that subject matter jurisdiction was lacking since the two claims aggregated by Paul to satisfy the "in excess of $75,000" requirement did not arise out of the same transaction or occurrence. The court could not obtain personal jurisdiction over Dan. Acme's motion was denied.

Acme then filed an answer which admitted Dan's statement, but denied that it was made within the scope of Dan's employment and asserted the affirmative defense of truth. Paul then filed a summary judgment motion, with his personal supporting affidavit describing facts which demonstrated that he had performed his job competently. Acme failed to respond to Paul's summary judgment motion.

94. Which of the following statements is correct?

    (A) Dan is an indispensable party.

    (B) Paul may not aggregate unrelated claims to meet the jurisdictional amount.

    (C) Dan is probably not an indispensable party.

    (D) (B) and (C), but not (A).

95. Paul's motion for a summary judgment should be:

(A) Granted, because Acme failed to respond with an affidavit which disputed Paul's assertions.

(B) Granted, because there is no genuine issue of fact.

(C) Denied, because the affidavit was made by a party to the action.

(D) Denied, because material issues of fact remain.

96. Assume for purposes of this question that (1) Paul never made a motion for summary judgment, (2) the jury rendered a general verdict in favor of Acme, and (3) the mutuality rule has been repudiated in this jurisdiction. If Paul now sued Dan for defamation, which of the following is correct?

(A) Dan could probably assert *res judicata* to avoid liability.

(B) Dan could probably assert collateral estoppel to avoid liability.

(C) Dan probably could **not** assert collateral estoppel principles to avoid liability.

(D) (A) and (B), but not (C).

97. Paul is a citizen of Idaho. He recently sued Deeter Corporation (which is incorporated in Delaware and has its principal place of business in Iowa) for $75,042.37. Paul's lawsuit, filed in a U.S. District Court in Idaho, claims that Deeter's President, Jack, recently caused Paul losses of $75,000 for defamation, and $42.37 for a dinner which the latter had promised to buy. The action emanates from a business dinner at a restaurant in Idaho. At that meeting, negotiations deteriorated to the point where Jack loudly called Paul a "con artist" and abruptly left without paying the bill. If Deeter Corporation contests the assertion of **subject matter jurisdiction** over it, will Paul prevail? (You may assume that personal jurisdiction requirements are satisfied.)

(A) Yes, because diversity jurisdiction is present.

(B) Yes, because (based upon the defamation) a federal question is present.

(C) No, because neither of Paul's claims **exceeds** $75,000.

(D) No, because the facts fail to indicate that Deeter Corporation has sufficient "minimum contacts" with Idaho.

98. Babco Publishing Co. is a New York corporation that prints and sells law school outlines. Babco's major sales are in New England, but it annually sells outlines in California via its exclusive distributor, Armco, a New Jersey corporation. Babco noticed that Dumbco, Inc., a Texas corporation, had recently published a series of outlines which closely resembled those of Babco. Dumbco also sells its outlines in California. California's long-arm statute permits its courts to exercise personal jurisdiction over non-personal injury defendant/tortfeasors, who are **not** domiciled in that state, if their business within the jurisdiction exceeds $80,000. Neither Babco or Dumbco's business in California exceeds $15,000. Can a U.S. District Court in California successfully exercise personal jurisdiction over Dumbco for copyright infringement if Babco sues Dumbco?

(A) Yes, if Dumbco has sufficient "minimum contacts" in California.

(B) Yes, despite the state statute, because "diversity" requirements are satisfied.

(C) No, because California requires that the defendant's business exceed $80,000, and federal courts ordinarily "borrow" the long-arm statute of the jurisdiction in which they reside.

(D) No, because the aggregate amount in controversy fails to exceed $75,000.

99. Arthur was a partner in the XYZ Public Relations Group, a Massachusetts general partnership, with offices in Boston, New York City and Los Angeles. XYZ was recently sued by KABD radio station. The suit alleged that XYZ had charged KABD $250,000 without disclosing that XYZ also represented a competitor of KABD, and that this resulted in a less than competent effort by XYZ. Arthur, who four months before this lawsuit had relocated from Boston to Los Angeles, was subpoenaed to have his deposition taken in New York City (at the offices of KABD's legal counsel.) While in New York, Arthur was personally served by Clarence, who owns the apartment that Arthur had lived in while in Boston. Clarence lives in New York City. Clarence's lawsuit was commenced in a U.S. District Court sitting in New York. The action, based upon diversity of citizenship, claims that Arthur had (1) held "wild parties" at the premises which damaged the rental unit (a private home), and (2) failed to pay rent, in an aggregate amount exceeding $75,000. Under these circumstances, is Arthur subject to personal jurisdiction in New York?

(A) Yes, because the requirements for diversity jurisdiction appear to be satisfied.

(B) Yes, because Arthur was personally served in New York.

(C) No, if Clarence subsequently fails to prove at trial that his damages, in fact, exceeded $75,000.

(D) No, because Arthur was in New York in response to a subpoena.

100. ABC Corporation, a relatively new Illinois entity, manufactures high powered motors which are installed into yachts manufactured by Defendant Inc., an Ohio corporation. ABC knew that Defendant sold most of its yachts in California and Florida, which abut major water bodies. A

yacht was sold by Defendant to Bonzo Watercraft Sales, Inc. (a Florida corporation), who then sold it to Paul. Due to a defect in the motor, the yacht capsized during its first "run." Paul was seriously injured. Paul sued Bonzo in the appropriate U.S. District Court in Florida. Four months later, after discovery, Paul sought to add ABC as an additional defendant. Florida's long-arm statute permits jurisdiction over non-residents when the person or entity involved has done business in Florida or sold personal property to a Florida domiciliary or entity. Under these circumstances, can the U.S. District Court assume personal jurisdiction over ABC? You may assume that ABC has never sold any of its motors directly to a Florida citizen or entity.

(A) Yes, if ABC could reasonably foresee that its motors might eventually be used in Florida.

(B) Yes, because ABC did business with Defendant, who sold the yacht in question to a Florida entity.

(C) No, because ABC never did any business in Florida or sold personal property to a Florida citizen or entity.

(D) No, because ABC clearly lacks sufficient minimum contacts with Florida.

Questions 101-102 are based upon the following facts.

Pat is domiciled in Los Angeles, California. While driving her car in Chicago, Pat collided with Dan, a Bar Review lecturer who lived in Chicago. Settlement discussions took place, but were not successful. Four months later, while Dan was giving a lecture in Los Angeles, California, he was personally served by Pat's process server. The lawsuit, filed in U.S. District Court, alleges that Dan's negligence caused the accident, and claimed damages exceeding $75,000.

101. Assuming Dan has no contacts with California other than lecturing there four days each year for the Bar Review course which employs him, can Pat successfully assert jurisdiction over Dan in California?

(A) Yes, because Dan was personally served within California.

(B) Yes, because Dan had adequate minimum contacts with California.

(C) No, because Dan lacked sufficient minimum contacts with California.

(D) No, because diversity of citizenship is lacking (Dan was served in California and Pat lives there).

102. Assume that Dan does not, initially, object to personal jurisdiction. He answers (denying liability) and counterclaims against Pat for the injuries he sustained in the accident. After some discovery, however, it appeared that Pat would probably prevail. Can Dan now contest personal jurisdiction?

(A) Yes, because a lack of personal jurisdiction can be raised at any stage of a federal litigation matter.

(B) Yes, because a lack of personal jurisdiction can be raised at any time prior to trial.

(C) No, because an objection to personal jurisdiction must be raised at the first available opportunity.

(D) No, because Pat, as the domiciliary/plaintiff, has the right to choose the forum.

103. Wanda brought an action in the applicable U.S. District Court in Idaho against XYZ insurance company. She was the sole beneficiary under a policy under which her ex-husband, Arthur, was the insured. XYZ answered that the policy was fraudulently procured, because Arthur misrepresented the condition of his health at the time the policy was issued. XYZ deposed both Wanda and Dr. Belton (who was Arthur's family doctor). At the trial, it is most likely that XYZ may:

(A) Use Wanda's deposition for any purpose.

(B) Use Wanda's deposition to impeach her own or Dr. Belton's credibility, *if* either testifies.

(C) Not use Wanda's deposition, because a deposition is merely a discovery tool.

(D) Not use Wanda's deposition, unless her attorney deposed one or more officers or employees of XYZ.

104. Pete commenced a lawsuit in U.S. District Court against Doe. The action alleged that Pete had been injured on Doe's premises about one month ago, and that Doe's negligence caused the injury. Doe filed an answer, and also claimed that Pete had breached a contract with Doe about nine months ago. The action was tried, and both Pete and Doe successfully prevailed upon their claims. About one month after these judgments, Pete commenced a breach of contract action against Doe, filed in U.S. District Court, alleging that the latter party had breached the contract upon which Doe's earlier judgment against Pete was based. (You may assume that all of the aforementioned actions were properly filed.) Under these circumstances, it is most likely that:

(A) Pete's action will be dismissed, because he should have counterclaimed against Doe in the earlier action.

(B) Pete's action will be dismissed, because the question of Doe's liability to Pete is settled under collateral estoppel principles.

(C) Pete's action will not be dismissed, because the question of Doe's liability to Pete under the contract is a distinct, new claim which is unrelated to Pete's initial lawsuit.

(D) Pete's action will not be dismissed, because (even though Pete's claim is related to the earlier action) it is not barred by collateral estoppel principles.

Questions 105-107 are based on the following facts:

P, seeking damages from D Inc., for patent infringement, sues D in a district court (which follows the discovery rules set forth in the FRCP). P's complaint alleges in part that D's agents knowingly copied P's patented electric generator and purposely made meaningless cosmetic changes to cover up the infringement. D answered by generally denying all of P's allegations.

105. D's research and development department keeps detailed records as well as models of all of its research projects. Must D disclose the existence of these items?

(A) No, these documents are privileged.

(B) No, a party need not perform discovery for its opponent.

(C) Yes, a party may discover any relevant, non-privileged material.

(D) Yes, a party must disclose the existence of documents and tangible things relevant to the disputed facts.

106. D retained 5 experts in anticipation of litigation. D procured reports from each expert, but does not plan to call the experts at trial. Instead, D plans to call two of its employees as experts. Can P obtain the identities and opinions of the non-employee experts?

(A) Yes, a party must disclose the identity and opinions of an expert it retains in anticipation of litigation.

(B) Yes, a party through interrogatories may discover the opinions of any expert the opposing party retains in anticipation of litigation.

(C) No, since the opinions are not admissible at trial they are not discoverable.

(D) No, unless the moving party can show exceptional circumstances which warrant discovery of the expert's opinions.

107. 20 days before trial, D learns that a retired employee developed the first sketches of its new generator. Must D divulge this information to P?

(A) Yes, since a party has a duty to supplement its initial mandatory disclosures.

(B) No, since the adverse party could find this person through its own discovery devices.

(C) No, unless D intends to use the employee as a witness.

(D) No. A party is not obligated to supplement its initial mandatory disclosures.

108. On March 21, 1996, Goldie Miner enlisted the services of the renowned law firm of Weare Phulla Bull & Associates. She claims that pesticides produced by Toxin, Inc. were sprayed next to her home and these insecticides have turned her skin deep purple. Bull looks at Ms. Miner and her skin is indeed a revolting deep purple hue. Bull helps his new client on with her coat and spots a box of dye hanging out of one of the pockets. He assures her that he can probably get Toxin to settle out of court to avoid adverse publicity for at least $10,000,000.

On April 1, Bull files a complaint in the district court alleging $100,000,000 in damages. Toxin answers and deposed Goldie on April 17, 1996. During the deposition Toxin's attorney becomes disgusted with Goldie and throws a glass of water at her. Remarkably, her skin pigment washes right off. The next day Toxin files several motions with the court including a motion to impose sanctions against Bull for filing a frivolous pleading. Bull withdraws his pleading 15 days after being served with the motion. May the court impose sanctions against Bull?

(A) Yes, because an attorney has a duty to conduct a reasonable inquiry to ensure the claim is not baseless.

(B) Yes, because the purpose of the claim was clearly to harass the defendant.

(C) No, because Bull withdrew the complaint before the court is allowed to impose sanctions.

(D) No, because an attorney cannot be punished for misrepresentations made by his client.

109. Gipetto, a famous comsetic surgeon domiciled in California, develops a hair growth formula to cure baldness. His initial tests on rats and wooden puppets show promise, so he test-markets his new product in the small town of Wannalie, Wyoming. 40 bald men try Gipetto's new tonic and all experience miraculous hair growth. Unfortunately, they all, to varying degrees, also experience terribly disfiguring nasal protrusions. The men join as plaintiffs in a suit against Gipetto in a district court in California. Their claims vary in value between $100,000 and $1,500,000.

Gipetto's attorney determines that it would be tactically advantageous to question the men before the effect of the tonic wears off. She serves the plaintiff with notice of the depositions. The plaintiffs move to prevent Gipetto from deposing all of them. The plaintiff's motion should be:

(A) Granted, since a party ordinarily may not take this many depositions.

(B) Granted, since parties to an action may not be deposed.

(C) Denied, because the information sought is relevant and not privileged.

(D) Denied, unless the court finds Gipetto's only intent is to harass the plaintiffs.

Multiple-Choice Answers

1. **A** ***U.S. district courts are competent*** to hear cases involving a federal claim (i.e., one arising under the Constitution, a treaty or the laws of the U.S.). (*See* ELO Ch.3-IV(A)(3).) Paul's claim is based upon violation of a state statute. It does **not** arise under the U.S. Constitution, a treaty or a federal law. Thus, Denton's motion should be granted. Choice **B** is incorrect because, while Denton is asserting a defense based upon the U.S. Constitution, competency based upon a "federal question" is analyzed only from the viewpoint of the claim being asserted by the plaintiff. Choice **C** is incorrect because no federal claim has been asserted by Paul. Finally, Choice **D** is incorrect because Paul's claim does not arise under the U.S. Constitution.

2. **C** For ***"diversity" subject matter jurisdiction*** to exist, (1) no plaintiff and no defendant may be citizens of the ***same state***, and (2) the amount in controversy ***must exceed $75,000***, exclusive of interest and costs. (*See* ELO Ch.3-II(A) & III(J).) [Note that in May, 1997, Congress raised the amount in controversy requirement from $50,000 to $75,000.] Since (1) the plaintiffs are citizens of Florida, and D is a citizen of Michigan and Delaware (a corporation is deemed to be a citizen of the states in which it is incorporated or has its principal place of business), and (2) each plaintiff is claiming damages in excess of $75,000, "diversity" subject matter jurisdiction is satisfied. Choice **D** is incorrect because D is also a citizen of Michigan. Choice **A** is incorrect because diversity subject matter jurisdiction is not dependent on the place of plaintiff's injury. Finally, Choice **B** is incorrect because a corporation is a citizen of the states in which it is incorporated or has its principal place of business. The fact that D was headquartered in Florida would not deprive the court of "diversity" subject matter jurisdiction.

3. **B** Cases based upon "federal question" subject matter jurisdiction must be commenced in the judicial district in which (1) any defendant resides, if all defendants reside in the same State, (2) a substantial part of the events or omissions on which the claim is based occurred or a substantial part of the property is located, or (3) any defendant may be found, if there is no district in which the action may otherwise be brought. 28 U.S.C. § 1391(b). When venue is improper, a U.S. district court may, on its own motion or on the motion of any defendant, transfer the action to another U.S. district court in which the matter could have originally been commenced, or dismiss the lawsuit; 28 U.S.C. § 1406(a). (*See* ELO Ch.2-VIII(E)(1-4) & (E)(10)(e).) Since the action could have been commenced in either California (where the defendant resides) or Texas (where the discrimination took place), it

may be transferred to the proper federal judicial district in either of those states. Choice **D** is incorrect because the court may not retain the action since the (1) defendant does not reside in Nevada, and (2) the cause of action did not arise in Nevada. Choice **A** is incorrect because the action may be transferred to either California or Texas. Finally, Choice **C** is incorrect because the action may be transferred to any U.S. district court where the litigation may have originally been commenced.

4. **C** Lack of subject matter jurisdiction may ordinarily be raised ***at any time*** throughout a legal proceeding. In state courts, an objection to personal jurisdiction is ordinarily deemed to be waived by a general appearance. (*See* ELO Ch.4-VI(A)(2) & VII(B)(2).) Since federal courts have exclusive subject matter jurisdiction with respect to ***admiralty claims***, the State A court was not competent to render a valid judgment (despite being a court of general jurisdiction). Choice **B** is incorrect because a lack of personal jurisdiction is ordinarily waived by a general appearance. Choice **A** is incorrect because Derek is likely to prevail only on the lack of subject matter jurisdiction issue. Finally, Choice **D** is incorrect because the State A court was not competent to render a judgment in this matter, even though any possible objection to personal jurisdiction was probably waived by Derek's general appearance.

5. **B** Where a suit is properly commenced in a state court and "federal claim" subject matter jurisdiction is satisfied, the action ***may be removed*** to the U.S. district court which is in the judicial district that encompasses the state court, if (1) ***all*** of the defendants join in the petition for removal, and (2) removal is sought ***within 30 days*** from the time the moving party received service of process. (*See* ELO Ch.3-VII(B)(2) & (K).) Since the action involves a federal claim, Defendant is ***entitled*** to have the litigation removed to the appropriate U.S. district court. Choice **A** is incorrect because where removal is otherwise proper, the fact that the action could not have originally been commenced in the U.S. district court to which it is removed is irrelevant. Choice **C** is incorrect because state courts of general jurisdiction are ordinarily competent to hear federal claims. Finally, Choice **D** is incorrect because citizenship is not pertinent where removal is based upon a federal claim.

6. **C** U.S. district courts are competent to hear cases involving a ***federal claim*** (i.e., one arising under the Constitution, a treaty or the laws of the U.S.). (*See* ELO Ch.3-IV(A).) Since Acme is asserting a federal

claim against the Steamroller's Union, subject matter jurisdiction exists — even though the amount in controversy does not exceed $75,000. Choices **A** and **B** are true in that (1) there is no diversity, since an unincorporated association is deemed to be a citizen of each state in which *any* of its members are domiciled (Acme and Steamroller's are therefore each citizens of Indiana), and (2) the amount in controversy does not *exceed* $75,000. *However,* subject matter jurisdiction still exists because a federal claim is involved (i.e., one arising under a U.S. statute). Finally, Choice **D** is incorrect because a federal, rather than state, claim has been asserted.

7. **C** Under *statutory* interpleader, a U.S. district court is competent where (1) any two of the defendant/claimants are citizens of *different* states, and (2) the amount involved is $500 or more. In a *statutory* interpleader action, venue is proper in any judicial district in which any of the claimants reside. (*See* ELO Ch.8-VII(C)(2).) Since venue is proper only in a judicial district in which a defendant/claimant resides, a U.S. district court would be *obliged to dismiss the action or transfer it* to a U.S. district court where the lawsuit could have been commenced. The citizenship of the plaintiff/stakeholder is *irrelevant* for purposes of determining subject matter jurisdiction in a statutory interpleader case. Choice **A** is incorrect because Sam's citizenship would not be imputed to Harvey. However, even if it were, diversity of citizenship for a statutory interpleader action would still exist. Choice **B** is incorrect because the jurisdictional amount for statutory interpleader cases is only $500 or more. Finally, Choice **D** is incorrect because Choices **A** and **B** are (as discussed, previously, above) erroneous.

8. **C** A summons and complaint may not ordinarily be delivered by a person who is *a party to the action*; FRCP 4(c)(2). Since Pete is the plaintiff and personally delivered the summons and complaint to Doris, service *should be quashed*. Choice **A** is incorrect because Big Time did receive actual notice of the pending lawsuit through the service upon Doris (service upon a corporate president is deemed to constitute notice). Choice **B** is incorrect because the fact that Doris was not an officer at the time at which the answer was due is irrelevant. Choice **D** is incorrect because service of the summons and complaint was made by Pete.

9. **A** A person who is not a party *should be joined* where failure to do so will leave any party to the action subject to a *substantial risk of incurring multiple liability* for a single obligation. If the court determines that in equity and in good conscience the action should be dismissed

in the non-party's absence, he is regarded as being **indispensable**. Where the joinder of an indispensable party will destroy subject matter jurisdiction, a federal court **must dismiss the action**; FRCP 19. Where an action is dismissed because of the failure to join an indispensable party, the court's decision is **not** deemed to be on the merits. Thus, dismissal of an action upon this ground would have no *res judicata* effect. (*See* ELO Ch.8-IV(D)(1-3) and Ch.9-II(C)(1).) Krooke would probably be considered an indispensable party, since failure to join him in the action would expose Bank to multiple liability (i.e., Krooke could subsequently sue Bank for the full amount of the savings account, since the decision in the *Plaintiff v. Bank* action would not be binding upon him). Choice **B** is incorrect because the fact that dismissal of the action will result (since diversity would be destroyed), is not, in itself, a justification to refuse to join an indispensable party. Choice **C** is incorrect because the fact that diversity exists between Plaintiff and Bank would not preclude dismissal for lack of subject matter jurisdiction if Krooke were joined (Plaintiff and Krooke are both citizens of the same state). Finally, Choice **D** is incorrect because (in addition to statement II being incorrect) there is no pendent jurisdiction in this instance. The pendent jurisdiction doctrine is applicable only when a state cause of action is appended to a federal claim which has been asserted in a U.S. district court. The facts do not indicate that Plaintiff's claim is based upon the Constitution, a treaty, or a federal law.

10. **C**   There **must** be subject matter jurisdiction with respect to a claim filed by the plaintiff against a **third-party defendant** (i.e., the impleaded party). (*See* ELO Ch.8-IX(F)(4)(a).) Since P and T are both citizens of Idaho, diversity subject matter jurisdiction is lacking. Choice **D** is incorrect because the fact that diversity exists between P and D is irrelevant to the plaintiff's action against T. Choice **A** is incorrect because the pendent jurisdiction doctrine is applicable only to situations where the plaintiff is attempting to attach a state cause of action to a federal claim. Here, P is attempting to assert an action against an additional party (rather than seeking to add a state cause of action to a federal claim). Choice **B** is incorrect because the U.S. Supreme Court has specifically rejected the application of ancillary jurisdiction to this type of situation; *Owen Equipment Co. v. Kroger*, 437 U.S. 365 (1978).

11. **B**   Under the federal concept of **supplemental jurisdiction**, if a federal claim exists, a U.S. district court may permit the plaintiff to append any state claims so related to the federal claim that they constitute the same "case or controversy" under Article III of the Constitution; 28

U.S.C. § 1367. (**Note**: In federal question cases this section essentially codifies the judge-made pendent jurisdiction standard, allowing a district court to hear state claims arising out of "a common nucleus of operative facts" with the federal claim; *United Mineworkers v. Gibbs*, 383 U.S. 715 (1966)). (*See* ELO Ch.3-VI(C)(1-2).) Choice **A** is incorrect because there is no amount in controversy requirement with respect to federal claims; 28 U.S.C. § 1331. Choice **C** is incorrect because the U.S. district court would not have subject matter jurisdiction based upon diversity since the amount in controversy does not exceed $75,000. Finally, Choice **D** is incorrect because Choice **B** is true.

12. **A** Full faith and credit *must be given* to an out-of-state default judgment obtained in a procedurally and constitutionally valid manner. (*See* ELO Ch.9-IV(B).) The court in California, even though one of general jurisdiction, was *not* competent to hear this matter (patent infringement cases are within the exclusive jurisdiction of federal courts). Thus, the California judgment is not procedurally sound and would not be entitled to full faith and credit by a New York court. Choice **B** is incorrect because service of process within a jurisdiction has traditionally been recognized as a valid means of obtaining personal jurisdiction over an out-of-state defendant. Choice **C** is incorrect because a defendant who fails to appear in an out-of-state action does not waive his right to later collaterally attack the constitutional and procedural aspects of that default judgment. Finally, Choice **D** is incorrect because Choice **A** (as discussed above) is true.

13. **D** Where (1) no plaintiff and no defendant are citizens of the same state, and (2) the amount in controversy *exceeds* $75,000, exclusive of interest and costs, *diversity subject matter jurisdiction exists*. The "amount in controversy" is usually satisfied if the benefit or cost to the plaintiff is *not*, to a "legal certainty," $75,000 or less. Since P has not alleged damages in *excess* of $75,000, the amount in controversy requirement is *not* satisfied. Also, *venue is not proper* because Arizona has *no connection* with the accident, the defendant does not reside there, nor is he subject to personal jurisdiction there. (*See* ELO Ch.3-V(D) & 2-VIII(E)(2-3).) Choice **A** is incorrect because, while venue is *not* proper, Statement II is also correct. Choice **B** is incorrect because, while Statement II is correct, Statement I is also true. Choice **C** is incorrect because P's claim does not satisfy the "amount in controversy" requirement.

14. A   In all averments of fraud or mistake, the circumstances constituting
fraud or mistake shall be stated with particularity; FRCP 9(b). While
the FRCP ordinarily requires only "a short and plain statement of the
claim showing that the pleader is entitled to relief" (FRCP 8), *fraud
claims must be stated with specificity.* (*See* ELO Ch.4-V(G)(1)(b).)
Choice **B** is incorrect because the assertion of a fraud constitutes an
exception to the general rules for pleading in federal court. Choice **C** is
incorrect because the manner of pleading prescribed by the FRCP
would be controlling in the event of conflict with an otherwise applicable state rule of pleading; *Hannah v. Plumer.* Finally, Choice **D** is
incorrect because Choice **A** is true.

15. D   The fact that two or more plaintiffs, or two or more defendants, are
citizens of the same state, does *not* destroy diversity. Choice **A** is incorrect because "diversity" requires that no plaintiff and no defendant be
citizens of the same state. Choice **B** is incorrect because plaintiffs are
not "compelled" to join their actions simply because their claims arise
out of the same transaction or series of transactions. Their joinder is
permissive. Finally, Choice **C** is incorrect because D's motion would
probably be denied (rather than granted) if the conditions described
in C are satisfied.

16. D   In an FRCP 23(b)(3) class action in federal court, each member of the
class must satisfy the "amount in controversy" requirement *where federal court competency is based upon diversity*; *Zahn v. International
Paper Co.*, 414 U.S. 291 (1973). (*See* ELO Ch.8-V(I). Choice **A** is incorrect because the diversity requirement is satisfied by the fact that no
plaintiff and no defendant are citizens of the same state. Choice **B** is
incorrect because a federal court is not *required* to dismiss the action
because the claims of most of the representatives are not in excess of
$75,000, exclusive of interest and costs. However, the representatives
and members of the class whose claims did not satisfy the "amount in
controversy" requisite would have to be deleted from the class. Finally,
Choice **C** is incorrect because the claims of the class representatives
cannot be aggregated to satisfy the amount in controversy requirement.

17. D   Where a suit is properly commenced in a state court and federal diversity requirements would be satisfied, the action can be removed to the
U.S. district court which is in the judicial district that encompasses the
state court, if: (1) *no defendant* is a citizen of the state in which the
action was brought, (2) *all of the defendants* join in the petition for
removal, and (3) *removal* is sought within *30 days* of the time the

party seeking removal received service of process. (*See* ELO Ch.3-VII(A-C) & (K).) Statement I is not correct because the *D v. P* action is not removable, since P is a citizen of the state (New York) in which the action has been commenced. Statement II is incorrect because, even if the state court was competent to hear this matter, P (being a citizen of New York) could not remove the action to the applicable U.S. district court. Finally, Statement III is correct because D's action against P does not appear to have arisen "out of the transaction or occurrence" which is the subject of P's lawsuit against D (the latter litigation involving the failure to manufacture and deliver restaurant equipment). Thus, it was not a compulsory counterclaim.

18. **D** A defendant *may implead* a person, not a party to the action, who is or may be liable to him/her for all or part of the plaintiff's claim against the defendant/impleading party; FRCP 14(a). An *impleaded party may assert against the impleading party* any counterclaims permitted under FRCP 13; FRCP 14(a). (*See* ELO Ch.8-(IX)(F)(1)(a).) Statement I is correct (a third party action is *not* proper), since Baker is not asserting an indemnity-type claim against Chance. Statement II is correct because, pursuant to FRCP 13(b), a defending party may assert as a counterclaim "any claim against an opposing party ... "; FRCP 13(b). Finally, Statement III is incorrect because (1) diversity in an impleader action is not analyzed from the viewpoint of the original plaintiff and the impleaded party (rather, it is examined from the perspective of the impleading and impleaded parties), and supplemental jurisdiction ordinarily extends to third party claims.

19. **A** A party asserting a claim against a single defendant *may join any independent causes* of action which he has against the latter; FRCP 18(a). Persons may be joined as defendants if (1) there is asserted against them jointly, severally, or in the alternative, *any right* arising out of the same transaction, occurrence, or series of transactions or occurrences, and (2) any question of law or fact common to *all defendants* will arise in the action; FRCP 20(a). A court may, however, order separate trials of any claim (or cross-claim) to (1) avoid prejudice, and (2) promote judicial economy; FRCP 42(b). (*See* ELO Ch.8-III(A), IV(B)(2) & (B)(7). Subject to FRCP 42(b), Paul could assert an unrelated breach of contract action against Mary. Statement II is incorrect because Peter's cross-claim must arise out of the transaction or occurrence for ancillary jurisdiction to apply. Thus, subject matter jurisdiction is lacking with respect to Peter's counterclaim since the "amount in controversy" requirement is not satisfied. Finally, Statement III is incor-

rect because a plaintiff may aggregate personal injury and property claims to satisfy the "in excess of $75,000" requirement necessary for diversity subject matter jurisdiction.

20. **B**   In a ***class action*** based on ***diversity subject matter jurisdiction***, no plaintiff and no defendant may be citizens of the same state; but only the citizenship of the representatives is considered. Since the plaintiff and the representatives of the defendant class are citizens of the ***same state*** (Pennsylvania), ***diversity does not exist***. Thus, the plaintiff's action would have to be predicated upon a federal claim to avoid dismissal. (*See* ELO Ch.8-V(A)(1)(a).) The proper venue in diversity cases is any judicial district where (1) any defendant ***resides***, if all defendants live in the same state, (2) a substantial part of the acts or omissions on which the claim is based took place or a substantial part of the property which is the subject of the action is located, or (if there is no jurisdiction where the suit may otherwise be brought) (3) any defendant is subject to personal jurisdiction when the case is commenced; 28 U.S.C. § 1391(a). Therefore, Choice **A** is incorrect because, while venue in Ohio is proper if that is where Union has sufficient contacts (*See* ELO Ch.2-VIII(E)(6-7), it is not the only judicial district in which the action could be brought. Since railroad property was destroyed in Pennsylvania, the action could have also been commenced in that state. Choice **C** is incorrect because there is no per se rule that actions involving unincorporated labor organizations are outside the subject matter jurisdiction of the federal courts. Choice **D** is incorrect because Statement I is wrong.

21. **C**   Where there has been ***a prior, valid judgment*** on the merits between the parties (or their privies) with respect to the cause of action being asserted in a subsequent lawsuit, the doctrine of *res judicata* precludes the latter action. The fact that John obtained a judgment against Bill would not preclude Matt from subsequently contesting John's claim, since Matt is ***not*** in privity with Bill. (*See* ELO Ch.9-III(C).) Choice **A** is incorrect because Bill could sue Matt for indemnity. Choice **B** is incorrect because a plaintiff is not required to sue every possible defendant in one action. Finally, Choice **D** is incorrect because John's claim against Bill for personal injuries is, in most jurisdictions, barred by *res judicata* because this action arose out of the same transaction as John's property loss.

22. **A**   A ***compulsory counterclaim*** arises out of the transaction or occurrence that is the subject matter of the opposing party's claim and does not require for its adjudication the presence of third parties over

whom the court cannot acquire jurisdiction; FRCP 13(a). There is *ancillary jurisdiction with respect to compulsory counterclaims*. (*See* ELO Ch.8-II(B)(2) & (F)(1). If Steamroller's counterclaim is deemed to be compulsory (as opposed to merely permissive) in nature, ancillary jurisdiction would apply to avoid an assertion by Acme that subject matter jurisdiction is lacking. Choice **B** is incorrect because, if Steamroller's claim is merely permissive in nature, there would have to be an independent basis of subject matter jurisdiction for it to be assertable in a federal court. Since there is no diversity and Steamroller's cause of action is not based on a federal statute, the U.S. Constitution or a treaty, the counterclaim could *not* be asserted in a U.S. district court. Choice **C** is wrong because the fact that a state claim is being asserted is irrelevant to determine if federal subject matter jurisdiction is satisfied. Finally, Choice **D** is incorrect because a lack of diversity would (but for supplemental jurisdiction) result in Acme prevailing on its motion.

23. **B**   A party may ordinarily obtain discovery of documents and other tangible items prepared in anticipation of litigation or for trial, (1) by or for another party, or (2) by or for that other party's representative (including her attorney), only upon a showing that (1) the party seeking such discovery has a *substantial need* for the items, and (2) she is *unable, without undue hardship*, to obtain the equivalent thereof by other means; FRCP 26(b)(3). (*See* ELO Ch.5-II(E)(7).) In effect, B restates the applicable provision of the FRCP. Choice **A** is incorrect because, even if the report had been prepared by Brown in anticipation of litigation or trial, it would still be discoverable if Paul could show a substantial need for the document and that he was unable to otherwise obtain it (or its equivalent) without undue hardship. Choice **C** is incorrect because the "work product" privilege extends to tangible items created by another party (not just to items prepared by that party's representative). Finally, Choice **D** is incorrect because the fact that Manco had obtained the report at the suggestion of counsel would not, by itself, make the item non-discoverable. It could still be obtained if Paul could persuade the court that (1) there was a substantial need for it, and (2) he was otherwise unable to acquire it without undue hardship (i.e., the machine was destroyed and Brown cannot be deposed).

24. **C**   In U.S. district courts, the judge *may* conduct the *voir dire* examination; FRCP 47(a). *Bias or prejudice* of a potential juror against one of the parties is usually a *proper subject for inquiry* at the *voir dire*. (*See* ELO Ch.7-VI(D).) The defendant's question with respect to prejudice

against corporations was probably an appropriate inquiry upon *voir dire*, and therefore the judge's refusal to ask potential members of the jury that question was probably **erroneous**. Choice **B** is incorrect because the fact that a party may exercise three challenges does not detract from the court's failure to inquire about a general prejudice against corporations. Choice **A** is incorrect because any question regarding a juror's ability to reach a fair and impartial verdict is appropriate at the *voir dire*. Questions in this context need bear no relationship to the factual issues which will be contested at trial. Finally, Choice **D** is incorrect because the judge may utilize his discretion in determining if questions which counsel requests are appropriate.

25. **C** A plaintiff who **accepts a remittitur** in federal court **may not** challenge the trial court's ruling on appeal. By accepting the remittitur, and thereby avoiding the delay and cost of a new trial, the plaintiff is deemed to have **relinquished** her **right to appeal** the court's order. (*See* ELO Ch.7-IX(H)(5).) If Paul was dissatisfied with the remittitur, he should have appealed the court's order on the basis that the judge had abused his discretion (i.e., there was no good faith basis for reducing the verdict of $75,000 to $25,000). The fact that Paul agreed to the reduction "under protest" is irrelevant. Choice **A** is incorrect because the Seventh Amendment argument is overcome by the fact that the plaintiff is considered to have agreed to the remittitur (i.e., the plaintiff was free to have rejected the remittitur and to have had the case retried by a jury). Choice **B** is incorrect because, whether the trial court abused its discretion or not in ordering a new trial, Paul waived his right to review the court's order by accepting the decreased sum. Finally, Choice **D** is incorrect because, where a legal claim is involved, the Seventh Amendment is applicable to damage issues.

26. **A** A U.S. district court is competent to hear federal claims (i.e., claims arising under the Constitution, a treaty, or the laws of the U.S.); 28 U.S.C. § 1331. (*See* ELO Ch.3-IV(A).) Since the plaintiffs are **asserting a right under the U.S. Constitution**, "federal claim" subject matter jurisdiction **exists** (regardless of diversity or the amount in controversy). Choice **B** is incorrect because the court would have subject matter jurisdiction whether or not (1) there is diversity of citizenship between the plaintiff's representative and the defendants, and (2) the "amount in controversy" requirement was satisfied. Choice **C** is incorrect because where a federal claim is involved, there ordinarily is no "amount in controversy" requirement. Finally, Choice **D** is incorrect because (1) for purposes of a class action, diversity of citizenship is analyzed from the viewpoint of the class representatives, on the one

hand, and the opposing party or parties, on the other hand, and (2) even if diversity was lacking, the motion would still be denied because competency in this instance is predicated upon a federal claim.

27. **C**   There are *four prerequisites* to a class action: (1) the class must be so large that *joinder* of all members is *not feasible*, (2) the claims or defenses of the representatives must be *typical* of the class they seek to represent, (3) there must be *common questions* of law and fact to the class, and (4) the representative must fairly and adequately represent the *interests of the class*; FRCP 23(a). (*See* ELO Ch.8-V(B).) Since there is the possibility that many potential members of the class (all college students in State X) would not be desirous of challenging the flag desecration statute, the defendants' "strongest" argument for denying certification of the class would probably be on this ground. Choice **A** is incorrect because the class would probably be sufficiently numerous (there are ordinarily thousands of college students within each state). Choice **B** is incorrect because there ordinarily is no amount in controversy requisite with respect to the assertion of a federal claim. Finally, Choice **D** is incorrect because plaintiffs' claim would probably be characterized as a FRCP 23(b)(2) class action, and notice is expressly mandated only with respect to a FRCP 23(b)(3) action. Additionally, (even if due process considerations mandated reasonable notice) it would probably not be impossible to notify the class because persons matriculating at a college presumably disclose their names and addresses to the institution. Finally, acceptable notice might be possible through college newspapers.

28. **B**   If a trial court *refuses to certify the class*, its finding is not a final order, and therefore, an immediate appeal may not be taken. The case must be tried as a *non-class action*, and only after a judgment is rendered can the correctness of the trial court's refusal to grant certification be reviewed. (*See* ELO Ch.8-V(J)(3).) The result in B is required as a consequence of the holding in *Coopers & Lybrand v. Livesay*, 437 U.S. 463 (1978). Choice **A** is incorrect because the "death knell" doctrine was specifically rejected in the *Coopers* decision. Choice **C** is incorrect because the opposite is true (the party seeking class certification must try the case on the merits before he can appeal the trial judge's refusal to permit the class action). Finally, Choice **D** is incorrect because the existing parties may litigate the case, even though certification of the class has been refused.

29. A   Where a state attempts to exercise personal jurisdiction over an out-of-state defendant, and no traditional basis of personal jurisdiction exists, there (1) must be an ***appropriate long-arm statute*** which permits service of process, and (2) the assertion of such personal jurisdiction must be ***consistent with due process.*** (*See* ELO Ch.2-I(D-E) & III(G).) Since Manco was served outside of State X and is not present in that forum, (1) service of process must be within the purview of the applicable long-arm statute, and the assertion of personal jurisdiction must comport with due process. The latter element is arguably satisfied because (1) it was reasonably foreseeable that Manco's machinery would ultimately reach State X (since Roe distributed Manco's products in that state), and (2) the impact of the contact (i.e., the injuries to Arnold and Bates) was significant. Choice **B** is incorrect because U.S. district courts ordinarily "borrow" (i.e., apply) the long-arm statute of the jurisdiction in which they are located. Thus, with rare exceptions (i.e., statutory interpleader), U.S. district courts do not have nationwide service of process. Choice **C** is incorrect because, even if the "amount in controversy" element is satisfied, that would merely establish the court's competency. Subject matter jurisdiction is irrelevant with respect to determining if the assertion of personal jurisdiction is appropriate. Finally, Choice **D** is incorrect because, where an action is brought in federal court, service of process may be accomplished in accordance with either the FRCP or the applicable state procedural rules; FRCP 4(e)(1).

30. C   A ***compulsory counterclaim*** arises out of the transaction or occurrence that is the subject matter of the opposing party's claim and does not require for its adjudication the presence of third parties over whom the court cannot acquire jurisdiction; FRCP 13(a). ***There is supplemental jurisdiction with respect to compulsory counterclaims.*** (*See* ELO Ch.8-II(B)(2) & II(F).) Storeco's counterclaim against Arnold is totally unrelated to the occurrence upon which the latter is contending that the former is liable. Since the amount involved does not exceed $75,000, the U.S. district court does not have subject matter jurisdiction over Storeco's counterclaim. Choice **D** is incorrect because Storeco's counterclaim is permissive (rather than compulsory) in nature. Choice **A** is incorrect because there is no supplemental jurisdiction with respect to permissive counterclaims. (*See* ELO Ch.4-V(B).) Finally, Choice **B** is incorrect because the fact that Arnold may have consented to personal jurisdiction in State X by commencing the action does not cure the lack of subject matter jurisdiction with respect to Storeco's counterclaim.

31. A A cross-claim arising out of the transaction or occurrence that is the subject matter of (1) the original action, or (2) a counterclaim therein, may be made by one party against another; FRCP 13(g). There is ancillary jurisdiction with respect to cross-claims. (*See* ELO Ch.8-X(B-C).) Since Manco's cross-claim against Storeco is **unrelated** to the plaintiffs' action, it is **not permissible** (even though there is an independent basis of subject matter jurisdiction). Choice **B** is incorrect because ancillary jurisdiction is ordinarily applied with respect to permissible cross-claims. However, in this instance, ancillary jurisdiction is not necessary because diversity and "amount in controversy" requirements are satisfied. Choice **C** is incorrect because Manco's cross-claim is not permissible, regardless of whether or not it might confuse the jury's determination of the original claim. Finally, Choice **D** is incorrect because, even though there is "diversity" subject matter jurisdiction between Manco and Storeco, this action is unrelated to the underlying claim and may not be asserted.

32. B Where the precise issue was actually litigated in a prior lawsuit by the party (or his/her privy) against whom issue preclusion is being asserted in a subsequent action, and that issue was essential to the decision which was rendered in the earlier lawsuit, *issue preclusion* will ordinarily be applied. (*See* ELO Ch.9-III(A-D).) Federal courts must ordinarily follow the issue preclusion rules of an earlier, valid state court decision; *Marrese v. American Academy of Orthopedic Surgeons*, 105 U.S. 1327 (1985). Since mutuality is not required in this jurisdiction, collateral estoppel may be asserted by Bank against Paul. This is because in the latter's action against Doris, it was decided that Carol had made a gift to Doris of the funds in question. This fact (Carol's gift) would also serve as a defense to Paul's action against the Bank for unauthorized withdrawals (if Carol had consented to the transfer, it cannot be said that the disbursement to Doris was not authorized). Choice **A** is incorrect because federal courts must give *res judicata* and collateral estoppel affect to an earlier, valid, state court decision. Choice **C** is incorrect because Bank and Carol are **not** in privity. Finally, Choice **D** is incorrect because Choice **B** is true.

33. C A *judgment* in an FRCP 23(b)(2) *class action is binding on the entire class*. (*See* ELO Ch.8-V(H)(1)(b).) X would be bound by the determination that there was insufficient proof that D had not read the exams; FRCP 23(c)(3). This issue is critical for both injunctive relief and monetary damages. Choice **A** is incorrect because a judgment rendered by a court which lacked subject matter jurisdiction can be collaterally attacked by a non-party. It therefore is not entitled to Full Faith and Credit. Choice **B** is incorrect because there was diversity. P and D are citizens of different states. Finally, Choice **D** is incorrect because Choice **C** is true.

34. **D**   The *assertion of personal jurisdiction* pursuant to an applicable *long-arm statute* must be consistent with *due process* (i.e., the defendant must have such "minimum contacts" with the forum as not to offend "traditional notions of fair play and substantial justice"); *International Shoe Co. v. Washington*, 326 U.S. 310 (1945). (*See* ELO Ch.2-I(D-E).) Neither Statement is correct. Even if State Y had a non-resident motorist statute which asserted personal jurisdiction over a non-resident who was involved in a motor vehicle accident *within the state*, such fact alone would *not* be an adequate basis for obtaining personal jurisdiction over D in State Y because the accident occurred in State X. Also, regardless of the language of a long-arm statute, the exercise of personal jurisdiction must still conform to due process. Choice **B** is incorrect because mere ownership of a vacant parcel of land, without any connection of that realty to the cause of action, is probably insufficient to constitute the defendant's "presence" within that state. The fact that D was personally served in State X is irrelevant to the determination of whether he has sufficient contacts with State Y for personal jurisdiction to be exercised over him in that state.

35. **D**   *Persons may join* in an action as plaintiffs if (1) they assert *any right* to relief jointly, severally, or in the alternative in respect of any claim arising out of the same transaction, occurrence or series of transactions or occurrences, and (2) *any question of law or fact* common to all plaintiffs will arise in the action; FRCP 20(a). (*See* ELO Ch.8-IV(B)(2).) Choice **B** is incorrect because there is no subject matter jurisdiction with respect to Q's claim against D. The amount claimed to be in controversy is not in excess of $75,000, exclusive of interest and costs. Supplemental jurisdiction is not applicable. It permits a plaintiff (when federal question jurisdiction exists) to append a state cause of action to a federal claim. It does not permit a party to append the claim to a different plaintiff's federal claim. Choice **A** is incorrect because joinder of claims would be appropriate, since there is a common issue of fact (i.e., whether P's termination from his employment was wrongful). C is incorrect because P's claim for damages to his car is unrelated to dismissal from his job. Thus, no claim-splitting would result from P's failure to assert the damage to his car in the present action, and *res judicata* is not applicable. If P had not asserted the

claim for damage to his car, subject matter jurisdiction based upon diversity would not exist for that claim (i.e., P's claim would not exceed $75,000).

36. **D**   In an impleader action, the third-party defendant (the impleaded party) may assert *any claim* against the plaintiff which arises out of the transaction or occurrence that is the subject matter of the plaintiff's claim against the third-party plaintiff (the impleading party). (*See* ELO Ch.8-IX(F)(1)(c).) Choice **A** is correct. The U.S. district court did *not* have subject matter jurisdiction in the initial action since P and D were citizens of the same state (State X) and no federal claim appears to have been involved. Choice **B** is correct because it conforms to the operative rule of law found in FRCP 14. Finally, Choice **C** is correct because under *res judicata* principles, (1) P could not split his claim against D (i.e., P was required to bring all causes of action arising out of the accident against D in the original lawsuit), and (2) D was required to file a counterclaim against P in the original lawsuit with respect to any claims arising out of the accident, or thereafter be barred therefrom. Even though P and D are citizens of the same state, ancillary subject matter jurisdiction would have permitted D to counterclaim against P. In any event, Choice **C** specifically directs the reader to disregard subject matter jurisdiction problems in the initial lawsuit.

37. **A**   Where a claim over which the *federal courts would have original jurisdiction* is brought in a state court, the action may be *removed to the U.S. district court* which is in the judicial district that encompasses the state court, if (1) *all the defendants* join in the petition for removal, and (2) removal is sought *within 30 days* from the time the moving party receives service of process; 28 U.S.C. § 1446(b). (*See* ELO Ch.3-VII(F) & (K).) Since federal courts have exclusive jurisdiction over copyright claims, the action is removable; the state court's lack of jurisdiction is *irrelevant* for removal purposes; 28 U.S.C. § 1441(e). Choice **B** is incorrect since subject matter jurisdiction is not lacking because the action is premised on a federal claim. Choice **C** is incorrect because a judgment by a court which was not competent can ordinarily be challenged on appeal. Finally, Choice **D** is incorrect because Choice **A** is true.

38. **C**   In a *statutory interpleader* action (1) only *minimal diversity* (i.e., diversity between any two claimants) is required, and (2) the obligation or property involved *must exceed $500 in value only*; 28 U.S.C. § 1335. Venue is proper in any judicial district in which any claimant resides. (*See* ELO Ch.8-VII(C)(2)(b-d).) Since venue in a statutory

interpleader action is proper where any claimant-defendant resides, Choice **C** is correct. Choice **A** is incorrect (a U.S. district court is competent to hear this matter), since there is diversity between D and E, and (2) the amount involved exceeds $500. Choice **B** is incorrect because the court would not be competent to hear E's claim against F (diversity and a claim in excess of $75,000 are lacking). E's claim against F is not an impleader action (in which event there would be supplemental jurisdiction), since E is *not* asserting an indemnity-type of claim against F. Finally, Choice **D** is incorrect because Choice **C** is true.

39. **B**   The parties in a *federal civil case* may stipulate to a jury of *less than twelve* persons. Unless the parties otherwise agree, the verdict in a federal civil trial must be unanimous; FRCP 48. (*See* ELO Ch.7-VI(B-C).) Since one of the jurors voted in favor of Defendant, the ruling was defective. Choice **A** is incorrect because the parties stipulated to a jury of less than twelve persons. Choice **C** is incorrect because the fact that a verdict fails to exceed $75,000 is irrelevant (the "amount in controversy" requirement is measured only at the time the action is filed). Finally, Choice **D** is incorrect because any lack of personal jurisdiction over Defendant appears to have been waived when the defendant failed to assert this alleged defect; FRCP 12(h)(1).

40. **B**   Where a suit is brought in a state court and federal competency requirements would be satisfied based upon diversity, the action *may be removed* to the U.S. district court which is in the judicial district that encompasses the state court, if (1) *no* defendant is a citizen of the state in which the lawsuit was commenced, (2) *all* of the defendants join in the petition for removal, and (3) the moving party seeks removal *within* 30 days of the time it receives service of process. (*See* ELO Ch.3-VII(A) & (K).) Where a diversity action is properly commenced, and the matter is transferred to another U.S. district court, the law (including the conflict of law rules) of the state in which the action was originally commenced must be applied. A *forum non conveniens* motion would probably be successful since (1) State W has no relationship to the litigation (it is merely a state in which D "resides" by doing business there), (2) the accident occurred in State Y, and (3) any witnesses to the accident probably reside in State Y. (*See* ELO Ch.2-VIII(D)(1-2) & VII(E)(10).) However, the law (including the conflict of law rules) of State W would be applied by the federal court in State Y. Choice **A** is incorrect because D is a citizen of State Y, since its principal place of business is there. Thus, removal is *not* possible.

Choice **C** is incorrect because, where a *joint* claim is involved, each plaintiff is viewed as asserting the entire sum requested. Finally, Choice **D** is incorrect because Choice **B** is true (as discussed above).

41. B Under the FRCP, a pleading must ordinarily contain (1) a *statement* of the court's *competency*, (2) a short and plain *statement* of the claim showing the pleader is entitled to *relief*, and (3) a *demand for judgment or relief* to which the pleader is entitled; FRCP 8(a). (*See* ELO Ch.4-V(B).) Phil's complaint is arguably defective in that he has failed to describe *why* Dowd is liable to him (i.e., Phil has failed to allege that Dowd *improperly* drove his car into Phil's vehicle, or even that Dowd was "negligent"). Phil has stated only that there was an accident and Dowd is liable to Phil in the amount of $85,000. Thus, while a court would probably overrule Dowd's motion, it might require Phil to more clearly set forth the factual basis upon which he is entitled to relief. Choice **A** is incorrect because a complaint will not be dismissed without leave to amend "unless it appears beyond doubt that the plaintiff can prove no set of facts in support of his claim which would entitle him to relief;" *Conley v. Gibson*, 355 U.S. 41 (1957). Choice **D** is incorrect because expiration of the statute of limitations *subsequent* to the lawsuit is irrelevant (commencement of the action tolls the statute of limitations). Finally, Choice **C** is incorrect because under the FRCP it is *not* necessary for a plaintiff to articulate the precise legal theory upon which relief is sought.

42. C A party *may set forth two or more claims alternatively*; FRCP 8(e)(2). (*See* ELO Ch.4-IV(C)(4).) Since the FRCP specifically authorizes separate claims, regardless of consistency, a complaint setting forth two different theories for recovery is permissible. In this instance, the inconsistency may be explainable by Phil's inability to recollect the exact circumstances of the accident. Choice **B** is incorrect because a federal pleading is not subject to dismissal for containing a legal conclusion. Finally, Choices **A** and **D** are incorrect because federal pleadings may contain inconsistent claims or defenses.

43. A In the absence of a traditional basis for obtaining personal jurisdiction, the assertion of personal jurisdiction over an out-of-state citizen must (1) conform to the applicable *long-arm statute*, and (2) be consistent with due process (i.e., the defendant must have sufficient minimum contacts with the forum as not to offend traditional *notions of fair play and substantial justice*). (*See* ELO Ch.2-I(D-E) & II(E).) Since E (1) could not foresee being haled into New York (D had misrepresented to E that this trip would terminate in New Jersey), and (2) apparently has no other contacts with New York, the assertion of personal jurisdiction over E would probably violate due process. Choice **D** is incorrect because expiration of the applicable statute of limitations *after* the lawsuit had commenced is irrelevant (the filing of the action tolls the statute of limitations). Thus, expiration of the statute of limitations after the action was commenced would not be a basis for granting D's motion. Finally, Choice **C** is incorrect because of the fact that the United States federal courts do not have the power of nationwide service of process.

44. C   In a *diversity* case, the proper judicial district to commence an action is one in which (1) any defendant resides, if all defendants reside in the same State, (2) a substantial part of the events or omissions on which the claim is based occurred or a substantial part of the property is located, or (if there is no jurisdiction where the suit may otherwise be brought) (3) any defendant is subject to personal jurisdiction when the case is commenced. 28 U.S.C. § 1391(a). (*See* ELO Ch.2-VIII(E)(1).) Statement I is correct because there is diversity subject matter jurisdiction (i.e., P is deemed to be a citizen of States X and Z, while D is a citizen of State Y) and there is alienage jurisdiction with respect to E; U.S. Constitution, Article III, Section 2. Additionally, venue is proper because (1) D "resides" in State Y (where it has its principal place of business), and (2) an alien who does *not* permanently reside in the U.S. may be sued in any judicial district; 28 U.S.C. § 1391(d). Statement II is correct because a "diversity" action may be removed to the applicable U.S. district court when (1) no defendant is a citizen of the jurisdiction in which the action was commenced, and (2) all of the defendants join in the petition for removal. Finally, Statement III is incorrect because all persons may be joined in one action as defendants if there is asserted against them jointly, severally, or in the alternative (1) any right to relief arising out of the same transaction, occurrence or series of transactions or occurrences, and (2) any question of law or fact which is common to all defendants will arise in the action; FRCP 20(a). Since P's action arises out of the fire which occurred at its plant and there is at least one common issue of fact (i.e., the exact amount of P's damages), joining D and E as defendants is proper.

45. D   Upon timely application, a person *may intervene* in an action as of right when (1) he *claims an interest* relating to the property or transaction which is the subject of the action, (2) he is so situated that disposition of the action *may*, as a practical matter, *impair* his ability to protect that interest, and (3) the applicant's interest is *not adequately* *represented* by the existing parties; FRCP 24(a)(2). (*See* ELO Ch.8-VI(B)(1).) Statement I is incorrect, since P is unquestionably the real party-in-interest in that she is seeking damages in excess of the maximum limit of her insurance policy. Statement II is incorrect because there is no diversity between D and E with respect to D's claim against E (both parties being citizens of State Y). Ancillary jurisdiction is not applicable in this instance, since D's action cannot be characterized as impleader (D is not asserting an indemnity-type of claim against E). Statement III is incorrect because E cannot intervene into the action as of right. Her interest would not be impaired by a successful judgment by P against D (since D and E are legally unrelated, there would be no collateral estoppel or *res judicata* effect in the event that P's action against D was successful).

46. A   Under the Seventh Amendment, *the right to a jury trial exists* as to any issue which pertains to a *legal* remedy. (*See* ELO Ch.7-XIII(C).) Since an action for trespass existed in 1791 (when the Seventh Amendment to the U.S. Constitution was ratified), it must be characterized as a "legal" claim. Thus, Delbert would be entitled to a jury trial with respect to all issues pertaining to this action. Choice **C** is incorrect because the "clean-up doctrine" (which allows a federal court to determine legal issues which were "incidental" to a primarily equitable claim) has been repudiated; *Dairy Queen, Inc. v. Wood*, 369 U.S. 469 (1982). Choice **B** is incorrect because in federal court, each party is entitled to a jury trial with respect to any legal issue (regardless of the "primary" relief which the plaintiff is seeking). Finally, Choice **D** is incorrect because the tort of trespass existed in 1791 (when the Seventh Amendment was ratified), and therefore would constitute a "suit at common law".

47. A   In *diversity cases*, the proper judicial district for *venue* purposes is one in which (1) any defendant resides, if all defendants reside in the same State, (2) a substantial part of the events or omissions on which the *claim* is based *occurred* or a substantial part of the *property* is *located*, or (if there is no jurisdiction where the suit may otherwise be brought) (3) any defendant is subject to personal jurisdiction when the case is commenced. 28 U.S.C. § 1391(a). If venue is improper, a U.S. district court may dismiss the case or transfer the action to another U.S. district court in which the matter could have originally been commenced; 28 U.S.C. § 1406(a). (*See* ELO Ch.2-VIII(E)(1) & (E)(10)(e).) Although D was improperly served, he apparently waived this error by not contesting venue and making a motion to transfer the case to State Z. Since the original venue was improper, the court could transfer the action to State Z where the suit could have originally been commenced. Choice **B** is incorrect because it is not a valid basis of dismissal — since D waived the right to object to venue. Choice **C** is incorrect because, despite D having been improperly served, his waiver of this defect allowed the court to transfer the action to State Z. Finally, Choice **D** is incorrect because Choice **A** is true.

48. C A party may generally discover *any matter*, not privileged, which is *relevant* to the action. However, documents and tangible items prepared in anticipation of litigation or trial, by or for (1) another party, or (2) that other party's representative (including his attorney), are discoverable *only upon a showing* that the party seeking discovery has a need for the materials and would otherwise be unable to obtain the substantial equivalent without undue hardship; FRCP 26(b)(3). (*See* ELO Ch.5-II(E)(7).) Jones's memorandum to the president of E is probably *not* within the "work product" privilege because there is no indication that it was " … prepared in anticipation of litigation." Rather, it appears to be an internal memorandum by one member of the Board of Directors to the president of his corporation. Jones was probably attempting to avoid prospective litigation by advising the president of E as to what Withers had said. Choices **A** and **B** are incorrect because the work product rule is probably not triggered (Jones's memorandum was probably not made in anticipation of trial or litigation). Finally, Choice **D** is incorrect because the work product privilege is assertable whether or not the attorney who prepared the document in question is actually representing the party in the current action.

49. D A party is entitled to *summary judgment* where, as a consequence of there being no "genuine issue of material fact," she is entitled to *judgment as a matter of law*; FRCP 56. (*See* ELO Ch.7-IV(D).) Choice **A** is correct because, even if Builder Corp. had utilized substandard materials in the construction, this alone would not prove E was negligent. E would be negligent only if (1) it failed to utilize reasonable care in overseeing the activities of Builder Corp., and (2) there was a causal relationship between the substandard materials and the building's collapse. Thus, genuine issues of fact would remain even if substandard materials had been utilized by Builder Corp. Choice **B** is correct because, for a plaintiff to prevail on a summary judgment motion, she must address any affirmative defenses raised by the defendant. Finally, Choice **C** is incorrect because a summary judgment probably would not be appropriate based upon Wither's affidavit.

50. C A party is entitled to a **summary judgment** where, as a consequence of there being no "genuine issue of material fact," he is entitled to **judgment as a matter of law**; FRCP 56. (*See* ELO Ch.7-IV(D).) Although a two-year statute of limitations is applicable, negligence actions ordinarily do not begin to run until an injury or damages have been sustained. Thus, E's summary judgment motion was properly denied. Choice **A** is incorrect because the fact that the building was constructed six years ago is irrelevant if the statute of limitations did not begin to run until the accident. Choice **B** is incorrect because one need not respond to a summary judgment motion if it, on its face, would be unsuccessful. Finally, Choice **D** is incorrect because the fact that E has the burden of proof on this issue is irrelevant in determining whether there is a triable issue of fact. E could have raised the statute of limitations defense through a motion for failure to state a claim upon which relief can be granted; FRCP 12. However, since E supported its motion with an affidavit, it must be treated as a summary judgment motion.

51. B **Default judgments** which are constitutionally or procedurally defective are subject to **collateral attack**. (*See* ELO Ch.2-VII(D).) Under FRCP 4 (which has been enacted in State X), if no acknowledgment is made to a summons and complaint which are sent by first-class mail, the defendant must be served as otherwise provided in that Rule. Since P failed to properly effectuate service of process, the State X judgment was subject to collateral attack. Choice **A** is incorrect because, despite actual receipt of the documents by D, he was not served in accordance with applicable law. Choice **C** is incorrect because, while a default judgment is usually deemed to be "on the merits," the State X judgment is **not** entitled to Full Faith and Credit (P having failed to conform to the statute pertaining to service of process). Finally, Choice **D** is incorrect because (1) Choices **A** and **C** are **not** correct, and (2) Choice **B** is true.

52. A **Quasi-in-rem** jurisdiction will ordinarily be tested by the **due process standard** applicable to personal jurisdiction (i.e., the defendant must have had sufficient minimum contacts with the forum as not to offend traditional notions of fair play and substantial justice); *Shaffer v. Heitner.* (*See* ELO Ch.2-V(C)(7).) If D does not have sufficient contacts with Texas as would support personal jurisdiction over him, the attachment should be quashed. Choice **B** is incorrect because prejudgment attachments are not *per se* unconstitutional; *Mitchell v. W.T. Grant Co.*, 416 U.S. 600 (1974). Assuming proper due process safeguards exist, a defendant's property can be seized prior to the time a judgment is actually rendered against him. Choice **C** is incorrect because even if the motion to quash was denied and the boat sold, A could only retain proceeds in an amount equal to his obligation. The balance would have to be remitted to D. Finally, Choice **D** is incorrect for the reasons described above.

53. B   Where a suit is commenced in a state court and federal diversity requirements are satisfied, the action can be removed to the U.S. district court where the lawsuit was commenced if (1) no defendant is a citizen of the state in which the action is brought, (2) all of the defendants join in the petition for removal, and (3) the defendants seek removal within 30 days of receiving service of process. (*See* ELO Ch.3-VII(K).) Removal would not be possible since C is a citizen of the forum in which the action has been commenced (i.e., a corporation is a citizen of the state in which it is incorporated *or* has its principal place of business). Choice **A** is incorrect because removal cannot occur when *any* defendant is a citizen of the state in which the action was commenced. Choice **D** is incorrect because C is a citizen of Utah. Finally, Choice **C** is incorrect because removal could not be granted (C being a citizen of the state in which the action has been commenced), even if C joined in the petition.

54. D   *Permissive counterclaims* may be joined only if there is an independent subject matter basis for such claims. Claims by a plaintiff against a third-party defendant (the impleaded party) must have an independent subject matter basis; *Owen Equipment Co. v. Kroger*, 437 U.S. 365 (1978). (*See* ELO Ch.8-II(F)(2) & IX(F)(4)(a).) The $1,000 counterclaim by Dumb against Pam is permissive in nature (i.e., not arising out of the transaction or occurrence which is the basis of the plaintiff's claim), and therefore supplemental jurisdiction would not exist. Since Dumb's claim does not satisfy the "amount in controversy" requirement (it is not in excess of $75,000), it could not be joined in this action; therefore, Statement I is incorrect. Statement II is also incorrect, since Pam's claim against Insurance Co. could not be joined — both parties are citizens of State B.

55. B   Where evidence is objected to at trial on the grounds that it is not within the pleadings, a court *may allow an amendment* when (1) presentation of the merits of the action will be subserved thereby, and (2) the objecting party fails to satisfy the court that admission of such evidence would prejudice her in maintaining her action or defense on the merits; FRCP 15(b). (*See* ELO Ch.4-X(B)(1).) Although B failed to raise anticipatory repudiation as a defense, he could be permitted by the court to amend his pleadings at trial to conform to the evidence which he wishes to introduce. Choice **A** is incorrect because there is no *per se* procedural rule in federal courts that evidence outside of the pleadings is never admissible. Choice **D** is incorrect because the admission of evidence outside the pleadings is discretionary with the court. In fact, FRCP 15(b) instructs a court to adopt a liberal approach in admitting such evidence. Finally, Choice **C** is incorrect because amendments to pleadings may be made after trial has commenced.

56. C A party *may amend* his/her pleadings once, as a matter of right, at any time before a responsive pleading has been served; FRCP 15(a). Since a motion under FRCP 12(b) *does not* constitute a "responsive" pleading, Paul was entitled to amend his complaint without leave of the court. (*See* ELO Ch.4-IX(B).) Choice **D** is incorrect because affidavits in support of a motion for summary judgment must be based upon *personal* knowledge; FRCP 56(e). Here, Bill's affidavit is based upon information related to him by Paul (rather than firsthand knowledge). Choice **A** is incorrect because a complaint in federal court need not articulate the particular legal theory being asserted. Finally, Choice **B** is incorrect because alternative claims may be asserted, regardless of consistency; FRCP 8(e)(2).

57. B A *contractual provision* stipulating a particular choice of forum in the event of litigation will ordinarily be observed. Where a motion to transfer venue is granted, the law of the transferring state will be applied in the transferree forum. (*See* ELO Ch.2-VIII(E)(10).) Choice **B** conforms to the applicable principles of law. Choice **A** is incorrect because a plaintiff's choice of forum will rarely be disturbed. The fact that litigation in Oregon is inconvenient to a party's employees is probably insufficient to transfer the action to such party's "home state." Y Corp.'s contention is further diminished by the contractual clause stipulating to litigation in Oregon. Choice **C** is incorrect because a "choice of forum" contractual provision would not be disregarded simply because it would otherwise be inconsistent with due process to assert personal jurisdiction over a party in that forum. While a court could refuse to exercise jurisdiction where (1) neither party nor the cause of the action has a nexus with the forum, or (2) the party asserting the clause had a grossly favorable bargaining position, neither of those situations is applicable here because X is a citizen of Oregon and Y Corp. is a "large" corporation. Finally, D is incorrect because Choice **B** is true.

58. B   In a class action asserted under FRCP 23(b)(3), the court is *required to give members of the class the best notice practicable under the circumstances*, including individual notice to members who can be identified through reasonable effort; FRCP 23(c)(2). (*See* ELO Ch.8-V(G)(1) & (N).) Since the names and addresses of purchasers of the Daleon automobile are unavailable (except for the buyers who are located in New Mexico and Delaware), notice by publication in major newspapers throughout the country will probably be adequate. Choice **A** is incorrect because, for diversity purposes, only the citizenship of the class representatives and the other party are analyzed. Choice **C** is incorrect because notice is mandated by FRCP 23(c)(2), which states that " ... the court *shall* ... " require notification to the class. Thus, a court cannot dispense with the notice requirement in a FRCP 23(b)(3) class action. Finally, Choice **D** is incorrect because Choice **B** is true.

59. C   A party may ordinarily obtain discovery of documents and tangible items prepared in anticipation of litigation or trial by or for another party, or that party's representative (including her attorneys), only by showing that the party seeking discovery (1) *has a need* for the materials, and (2) is *otherwise unable* to obtain them (or the substantial equivalent) without undue hardship; FRCP 26(b)(3). However, FRCP 26(a)(2) mandates that an expert, whose opinions may be presented at trial, prepare a report containing his opinions and the basis for them (as well as other specified information). (*See* ELO Ch.5-II(E)(7) & (F)(2)(a-b).) Thus, the mandatory pretrial report and subsequent depositions of the locksmith could suffice as a substantial equivalent for the original report making it undiscoverable. Conversely, since the lock was repaired prior to the time that Amusement Co.'s attorney had an opportunity to examine it, the pictures taken by P's boyfriend are likely discoverable (even though they are arguably prepared in anticipation of litigation and thus "work product"). Accordingly, choice C is the only selection which correctly describes what Amusement Co. may discover.

60. C   Where a suit is commenced in a state court and federal subject matter jurisdiction would be satisfied based upon a federal claim, the action is removable to the U.S. district court which is in the judicial district that encompasses the state court if (1) all of the defendants join in the petition for removal, and (2) removal is sought within 30 days from the date the moving party received service of process; 28 U.S.C. § 1441(b). (*See* ELO Ch.3-VII(K).) Since Polly's claim is based on a federal claim, Acme may remove the case to the appropriate U.S. district court. *Diversity is not pertinent where a federal claim is involved*. Choice **D**

is incorrect because there is no diversity of citizenship because Polly and Acme are both citizens of Georgia. Choice **B** is incorrect because, while there is a lack of diversity, removal is appropriate since Polly is asserting a substantial federal claim. Finally, Choice **A** is incorrect because (1) becoming a citizen of a different state for litigational purposes is usually permissible, and (2) in any event, the citizenship of Polly is irrelevant for purposes of removal since she is asserting a federal case.

61. **A**   Where a *class action is based upon a federal claim*, there is *no* diversity or "amount in controversy" requirement. (*See* ELO Ch.8-V(I). A class action based upon diversity subject matter jurisdiction is not possible here because none of the plaintiffs possesses a claim in excess of $75,000. Thus, an action could be commenced in federal court only if the plaintiffs can premise their right to recovery upon a federal statute (or the U.S. Constitution or a treaty). Choice **B** is incorrect because separate plaintiffs may not aggregate their claims in a class action to satisfy the "amount in controversy" requirement. Choice **C** is incorrect because, where a class action is based upon diversity, each plaintiff must claim damages in excess of $75,000. Finally, Choice **D** is incorrect because, even if there is diversity between the class representative and the defendant, the "amount in controversy" requirement is not satisfied.

62. **C**   A person who is not a party *should be joined* where failure to do so will leave any party to the action subject to a *substantial risk* of incurring multiple liability for a single obligation. If the court determines that in equity and in good conscience the action should be dismissed in the non-party's absence, he is regarded as "indispensable". Where the joinder of an indispensable party will destroy subject matter jurisdiction, a federal court must dismiss the action; FRCP 19. A plaintiff is not required to join every potential defendant. (*See* ELO Ch.8-IV(D).) In this instance, complete relief can be afforded P on the basis of his lawsuit against Y (i.e., P could obtain a judgment for the full amount of his injuries against Y, if (1) Y were negligent, and (2) Y's conduct contributed to P's injuries). Even if X was a joint tortfeasor, Y could not complain of being exposed to multiple liability because he and X would (in addition to being jointly liable) each be severally liable to P for the full amount of the latter's injuries. While Y might lose contribution rights from X as a result of P's failure to also name X as a defendant, this fact alone does *not* make X an indispensable party. A defendant who is individually liable to the plaintiff has no expectation that the latter will name every possible party. Choice **A** is incorrect because "a common nucleus of operative facts" is not the standard used in determining if an unnamed party is indispensable. Choice **B** is incorrect because, even if X was wholly or partially responsible for the accident, Y cannot insist that X be included in the litigation. Choice **D** is incorrect because a party is either indispensable or not, whether or not his joinder destroys diversity.

63. C   Where the precise issue was actually litigated in a prior action by the party against whom issue preclusion is asserted, and that issue was essential to the decision rendered in the prior lawsuit, *issue preclusion may be permitted*. (*See* ELO Ch.9-III(B)(1-3).) If Arnold prevailed, Chuck would probably be able to assert collateral estoppel against Bill. Choice **A** is incorrect because the action against Chuck (based upon the guarantee) is different from that asserted against Bill (based upon non-payment of the promissory note). Choice **B** is incorrect because Chuck was not a party to the *Bill v. Arnold* action. Finally, Choice **D** is incorrect because Choice **C** is true.

64. D   Upon *timely* application, a person *may* intervene in an action as of right when he (1) *claims an interest* relating to the property or transaction which is the subject of the action, (2) he is so situated that disposition of the action may, as a practical matter, *impair* his ability to protect that interest, and (3) the applicant's interest is *not adequately represented* by the existing parties; FRCP 24(a)(2). (*See* ELO Ch.8-VI(B)(1).) Choice **A** is incorrect because Paul should be able to obtain full relief against Jim as prime obligor. Choice **B** is incorrect because, while Ralph has an interest in the action, permitting him to intervene would destroy diversity. It is therefore unlikely that permissive intervention would be permitted in this instance. Finally, Choice **C** is incorrect because Ralph's ability to protect his interest would not be impaired or impeded by a judgment in the outstanding action. Any judgment against Jim would probably *not* have a *res judicata* or collateral estoppel effect on Ralph if Paul subsequently sued him under the guarantee.

65. B   A party *may implead another person*, not a party to the action, who is or may be liable to him for all or part of the plaintiff's claim against the impleading party; FRCP 14(a). An impleaded party may assert against the impleading party any counterclaims permitted under FRCP 13; FRCP 14(a). (*See* ELO Ch.8-IX(A) & (F)(1)(a).) Statement II is correct because Don has an indemnity-type claim against ABC. Since there is supplemental jurisdiction for impleader actions, Don's claim against ABC is proper (even though diversity and "amount in controversy" requisites would otherwise not be satisfied). Statement I is not correct. Polly's personal injury action against Don does not arise from the same nucleus of operative facts which constitutes the basis of her federal claim against him. Thus, supplemental jurisdiction is *not* applicable. "Diversity jurisdiction" is lacking for the car accident claim, since (1) Polly and Don are both citizens of the same state, and (2) the amount in controversy does not exceed $75,000.

66. C When the mental or physical condition of a *party* is in controversy, the *court may order* that party to *submit* to a physical or mental examination by a physician. Such an order will be made only upon motion, for good cause shown, and prior notice to the person to be examined and all other parties; FRCP 35. (*See* ELO Ch.5-III(I).) Since Wanda is *not* a party to the action, an eye examination of her by P cannot be ordered. Choice **D** is incorrect because, while the order requiring the examination must be issued by the court, it is not necessary that the judge actually select the physician (i.e., she might approve a physician recommended by one of the parties). Choice **A** is incorrect because Wanda, who is not a party, cannot be ordered to submit to a physical examination. Finally, Choice **B** is incorrect because, although Wanda's vision is important to the question of whether D's alibi can be sustained, an eye examination cannot be ordered since she is not a party.

67. C *U.S. district courts are competent* to hear cases involving a federal claim (i.e., one arising under the Constitution, a treaty or the laws of the U.S.). (*See* ELO Ch.3-IV(A)(3).) There is no "federal question" because Polly has alluded to a violation of the U.S. Constitution only in the context of anticipating a possible defense which might be raised by Denny. However, a defense based upon the U.S. Constitution or a federal statute cannot serve as the basis for subject matter jurisdiction in federal court. Additionally, there is no "diversity" because Polly's claim is only for $3,000 (six months of rent at $500.00 per month). Thus, Choice **C** represents the only correct selection.

68. C Where the precise issue was actually litigated in a prior action by the party against whom *issue preclusion* is being asserted, and that issue was essential to the decision rendered in the prior lawsuit, issue preclusion *may be* permitted. (*See* ELO Ch.9-III(B)(2).) Since Ball recovered a default judgment against Mel in the initial lawsuit, it would have no collateral estoppel effect (i.e., obviously, the issues were not actually litigated). Also, since Wine and Ball are not in privity, the initial judgment would have no *res judicata* effect. Choice **A** is incorrect because Wine and Ball are not in privity with each other; they are complete strangers. Choice **B** is incorrect because the issues in Ball's action against Mel were not actually litigated. Finally, Choice **D** is incorrect because Choice **C** is true.

69. D   *Notice* of a proposed settlement of a class action *must be* approved by the court; FRCP 23(e). (*See* ELO Ch.8-V(K).) Choice **A** is incorrect because a decision to refuse to certify a class action is *not* a final order, and consequently an immediate appeal therefrom may *not* be taken; *Coopers & Lybrand v. Livesay*, 437 U.S. 463 (1978). Choice **B** is incorrect because a class action settlement must be approved by the court; FRCP 23(e). Finally, Choice **C** is incorrect because where a class action is successful (or a favorable settlement is arranged), federal courts often award the class representative reasonable attorney fees. However, if a class action is predicated on a specific federal statute, attorney fees are awarded only if the enactment explicitly permits them to be recovered; *Alyeska Pipeline Service Co. v. Wilderness Society*, 421 U.S. 240(1975).

70. C   When diversity is the basis for jurisdiction, intervention does not fall within the federal courts' supplemental jurisdiction; 28 U.S.C. § 1367(b). An intervenor must independently satisfy subject matter jurisdiction requirements. (*See* ELO Ch.8-VI(B)(6).) Since Bob and Oscar are citizens of the same state (Ohio), competency based upon diversity would not be satisfied. Choice **D** is incorrect because Bob's belief as to the potential damages is irrelevant, since diversity does not exist. Choice **A** is incorrect because there is no supplemental jurisdiction, as stated above. Finally, Choice **B** is incorrect because Bob is not an indispensable party. Art can obtain complete relief without Bob joining as a party, and Bob's absence would not expose Oscar to a risk of multiple liability for the same obligation; FRCP 19(a). Oscar owes Art a separate and distinct obligation from that owed to Bob.

71. A   *Statutory interpleader* is appropriate where: (1) there is *diversity* between at least two of the defendant/claimants, and (2) the obligation or property involved *exceeds $500* in value; 28 U.S.C. § 1335. There is nationwide personal jurisdiction for statutory interpleader; 28 U.S.C. § 2361. For "rule" interpleader, the ordinary rules of subject matter and personal jurisdiction apply. Since there is minimal diversity amongst the claimant/defendants (i.e., they are not all citizens of the same state) and the amount in controversy exceeds $500, a "statutory" interpleader action is appropriate. *Venue* is proper in any district in which any claimant/defendant resides. There is a federal statute authorizing nationwide personal jurisdiction for statutory interpleader. (*See*

ELO Ch.8-VII(C-D).) Choice **B** is incorrect because "rule" inter-pleader is not appropriate since diversity does not exist (Insurco is a citizen of the same states as Bill, Carl and Melvin). Choice **C** is incorrect because, under "rule" interpleader, there is nationwide personal jurisdiction; 28 U.S.C. § 2361. Finally, Choice **D** is incorrect because the party commencing an interpleader action may claim that he has no liability, whatsoever, to the claimant/defendants.

72. **C** A motion for a ***directed verdict*** should be granted where there is no sufficient legal basis for any other judgment. (*See* ELO Ch.7-VII(B).) Since it is entirely possible that a jury could conclude that Joan's physical problems were the consequence of the infection (rather than the inadvertent application of an acidic substance by Dr. Brown), a directed verdict would not be appropriate. Choice **A** is incorrect because the fact that Dr. Brown admitted that the perforium bottle was located near a container holding an acidic substance would not preclude the jury from reasonably concluding that the wrong bottle had ***not*** been used. Choice **B** is incorrect because it cannot be said that there was no sufficient legal basis for concluding that Dr. Brown was ***not*** negligent. Finally, Choice **D** is incorrect because Choice **C** is true.

73. **A** A ***motion for a directed verdict*** should be granted where there is no legally sufficient basis for any other judgment. (*See* ELO Ch.7-VII(B).) Since a jury could reasonably conclude that Dr. Brown inadvertently applied an acidic substance to Joan's ear, a directed verdict in favor of the former would be inappropriate. Thus, the trial court's judgment should be reversed and a new trial ordered. If the trial court had withheld its decision upon the motion for a directed verdict until the jury had rendered its decision, it might not have been necessary to order a new trial (i.e., the jury verdict could be in conformity with the directed verdict). For this reason, a determination upon a motion for a directed verdict ***will ordinarily be withheld*** until after the jury's verdict has been returned. Choice **B** is incorrect because, as described in the answer to the preceding question, a jury could reasonably find that Dr. Brown was ***not*** at fault. Choice **C** is incorrect because a jury could reasonably render a verdict for Joan. Finally, Choice **D** is incorrect because Choice **A** is true.

74. **D** ***A motion for a directed verdict is a prerequisite for a JNOV;*** FRCP 50(b). A motion for a new trial may be joined with a motion for a JNOV ("judgment as a matter of law"); FRCP 50(b). (*See* ELO Ch.7-XI(A)(2)(a) & XII(A).) Since Dr. Brown did not make a motion for a directed verdict at the close of the evidence, a JNOV cannot be

granted. Since the trial court denied the motion for a new trial and Dr. Brown did not appeal this decision, the jury verdict must be reinstated. Choice **A** is incorrect because a motion for a new trial may be joined with a JNOV motion. Choice **C** is incorrect because no appeal was taken by Dr. Brown from the order denying a new trial. Thus, a new trial cannot be ordered. Finally, Choice **B** is incorrect because no motion for a directed verdict was made, so a JNOV cannot be sustained.

75. **D**   A person who is not a party ***should be joined*** where failure to do so will leave any party to the action subject to a substantial risk of incurring multiple liability for a single obligation. If the court determines that in equity and good conscience the action should be dismissed in the non-party's absence, he is regarded as being indispensable. Where the joinder of an indispensable party will destroy subject matter jurisdiction, a federal court must dismiss the action; FRCP 19. (*See* ELO Ch.8-IV(D)(1-5).) Z is probably ***not*** an indispensable party because (1) any decision in the *Y v. X* lawsuit would not have a collateral estoppel effect upon him, and (2) since Y was aware of Z's interest in the vehicle, Z could still pursue an action against Y in the event that Y was victorious against X. Additionally, X would be subjected to multiple liability for a single obligation. By entering into separate transactions with two different persons for the same item, X accepted the risk that each buyer would have an action against him if the vehicle were not delivered. Choice **C** is incorrect because supplemental jurisdiction does ***not*** extend to indispensable parties. 28 U.S.C. § 1367(b). Choice **A** is incorrect because, even though Z has an interest in the vehicle, that interest cannot be seriously impaired by the *Y v. X* lawsuit. Finally, Choice **B** is incorrect because the fact that the X-Z agreement preceded the X-Y agreement is irrelevant in determining if a person is an indispensable party.

76. **B**   Upon timely application, a person may intervene in an action as of right when she (1) ***claims an interest*** relating to the property or transaction which is the subject of the action, (2) she is so situated that disposition of the action may, as a practical matter, ***impair her ability to protect that interest***, and (3) the applicant's interest is ***not adequately represented*** by the existing parties; FRCP 24(a)(2). (*See* ELO Ch.8-VI(B)(1).) Since Construction Company might have an indemnity-type claim against Big Builders (arguably, the latter entity is more at fault than the former for providing the defective scaffolding), impleader would be appropriate if personal jurisdiction and venue requisites were satisfied. Subject matter jurisdiction is ***not*** a consider-

ation because supplemental jurisdiction extends to the action by Construction Company against Big Builders. Choice **A** is incorrect because, while Big Builders arguably has an interest in the *Mary v. Construction Company* lawsuit, there appears to be no reason to believe that Construction Company could not effectively contest Mary's claim. Additionally, any judgment obtained by Mary would not have a collateral estoppel or *res judicata* effect in a subsequent action by Construction Company against Big Builders. Choice **C** is incorrect because, Construction Company's counterclaim being permissive in nature, the "amount in controversy" requirement would not be satisfied. Finally, Choice **D** is incorrect because Choice **B** is true.

77. **A**   Where the party against whom a presumption operates has introduced proof sufficient for the fact finder to resolve the factual proposition embodied by the presumption in his favor, ***the party in whose favor the presumption operated must carry the burden of proof with respect to such factual proposition***; Federal Rules of Evidence 301. (*See* ELO Ch.7-II.) Since Construction Company has introduced sufficient proof for a fact finder to determine that it had inspected the scaffolding (i.e., the supervisor had told Paul it looked "unsafe"), Mary had to produce proof adequate for a fact finder to conclude that Construction Company had not inspected the scaffolding. However, Mary did not do this; her proof indicated only that Paul was apprehensive about working near the scaffolding. Choice **B** is incorrect because the evidence introduced by Mary does not pertain to Construction Company's alleged failure to inspect the scaffolding. Since Mary (as the plaintiff) would have the burden of proof on this issue, a verdict must be directed for Construction Company. Choice **D** is incorrect because Construction Company introduced enough evidence to rebut the presumption against it (i.e., for a jury to conclude it had inspected the scaffolding). Finally, Choice **C** is incorrect because, under these circumstances, the court is obliged to direct a verdict in favor of Construction Company.

78. **D**   Where the party against whom a presumption operates has introduced proof sufficient for the fact finder to resolve the factual proposition embodied by the presumption in her favor, the party in whose favor the presumption operated must carry the burden of proof with respect to such factual proposition; Federal Rules of Evidence 301. ***A verdict cannot be set aside if there is substantial evidence to support it***. (*See* ELO Ch.7-II & V(E).) Since Construction Company introduced enough evidence to rebut the presumption (i.e., to cause Mary to introduce evidence sufficient to carry her burden of proof on the issue

of whether Construction Company was negligent in its inspection of the scaffolding), the court's factual determination and corresponding judgment could *not* be set aside. Choice **A** is incorrect because, since substantial evidence pertaining to the factual proposition embodied by the presumption was introduced by each side, the presumption could be overcome. Thus, the court's judgment should be sustained. Choice **B** is incorrect because the presumption was rebutted when Construction Company introduced proof sufficient for a jury to infer that it had made a reasonable inspection of the scaffolding. Finally, Choice **C** is incorrect because a finding of fact may not be set aside when there is substantial evidence to support it.

79. A   A *cross-claim may be asserted* against a co-party if the cause of action arises out of the transaction or occurrence which is the subject matter of the original action; FRCP 13(g). (*See* ELO Ch.8-X(B)(1).) Since Mary's cross-claim against John (presumably for indemnity) arises from the accident, it may be asserted in this action. Although Mary and John are both citizens of Maine, there is ancillary jurisdiction with respect to cross-claims. Choice **B** is incorrect because cross-claims are not compulsory under the FRCP. Thus, an action is not barred if no cross-claim is made in the original lawsuit. Choice **C** is incorrect because Mary may assert a cross-claim against John under these circumstances. Finally, Choice **D** is incorrect because Mary's suit against John is a cross-claim, rather than a counterclaim (John is a co-party and has not commenced an action against Mary).

80. D   A defendant may implead another person, not a party to the action, who is or may be liable to it for all or part of the plaintiff's claim against the defending/impleading party; FRCP 14(a). An *impleaded party may assert against the impleading party* any counterclaims permitted pursuant to FRCP 13; FRCP 14(a). (*See* ELO Ch.8-IX(A) & (F)(1)(a).) *The Star* would probably have an indemnity-type claim against Albert if the information which the latter supplied to it was incorrect. The fact that *The Star* and Albert are citizens of the same state would *not* prevent the lawsuit, since there is supplemental jurisdiction for impleader actions. Choice **C** is incorrect because an impleader action may be instituted for an indemnity-type of claim. If *The Star* were asserting that Albert alone was liable to Beacon House, it would *not* satisfy this requisite. Choice **A** is incorrect because courts have supplemental jurisdiction over impleader actions. Finally, Choice **B** is incorrect because (1) any judgment by Beacon House against *The Star* would not have a collateral estoppel or *res judicata* effect upon Albert in the event of a subsequent action against the latter, and (2)

Albert's interests will probably be adequately represented by *The Star*.
Thus, intervention into the action by Albert would be permissive
(rather than "as of right").

81. **C**   Where the precise issue was actually litigated in a prior suit by the person against whom issue preclusion is being asserted, and that issue was
essential to the decision rendered in that action, ***issue preclusion may
be permitted***. (*See* ELO Ch.9-III(B)(1-3). Since *The Star* would have
actually litigated the issues pertaining to whether the statements in its
article were true or not, a finding that such statements were untrue
would presumably be binding upon *The Star* in a subsequent action
against it by Don. A court could, however, refuse to allow Don to
assert collateral estoppel if it felt that he had "hung back" by failing to
commence litigation until the initial lawsuit was completed. Choice **D**
is incorrect because one is never required to intervene in an action
(even if he could have done so as of right). Thus, a party who fails to
intervene in an existing action does not forfeit his right to assert an
action against a party in the initial lawsuit. Choice **B** is incorrect
because, even though an action for an accounting has traditionally
been viewed as being equitable in nature, it is now viewed as one for
damages; ***Dairy Queen v. Wood***, 369 U.S. 469 (1962). Thus, Albert
probably would be entitled to a jury trial on this question. Finally,
Choice **A** is incorrect because courts have supplemental subject matter
jurisdiction over cross-claims.

82. **B**   *A court may re-align parties to reflect their true interests in the litigation for diversity purposes.* (*See* ELO Ch.3-III(B)(4).) Although D
has an interest in the action (i.e., D wishes the trust to continue) which
might be impaired if the plaintiffs are successful (i.e., D would pay a
greater amount of taxes), diversity probably would ***not*** be destroyed by
D's joinder. This is because D should be aligned with T (rather than
made an involuntary plaintiff) since, as a practical matter, his interests
coincide with those of T; they both desire to maintain the trust. Thus,
complete diversity would exist even if D were compelled to join the litigation. Choice **A** is incorrect because for diversity to be satisfied, no
plaintiff and no defendant may be citizens of the same state. Choice **D**
is incorrect because, while D may be an indispensable party, he would
probably be aligned with T. Thus, diversity would still exist. Finally,
Choice **C** is incorrect because, even if D was aligned with T, diversity
still exists.

83. A   Where the jury's answer to written interrogatories are inconsistent with a general verdict rendered by the jury, ***the judge may*** (1) ***enter a verdict*** in accordance with the answers to the interrogatories, (2) ***return the answers*** to the jury for further consideration and verdict, or (3) ***order a new trial***; FRCP 49(b). A party may ordinarily dismiss a lawsuit after the other side has filed an answer by filing a stipulation of dismissal which is signed by all the parties who have appeared in the action. (*See* ELO Ch.7-VIII(C) & IV(B)(2).) Unless otherwise stated in the notice of dismissal or stipulation, a dismissal by consent is without prejudice; FRCP 41(a)(1). Since the dismissal was signed by Defendant, it would be deemed to be without prejudice to Plaintiff's right to subsequently initiate a similar action against Defendant. Choice **B** is incorrect because a court is not obliged to render a judgment in strict conformity with the jury's answers to interrogatories. Choice **C** is incorrect because (1) the court cannot enter a general verdict inconsistent with the jury's answers to interrogatories, and (2) the court may send the interrogatory answers and verdict back to the jury for further consideration. Finally, Choice **D** is incorrect because Choice **A** is true.

84. C   Unless the parties or local rules stipulate otherwise, a ***party must disclose without waiting for a discovery request any insurance policy under which any person carrying on an insurance business may be liable to satisfy part or all of a judgment***; FRCP 26(a)(1)(D). (*See* ELO Ch.5-II(I)(1)(a)(iv).) Thus, the insured party must disclose the insurance policy even if it would not be admissible at trial. Choice **D** is incorrect because the existence of insurance by a party will rarely be relevant to the issues of the case. Choices **A** and **B** are incorrect because Choice **C** is true.

85. A   If a ***deposition*** is conducted in bad faith or in such a manner as to annoy, embarrass or oppress the deponent, ***the court may order*** the officer conducting the ***examination to cease*** forthwith from taking the deposition or limit the scope and manner of the deposition. In such event, the court may order the party conducting the deposition to pay the attorneys' fees of the objecting party; FRCP 30(d)(3). If the party who scheduled the deposition fails to attend, the court may order that party to pay the other the reasonable expenses incurred by the latter, including reasonable attorneys' fees; FRCP 30(g)(1). (*See* ELO Ch.5-IV(D).) If Andy (1) conducted a deposition in a manner designed to embarrass the deponent, or (2) failed to attend a deposition which he had scheduled, the aggrieved party is entitled to obtain his reasonable expenses associated with the depositions, including attorneys' fees. Statement III would not be a cause for sanctions against Andy. If the deposed person or party can show that she was unable (despite the exercise of diligence) to obtain counsel to represent her at a deposition, the testimony may be precluded from being used against such party at trial; FRCP 32(a)(3). Finally, Statement IV does not justify sanctions unless the objections were made in an argumentative or suggestive manner; FRCP 30(b)(1).

86. C In a FRCP 23(b)(3) class action, the notice must advise each class member that (1) any member *may opt out* of the class, (2) any member who does *not* opt out of the class will be bound by the final judgment, and (3) any member who remains in the class *may appear* in the action through an attorney; FRCP 23(c)(2). (*See* ELO Ch.8-V(G)(2).) Since the notice fails to indicate that a final judgment is binding upon all members of the class, it is inadequate. Choice **A** is incorrect because the plaintiff (rather than the defendant) must pay the costs of mailings to class members. If he fails to do so, the action will be dismissed. Choice **B** is incorrect because a class action judgment has no negative collateral estoppel effect with respect to individuals who decided to opt out of the class. Finally, Choice **D** is incorrect because Choice **B** is true.

87. A Parties may obtain discovery regarding any matter, not privileged, which is relevant to the subject matter of the pending action. It is *not a ground for objection* that the information sought will *not be admissible* at trial, if such information is reasonably calculated to lead to the discovery of admissible evidence; FRCP 26(b)(1). (*See* ELO Ch.5-II(C-D).) If information sought is (1) privileged, or (2) not reasonably calculated to lead to admissible evidence, it need not be disclosed. Thus, Statements I and III embody valid objections. Statement II is incorrect because factual information relating to the claims of a party is discoverable. Finally, Statement IV is not a valid objection because, although the evidence might be obtained from a less expensive source, this type of limitation upon the ordinary rights of discovery must be embodied in a court order; FRCP 26(b)(1).

88. B Opinions of experts retained by counsel in anticipation of litigation who are not to be called as witnesses are discoverable only "upon a showing of *exceptional circumstances*" (where the party would otherwise be unable to obtain the same facts or opinions by other means). FRCP 26(b)(4)(B). (*See* ELO Ch.5-II(F)(2-3).) Thus, the economist's opinion is not discoverable because there are no indications that the other party was unable to access the facts or opinions through other means. Choice **D** is incorrect because no privilege appears to be applicable to the economist's opinion. Choice **C** is incorrect, since the time at which an expert forms his opinion is irrelevant to its discoverability. Finally, Choice **A** is incorrect because B is true.

89. D   Under Article 4, Section 1 of the U.S. Constitution, each *state must ordinarily give the judgments of other states the same effect* (i.e., Full Faith and Credit) which the earlier judgment would have in the state in which it was rendered. (*See* ELO Ch.9-IV(B). The State Y court would be obliged under Full Faith and Credit principles to recognize the decision rendered in the State X court. Choice **A** is incorrect because, while the earlier judgment would prevent Defendant from *re-litigating* the claim, plaintiff is seeking only to enforce the prior judgment. Choice **B** is incorrect because the State Y court cannot constitutionally disregard the State X judgment. Finally, Choice **C** is incorrect because the State Y court must give effect to the earlier judgment, even though it was based upon a doctrine which is not adhered to in State Y.

90. C   *Where the precise issue was actually litigated* in a prior action by the person against whom issue preclusion is being asserted, and that issue was essential to the decision rendered in that lawsuit, *issue preclusion may be permitted*. (*See* ELO Ch.9-III(B-C).) Since C was not in privity with A, the judgment against A could not preclude C from re-litigating the question of B's negligence. The application of collateral estoppel here would violate C's due process rights. Choice **A** is incorrect because the application of collateral estoppel principles would violate C's due process rights. Choice **B** is incorrect because (1) a different action is involved (C's rights of recovery, rather than A's), and (2) A and C are not in privity. Finally, Choice **D** is incorrect because collateral estoppel may not constitutionally be applied, whether or not the mutuality rule has been repudiated in this state.

91. B   For purposes of diversity, a *partnership is deemed to be a citizen of the states in which any one of its partners is domiciled*. (*See* ELO Ch.3-III(J)(2).) It would be helpful to know where Paul is domiciled to determine if that state is the same one in which (1) either of Dodo's partners is domiciled (State X), or (2) Dominic's is a citizen for diversity purposes (State Z). Thus, Statement II is important since, if Paul were a citizen of either State X or State Z, diversity subject matter jurisdiction would not exist. It would also be helpful to know the extent of Paul's injuries to determine if the "in excess of $75,000" requirement is satisfied. Statement I is unimportant because the citizenship of a corporation is determined by its states of incorporation and principal place of business. The place of domicile of its shareholders is irrelevant for diversity purposes. Finally, Statement IV is important for purposes of personal jurisdiction, but is unrelated to determining the court's competency.

92. A   Under FRCP 4, notice with respect to actions commenced in a U.S. district court must be accomplished in accordance with the FRCP or the applicable local law. However, as a matter of due process, *notice must always be reasonably calculated* under the circumstances to apprise the defendant of the outstanding action. (*See* ELO Ch.2-VI(C)(4-5).) There is little doubt that a procedure which permits notification by posting in a situation where personal service could probably be effectuated would be unconstitutional; *Schroeder v. City of New York*, 371 U.S. 208(1962), *Walker v. City of Hutchinson*, 352 U.S. 112 (1956). Since the names of the officers or directors of Dominic's could presumably be ascertained from the State Z corporate records, the State Z notice statute would be unconstitutional as applied to these circumstances. Choice **C** is incorrect because actual receipt of notice by a defendant does not cure a statutorily invalid statute; *Wuchter v. Pizzutti*, 276 U.S. 13 (1928). Choice **B** is incorrect because notice in a federal court proceeding may be given in accordance with the applicable state service of process statute (provided, of course, it is valid). Finally, Choice **D** is factually true but incorrect because the state notice statute must be constitutional as applied to the existing circumstances.

93. A   Unless a traditional basis of personal jurisdiction exists, *personal jurisdiction may not be taken over an out-of-state defendant unless it is statutorily and constitutionally permissible*. (*See* ELO Ch.2-I(D-E).) Since Dodo's is not physically present in State Z (i.e., it has no personnel in the jurisdiction), the existence of a long-arm statute which empowered State Z courts to assert personal jurisdiction over a defendant in circumstances such as these would be a very significant question. Thus, Statement I is pertinent. Statement II is pertinent because Dodo's awareness that the oven would be utilized in State Z would certainly make it more likely that it should have reasonably foreseen being haled into court in the state; *World-Wide Volkswagen Corp. v. Woodson*, 444 U.S. 286(1980). Statement III is pertinent because the greater volume of business by Dodo in State Z, the less likely it is that "traditional notions of fair play and substantial justice" would be "offended" by making the defendant stand trial in that state; *International Shoe Co. v. Washington*, 326 U.S. 310 (1945). Finally, the physical health of the parties involved in litigation has never been cited as a relevant factor in the determination of whether personal jurisdiction exists or not (it could presumably be considered in the context of a *forum non conveniens* motion).

94. C   *A person who is not a party should be joined* where failure to do so will leave any party to the action subject to a substantial risk of incurring multiple liability for a single obligation. If the court determines that in equity and in good conscience the action should be dismissed in the non-party's absence, he is regarded as being indispensable. Where the joinder of an indispensable party will destroy subject matter jurisdiction, a federal court must dismiss the action; FRCP 19. (*See* ELO Ch.8-IV(D)(1-3).) Paul can obtain complete relief (a judgment for the full amount of his damages) without the necessity of joining Dan. Additionally, Acme will not be exposed to multiple liability for the same obligation since (1) Paul can only obtain one recovery for his injuries, and (2) where the potential defendants are joint tortfeasors, neither is prejudiced by a plaintiff's decision to refrain from suing every person who could possibly be liable. The risk that a particular defendant could have to bear the entire amount of the plaintiff's recovery always exists where there are joint tortfeasors. Choice **B** is incorrect because a plaintiff in a U.S. district court suing a single defendant may aggregate totally unrelated claims to meet the jurisdictional amount. It is only where plaintiff asserts actions against more than one defendant that the plaintiff must show that at least one of his claims (1) arises from a common transaction or occurrence, and (2) possesses a common question of law or fact. Choice **A** is incorrect because (as explained above) Dan is not an indispensable party. Finally, Choice **D** is incorrect because Choice **B** is not true.

95. D   A party is *entitled to summary judgment* where, as a consequence of there being no "genuine issue of material fact," he is *entitled to judgment as a matter of law*; FRCP 56. (*See* ELO Ch.7-IV(D).) Even though Acme neglected to respond to Paul's affidavit, Paul would only be entitled to a partial summary judgment on the issue of his job competency. His affidavit does not address the issues of (1) whether Dan's statement about Paul was within the scope of Dan's employment, and (2) whether Paul was entitled to recover for the unused vacation pay. Choice **C** is incorrect because the affidavit necessary to support a summary judgment motion may be made by the moving party, personally. Although Choice **A** is factually accurate, it is incorrect because it would only entitle Paul to a summary judgment on the issue of his competence. Finally, Choice **B** is incorrect because (as explained above) genuine issues of fact still exist.

96. C Where the precise issue was actually litigated in a prior lawsuit by the party (or his privy) against whom issue preclusion is being asserted in a subsequent action, and that issue was essential to the decision which was rendered in the earlier lawsuit, *issue preclusion will ordinarily be applied*. (*See* ELO Ch.9-III(B)(3).) Neither issue (whether Dan's statement was true, and whether it was within the scope of Dan's employment), independently, was essential to the judgment. Acme would have been victorious if it had prevailed on either of the issues. Some states apply offensive collateral estoppel where a specific factual finding was made on an issue (even if that issue was not essential to the judgment). However, since only a general verdict was rendered here, this view is not pertinent. Choice **B** is incorrect because (as explained above) collateral estoppel is not applicable. Finally, Choice **A** is incorrect because (1) a different cause of action is involved (*Paul v. Dan*), and (2) Dan is probably *not* in privity with Acme.

97. A A federal district court is competent to hear matters that (1) involve a federal question, or (2) satisfy diversity requirements (i.e., no plaintiff and no defendant are citizens of the same state and the plaintiff's claim exceeds $75,000). The correct answer is Choice **A**. Because Paul and Deeter Corporation are citizens of different states and the aggregate amount of the plaintiff's claim exceeds $75,000, diversity requirements are met and the district court may properly exercise subject matter jurisdiction. Choice **B** is incorrect because no federal question exists (i.e., the plaintiff is not suing pursuant to a federal statute). Choice **C**, while factually true, is incorrect, because the plaintiff's claims must only *aggregate* "in excess of $75,000." It is not necessary for each claim to exceed $75,000. Finally, Choice **D** is incorrect because the sufficiency of "minimum contacts" relates to personal jurisdiction, and the facts stipulate that personal jurisdiction requirements are satisfied.

98. A Where the basis for competency is a *federal question*, the matter may be heard in any jurisdiction in which the defendant is present or has sufficient minimum contacts (regardless of a more restrictive state long-arm statute). The correct answer is Choice **A**. Since the controversy is premised upon a *federal question* (i.e., Babco is suing under federal copyright law), California is an appropriate jurisdiction, *if* Dumbco has sufficient minimum contacts (or is deemed to be present) in that state. Regularly conducting business within California should satisfy that standard. Choice **B** is incorrect. Even if the elements of diversity subject matter jurisdiction are satisfied, the California long-arm statute would not permit its courts to assume personal jurisdiction over Dumbco (the out-of-state defendant). In a "diversity" (as opposed to federal question) situation, the state's long-arm statute is applicable, and Dumbco's business in California does **not** exceed $80,000. Choice **C** is incorrect, because a U.S. district court is **not** obliged to "borrow" the state long-arm statute when a federal question is involved. Finally, Choice **D** is incorrect because the basis of competency (i.e., subject matter jurisdiction) is a federal claim, not diversity of citizenship; the requirement that claims exceed $75,000 (exclusive of interest and costs) applies only in diversity cases.

99. **D**   In federal cases, the amount in controversy stated by the pleader in diversity cases controls, unless it appears to a legal certainty that the claim fails to exceed $75,000. Where an out-of-state defendant is personally served while in the jurisdiction to assist in the administration of justice, courts often quash a service of process upon that person. This action is discretionary with the court. The correct answer is Choice **D**. Because Arthur was in New York to assist in the administration of justice (i.e., complying with a subpoena), he will probably be able to quash the service of process made upon him. Choice **C** is incorrect, because the damages actually established (even if proven to not exceed $75,000) would not result in the failure of Clarence's lawsuit. A plaintiff in diversity cases must only demonstrate at the commencement of the litigation (if challenged) that there is no "legal certainty" that his damages will not exceed $75,000. Choice **A** is incorrect, because (although diversity requirements appear to be satisfied) the service of process upon Arthur will probably be quashed. Finally, Choice **B** is incorrect, because the service of process will probably be quashed.

100. **C**   Where competency (i.e., subject matter jurisdiction) is premised upon diversity of citizenship, a U.S. District Court "borrows" the long-arm statute of the jurisdiction in which it is located. The correct answer is Choice **C**. Although ABC **arguably** had minimum contacts with Florida as a consequence of its knowledge that its motors were integrated into yachts which were sold in that state, the Florida long-arm statute precludes personal jurisdiction in this situation because ABC neither sells products in Florida, nor to Florida domicilliaries. (Note: where subject matter jurisdiction is premised upon a **federal question**, the state long-arm statute can be disregarded as long as "minimum contacts" exist.) Choice **D** is incorrect because ABC's knowledge that its motors might be operated in Florida could constitute "sufficient minimum contacts" with Florida if this were a federal question rather than a diversity situation. Choice **A** is incorrect, since Florida's long-arm

statute precludes the assertion of personal jurisdiction in this instance. Finally, Choice **B** is incorrect, because the fact that ABC did business with the party who sold the item in question to a Florida domicilliary does not permit a court of that state to assume personal jurisdiction over ABC.

101. A Courts may exercise personal jurisdiction over a defendant who is served while physically present in the jurisdiction. The correct answer is Choice **A**. Because Dan was personally served while within California, he can be required to stand trial in that jurisdiction. The fact that he was served while performing an activity completely different from the one during which Pat was injured is irrelevant. Choice **B** is incorrect, because Dan probably lacks adequate minimum contacts with California; he is there only four days per year and at the discretion of his employers. Choice **C** is incorrect because, although Dan probably lacked minimum contacts with California, he was personally served in the jurisdiction. As explained above, personal service within the jurisdiction can be sufficient. Finally, Choice **D** is incorrect because diversity of citizenship does exist (Pat is a California citizen and Dan is a citizen of Illinois, and the amount claimed exceeds $75,000).

102. C Under FRCP 12(b), "[e]very defense . . . to a claim for relief in any pleading shall be asserted in the responsive pleading . . . except that the following defenses may at the option of the pleader be made by motion: . . . (2) lack of jurisdiction over the person. . . . A motion making any of these defenses shall be made before pleading if a further pleading is permitted." Since Dan failed to object to personal jurisdiction in his first pleading (his answer and counterclaim), he has waived this defense, and thus the correct answer is Choice **C**. Choice **D** is incorrect because a plaintiff's choice of forum remains subject to the proper exercise of personal jurisdiction over the defendant. Choices **A** and **B** are incorrect, since a lack of personal jurisdiction must by raised in the initial response of the objecting party, or it is waived.

103. A Under FRCP 32(a)(2), "[t]he deposition of a ***party*** . . . may be used by an adverse party for any purpose." Thus, the correct answer is Choice **A**. XYZ can use Wanda's deposition for any purpose (i.e., as direct evidence or to impeach her). Choice **B** is incorrect, because the deposition ***of a party*** to the action can be used for purposes other than impeachment. Choice **C** is incorrect, since Wanda's deposition may be used for substantive purposes by XYZ. Finally, Choice **D** is incorrect, because XYZ can use Wanda's deposition, whether or not her attorney deposed any of XYZ's officers or employees.

104. A   A pleading shall state as a counterclaim any claim which, at the time of serving the pleading, the pleader has against any opposing party, if it (1) arises out of the transaction...that is the subject matter of the opposing party's claim, and (2) does not require for its adjudication the presence of third parties of whom the court cannot acquire jurisdiction; FRCP 13(a). The correct answer is Choice **A**. Doe's action against Pete for breach of contract required Pete to assert any counterclaim that he (Pete) might have against Doe under the specific agreement in question. When Pete failed to assert a counterclaim, any action against Doe under that contract was forfeited. Choice **B** is incorrect, because collateral estoppel is not applicable. Collateral estoppel comes into play when an issue has arguably been decided in an earlier action. The specific issue of Doe's possible liability to Pete under the contract was presumably *not* litigated in the earlier case. Choice **C** is incorrect, because Pete was required to counterclaim against Doe when he (Pete) was sued by Doe under the agreement. Finally, Choice **D** is incorrect because, even though Pete's claim is not barred under collateral estoppel principles, it can no longer be asserted. Pete was obliged to file a counterclaim against Doe when the latter asserted a breach of contract action under that agreement against Pete.

105. D   Before discovery begins a party must disclose the following information if relevant to the disputed facts *pleaded with particularity:* (1) the name, address and telephone number of every person likely to have discoverable information, and (2) a copy of, or a description of all tangible things and documents; FRCP 26(a)(1) (*See* ELO Ch.5-II(I)(1).) Since the documents and model would be relevant to P's allegation as stated in her complaint, D was required to disclose these documents to P by copying them or describing them by category and location (unless the court had opted out of the mandatory pre-discovery disclosure). Choice **C** is a correct statement of the law. However, this alone would not require a party to *voluntarily disclose* known sources of discoverable information. There is no indication of any privilege here so Choice **A** is wrong. Lastly, Choice **B** is incorrect because **D** is true.

106. D   A party may discover experts retained by counsel who will not be called at trial only upon a showing of *exceptional circumstances* (that it is impossible for the moving party to obtain these facts or opinions by another means): FRCP 26(b)(4)(B). (*See* ELO Ch.5-II(F)(3).) Since there is no indication of such circumstances here, P may not discover the identities and opinions of D's retained experts. Thus Choice **A** is false. Choice **B** is incorrect because it states the law prior to the 1993 amendments to the FRCP. Choice **C** is a misstatement of the law, since evidence need only be relevant not admissible to be discoverable; FRCP 26(b)(1).

107. A   A party must supplement its initial mandatory disclosure if it discovers they are no longer complete or accurate; FRCP 26(e)(1). (*See* ELO Ch.5-II(J).) Thus, the existence of a new witness who may have discoverable information regarding disputed facts pleaded with particularity would have to be disclosed by D. Choices **B**, **C**, and **D** are all incorrect because they fail to recognize this mandatory requirement to supplement initial disclosure.

108. C   FRCP 11 provides that attorneys who file frivolous or harassing pleadings may be sanctioned by the court. However, the rule allows attorneys a *"safe harbor"* of 21 days from the date the adverse party serves a motion on him to withdraw or correct the offending pleading; FRCP 11(c)(1)(A). Thus, no matter how outrageous the pleading Bull cannot be sanctioned because he withdrew the complaint within the "safe harbor" period. (*See* ELO Ch.4-IV(C)(3).) An attorney must make a reasonable inquiry before signing the pleading. Bull's failure to ask about the dye probably fails this standard. However, Choice **A** is incorrect because Bull withdrew the complaint in a timely fashion. Similarly, Choice **B** is incorrect because the outrageousness of the attorney's conduct is irrelevant as long as the pleading is withdrawn within the 21 day period. Choice **D** is not true. Since an attorney swears to the pleading, he is responsible to make reasonable inquiries to determine the veracity of the complaint. If he fails to do this he is open to sanctions under FRCP 11.

109. A   FRCP 30(a)(2)(A) sets a presumptive limit of *10 depositions* for each party. However, the parties can agree to more depositions or the court can order more. (*See* ELO Ch.5-III(D)(6).) Since there is no evidence that this limit has been lifted, P's motion should be granted. Choice **B** is incorrect because parties may be deposed. Since the limit is imposed irrespective of whether added depositions are likely to lead to relevant information, Choice **C** is not right (but a court might consider this in deciding whether to issue an order permitting more depositions). Choice **D** is incorrect because Choice **A** is true.

Table of References to the Federal Rules of Civil Procedure

Table of References to Title 28, United States Code

Index

References are to the number of the question raising the issue.
"E" indicates an Essay Question; "M" indicates a Multiple-Choice Question

Law In A Flash Flashcards

Flashcards

Civil Procedure 1 ◆	$16.95
Civil Procedure 2 ◆	16.95
Constitutional Law ▲	16.95
Contracts ◆▲	16.95
Corporations	16.95
Criminal Law ◆▲	16.95
Criminal Procedure ▲	16.95
Evidence ▲	16.95
Future Interests ▲	16.95
Professional Responsibility (953 cards)	32.95
Real Property ◆▲	16.95
Sales (UCC Article 2) ▲	16.95
Torts ◆▲	16.95
Wills & Trusts	16.95

Flashcard Sets

First Year Law Set	95.00

(includes all sets marked ◆ *plus* the book
Strategies & Tactics for First Year Law.)

Multistate Bar Review Set	165.00

(includes all sets marked ▲ *plus* the book
Strategies & Tactics for MBE)

Law In A Flash Software

(for Windows® 3.1 and Windows® 95 only)

- Contains the complete text of the corresponding *Law In A Flash* printed flashcards
- Side-by-side comparison of your own answer to the card's preformulated answer
- Fully customizable, savable sessions – pick which topics to review and in what order
- Mark cards for further review or printing

Every *Law In A Flash* title and set is available as software.

Requirements: 386, 486, or Pentium-based computer running Windows® 3.1, Windows® 95, or Windows® 98; 16 megabytes RAM; 3.5" high-density floppy drive; 3MB free space per title

Individual titles	$19.95
Professional Responsibility (covers 953 cards)	34.95
First Year Law Set*	115.00
Multistate Bar Review Set*	195.00

* These software sets contain the same titles as printed card sets *plus* the corresponding *Strategies & Tactics* books (see below).

Law In A Flash Combo Packs

Flashcards + software, together at a substantial saving.

Individual titles in combo packs	$29.95
Professional Responsibility combo pack	46.95

(Sorry, LIAF Combo packs are not available in sets.)

Strategies & Tactics Series

Strategies & Tactics for the MBE

Packed with the most valuable advice you can find on how to successfully attack the MBE. Each MBE subject is covered, including Criminal Procedure (part of Criminal Law), Future Interests (part of Real Property), and Sales (part of Contracts). The book contains 350 actual past MBE questions broken down by subject, plus a full-length 200-question practice MBE. Each question has a *fully-detailed answer* which describes in detail not only why the correct answer is correct, but why each of the wrong answer choices is wrong. Covers the MBE specifications tested on and after July, 1997.

$34.95

Strategies & Tactics for the First Year Law Student

A complete guide to your first year of law school, from the first day of class to studying for exams. Packed with the inside information that will help you survive what most consider the worst year of law school and come out on top.

$12.95

Strategies & Tactics for the MPRE

Packed with exam tactics that help lead you to the right answers and expert advice on spotting and avoiding the traps set by the Bar Examiners. Contains actual questions from past MPRE's, with detailed answers.

$19.95

Products for 1998-99 Academic Year

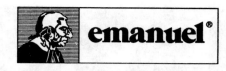
emanuel®

Emanuel Law Outlines

Steve Emanuel's Outlines have been the most popular in the country for years. Over twenty years of graduates swear by them. In the 1997–98 school year, law students bought an average of 3.0 Emanuels each – that's 130,000 Emanuels.

Civil Procedure ◆	$18.95
Constitutional Law	23.95
Contracts ◆	17.95
Corporations	18.95
Criminal Law ◆	14.95
Criminal Procedure	15.95
Evidence	17.95
Property ◆	17.95
Secured Transactions	14.95
Torts (General Ed.) ◆	17.95
Torts (Prosser Casebook Ed.)	17.95
Keyed to '94 Ed. Prosser, Wade & Schwartz	

Special Offer...First Year Set

All outlines marked ◆ *plus* Steve Emanuel's 1st Year Q & A's *plus* Strategies & Tactics for the First Year Law Student. Everything you need to make it through your first year.　$97.50

Lazar Emanuel's *Latin for Lawyers*

A complete glossary and dictionary to help you wade through the complex terminology of the law.

New title　　　　　　　　　　　　　　　　*$15.95*

The Professor Series

All titles in these series are written by leading law professors. Each follows the Emanuel style and format. Each has big, easy-to-read type; extensive citations and notes; and clear, crisp writing. Most have capsule summaries and sample exam Q & A's.

Agency & Partnership	$15.95
Bankruptcy	15.95
Environmental Law	15.95
Family Law	15.95
Federal Income Taxation	15.95
Intellectual Property	17.95
International Law	16.95
Labor Law	15.95
Negotiable Instruments & Payment Systems	14.95
Products Liability	13.95
Professional Responsibility (*new title*)	17.95
Property (*new title*)	17.95
Torts	13.95
Wills & Trusts	15.95

Question & Answer Collections

Siegel's Essay & Multiple–Choice Q & A's

Each book contains 20 to 25 essay questions with model answers, plus 90 to 110 Multistate-style multiple-choice Q & A's. The objective is to acquaint the student with the techniques needed to handle law school exams successfully. Titles are:

Civil Procedure ◆	Evidence
Constitutional Law	Professional Responsibility
Contracts ◆	Property ◆
Corporations	Torts ◆
Criminal Law ◆	Wills & Trusts
Criminal Procedure	

Each title　　　　　　　　　*$15.95*

Siegel's First Year Set - All titles marked ◆, at a discounted price.

$79.95 if purchased separately　　　　　　　　*$59.95*

The Finz Multistate Method

967 MBE (Multistate Bar Exam)–style multiple choice questions and answers for all six Multistate subjects, each with detailed answers – *plus* a complete 200 question practice exam modeled on the MBE. Perfect for law school and **bar exam** review.

　　　　　　　　　　　　　　　　　　$33.95

Steve Emanuel's First Year Q&A's

1,144 objective–style short-answer questions with detailed answers, in first year subjects. A single volume covers Civil Procedure, Contracts, Criminal Law, Criminal Procedure, Property, and Torts.

　　　　　　　　　　　　　　　　　　$18.95

LEXIS®·NEXIS®

NOW brings to you...

SHEPARD'S® UPDATED DAILY!

LEXIS-NEXIS is your best online source for SHEPARD'S legendary history and treatment analysis. New citing references and analyses are updated every day upon receipt from SHEPARD'S.

Wider Coverage
This unsurpassed level of SHEPARD'S currentness extends to all citations series on LEXIS-NEXIS...and LEXIS-NEXIS gives you wider coverage than any other online source, including all 50 state statutes, the U.S. Code, the CFR, patents, Federal Rules of Court, law reviews, and of course caselaw.

Quick Rating Codes
Take advantage of the SHEPARD'S Signal on LEXIS-NEXIS—three concise codes that quickly rate the strength of your cited case.

Faster Research
SHEPARD'S on LEXIS-NEXIS has been streamlined to reduce research steps, improving your productivity like never before.

Be sure you've built your case on a solid foundation by using SHEPARD'S on LEXIS-NEXIS. For a free brochure or to learn more,

CALL 1-800-528-1891.

LEXIS·NEXIS®
A member of the Reed Elsevier plc group

SHEPARD'S®

It's all you need to know

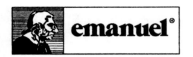 **emanuel**®

We'd like to know . . . .
Siegel's Civil Procedure (4th ed.)

We value your opinions on our study aids. After all, we design them for *your* use, and if you think we could do something better, we want to know about it. Please take a moment to fill out this survey and feedback form and return it to us. We'll enter you in our monthly drawing where 5 people will win the study aid of their choice! If you don't want to identify yourself, that's OK, but you'll be ineligible for the drawing.

Name: _____ Address: _____

City: _____ State: _____ Zip: _____ E-mail: _____

Law school attended: _____ Graduation year: _____

Please rate this product on a scale of 1 to 5:

General readability (style, format, etc.)............................. *Poor* ① ② ③ ④ ⑤ *Excellent*

Length of book (number of pages) .... *Too short* ① ② ③ ④ ⑤ *Too long*

Essay questions.. *Poorly written* ① ② ③ ④ ⑤ *Well written*

Multiple-choice questions .... *Poorly written* ① ② ③ ④ ⑤ *Well written*

End-of-book aids (tables & index) .... *Not useful* ① ② ③ ④ ⑤ *Useful*

Book's coverage of material presented in class .... *Incomplete* ① ② ③ ④ ⑤ *Complete*

OVERALL RATING... *Poor* ① ② ③ ④ ⑤ *Excellent*

Suggestions for improvement: _____
_____
_____

☛ **What other study aids did you use in this course?** _____
_____

☛ **If you liked any features of these other study aids, describe them:** _____
_____
_____

☛ **What casebook(s) did you use in this course?** _____

☛ **What study aids other than Emanuel do you use, and what features do you like about them?** _____
_____
_____

☛ **Please list the items you would like us to add to our product line:**

Outline subjects: _____

Flashcard subjects: _____

Other products (e.g., software, multimedia, etc.): _____

☛ **If you win our drawing, what one study aid would you like?** _____

Send to: *Emanuel Law* **Survey**   OR   Fax to: *(914) 834-5186*
          1865 Palmer Avenue, Suite 202
          Larchmont, NY 10538

✂ Cut here ✂

Please complete & return the Survey Form on the other side

NOTES

NOTES

NOTES

NOTES

NOTES

NOTES

NOTES

NOTES